Revolt of the Peasantry 1549

The Author

Julian Cornwall is Subject Leader of History at Colchester Institute of Higher Education. He is a specialist in English economic and social history of the early sixteenth century and has written many articles on the subject.

CORNWALL, Julian. Revolt of the peasantry, 1549. Routledge & Kegan Paul, 1978 (c1977). 254p maps bibl index 77-30119. 14.25 ISBN 0-7100-8676-8. C.I.P.

CHOICE JULY/AUG.' *History, Geography &* *Travel* *Europe*

Popular revolts were endemic in Tudor England. Lacking a standing army and having discouraged the nobility from maintaining their own armed retainers, the Tudor state relied on local gentry to prevent riots from escalating into insurrections and upon the vigilance of national authorities to prevent insurrections from developing into full-scale rebellion. The revolts of 1549 show what could happen when local leadership was weak and indecisive and Lord Protector Somerset's attention was directed elsewhere. Cornwall's account of the Prayer Book Rebellion in Cornwall and Devon and of Kett's Rebellion in Norfolk provides a detailed explanation of these distinct and separate revolts, and of the ways in which Somerset sought to deal with them. The author's narration is unmarred by footnotes or even many textual references to the sources of his quotations. He does, however, include a brief bibliographical essay and seems aware of much of the more recent scholarly thinking about Somerset and the rebels' social make-up. This book is unsuitable for advanced undergraduates but may well prove useful to those taking introductory history courses. Libraries lacking the now o.p. accounts of the revolts may wish to have this one.

Revolt
of the
Peasantry 1549

Julian Cornwall

Routledge & Kegan Paul
London, Henley and Boston

First published in 1977
by Routledge & Kegan Paul Ltd
39 Store Street,
London WC1E 7DD,
Broadway House,
Newtown Road,
Henley-on-Thames,
Oxon RG9 1EN and
9 Park Street,
Boston, Mass. 02108, USA
Set in IBM Press Roman by
Express Litho Service (Oxford)
and printed in Great Britain by
Redwood Burn Ltd
Trowbridge and Esher
© Julian Cornwall 1977

British Library Cataloguing in Publication Data

Cornwall, Julian

Revolt of the peasantry, 1549.
1. Peasant uprisings – England 2. Kett's Rebellion,
1549 3. Great Britain – History – Edward VI,
1547–1553
I. Title
942.05'3   DA345   77–30119

ISBN 0 7100 8676 8

To Margaret

Contents

Maps

Acknowledgments

I am greatly indebted to my colleague David Stephenson for reading and commenting on the draft, to Jack Millar of Longwood College, Virginia, for advice on military details, and most of all to my wife who compiled the index and generally encouraged me to complete the work.

WALES

Bristo

BRISTOL CHANNEL

SOMERSET

Bridgwater · King's W·
· Br·
· Torrington · Taunton · Shaftesb·
· Sh·
Tiverton · Mohuns Ottery · Hinton St
Sampford Courtenay · Crediton Honiton · Fenny Bridges DO·
· Okehampton · Rockbeare · Ottery St Mary
Launceston · EXETER · Clyst St Mary Dor·
· Topsham
· Helland DEVON
CORNWALL · Bodmin
Trematon · Plymouth
· Fowey
Penryn · ·
· Constantine
St Michael's Mount · Helston

Map 1 Southern England

Introduction

The two rebellions which convulsed England in the summer of 1549 are well trodden ground for students of sixteenth-century history, although much less familiar to the wider reading public, sometimes amounting to little better than dimly recollected facts from some long-forgotten school lesson. These episodes deserve to be better known. In the writing of history nowadays there is a significant trend away from exclusive pre-occupation with affairs of state towards a greater emphasis on the lives and struggles of ordinary people. Oddly enough, popular history designed for mass consumption has yet to catch up with this development. Recent television excursions into the Tudor age have been devoted exclusively to the lives of three of the monarchs, Henry VII, Henry VIII and Elizabeth I. It is of further interest to observe the neglect of the stormy and fascinating 11 years which separated the reigns of the two latter rulers when the throne was occupied successively by a sickly child and a faded middle-aged woman: an unglamorous interlude in a romantic epoch! And not only is it accepted that the history of England comprehended the 'country' as well as the 'court', it is also recognised that the kingdom was in many respects the sum of the counties, each of which to a greater or lesser degree constituted a self-conscious community in its own right. Until at least the second half of the seventeenth century it is necessary to pursue the history of the nation through the structure and activities of these local communities. Both the risings of 1549 were motivated primarily by local issues.

In contrast with the opening and closing decades, the middle 30 years or so of the sixteenth century were restless and intermittently violent. Not the least of the achievements of the founders of the Tudor dynasty was the liberating of England from the scourge of civil strife. Apart from one brief flare-up in 1487, the accession of Henry VII had terminated the armed struggles for possession of the Crown commonly known as the Wars of the Roses. Subsequent upsurges of violence during his reign took the form of resistance in remote regions to his policy of enforcing uniform administration throughout the realm, and were specifically protests against taxation. Only the two Cornish risings of 1497 involved fighting on any scale, and after they had been crushed the nation enjoyed relative freedom from disorder for almost four decades until, in 1536, a serious rebellion broke out in the North, to be followed by four more during the next 33 years, with no less than three in the space of five years 1549–54.

The Pilgrimage of Grace began in Lincolnshire in October 1536 as a rising of the peasants provoked by a variety of causes of which the most immediate were taxes and hostility to the dissolution of the monasteries. It came to nothing. Several thousands of sketchily armed country people wandered about the Parts of Lindsey for a few days accompanied, perhaps reluctantly, by a handful of gentlemen, and eventually came to a stop outside the walls of Lincoln which refused to open its gates and make common cause with them. Then, as hastily assembled royal forces began to converge on them, the gentlemen seized the opportunity to decamp, leaving the peasants leaderless, with nothing to do but disperse.

Meanwhile the revolt had spread to Yorkshire where a potentially far more menacing movement developed. Similarly originating in a medley of local grievances, largely economic in character, coupled with reaction against Henry VIII's policy towards the Church, which had just culminated in the deprivation of the county of a large number of religious houses, the Pilgrimage drew in not merely the common folk, but the gentry as well, found a dissident peer, Lord Darcy, to lead it, and an able organiser and articulate spokesman in a lawyer named Robert Aske. Momentarily too weak to confront the insurgents, the King's Lieutenant, the duke of Norfolk, had no recourse but to negotiate. Fortunately they did not aspire to overthrow the government, indeed the gentry were soon looking for a pretext to back down, and willingly accepted promises which effectively bound the King to nothing. In the end all the rising seemed to have proved was that it was impossible to mount a successful challenge to Henry VIII or deflect him from his course. In retrospect it was bound to fail against a régime which, despite (maybe because of) its despotic complexion, commanded the loyalty of the majority of the nation.

If anyone was responsible for this, the first armed revolt for 40 years, it was Henry himself. It was he alone who, in order to subject the Church to his authority, had upset the equilibrium of the state and driven conservative elements to take up arms in defence of their convictions. The process he had begun he could not halt. Widespread and bitter grievances, the preconditions for rebellion, existed in abundance. In 1547 Henry died, leaving a sickly child as his heir and entrusting the affairs of the kingdom to a government that was inherently weak. Further, he left a country seething with discontent — a frustrated desire for radical changes in religion complicated by a formidable array of social problems which he had ignored in his absorption with purely political and constitutional problems.

Within two years the regency had to face two rebellions simultaneously, provoked by the very reforms it had itself initiated. These, both religious and social, were at one and the same time insufficient to satisfy demand, yet more than enough to undermine the confidence of many people and, in conjunction with long festering discontents, to drive others to open rebellion which was only put down by massive military action.

Neither revolt sought the downfall of the government. In 1554 Sir Thomas Wyatt attempted just that in order to prevent Queen Mary going ahead with her plan to marry Philip of Spain and re-establish Catholicism in England. He too failed, but his rebellion brought to three the total for the 11 years 1547–58, not to mention a rash of lesser disorders and several conspiracies. It fell to Elizabeth I to restore tranquillity and confidence after more than 20 years of unrest, and significantly she chose to do so by means of a compromise settlement which, while accepting that many developments had gone too far to be reversed, was none the less firmly grounded in conservatism, and by fudging the most contentious issues sought to avoid further change. The appeal was to the moderate majority. Of course the extremists remained unsatisfied. There was one more revolt to come, the Rebellion of the Northern Earls in 1569 which proved in the event to be nothing more than an empty gesture on the part of a couple of dissident Catholic noblemen in the remotest part of England, and fizzled out after a few days. From this point onwards the peaceful conditions of the early years of the century were finally restored.

The turbulent middle years of the period coincide almost exactly with the time during which the Reformation, and briefly the Counter-reformation, were taking place. It was as though in breaking with Rome and implementing radical changes in the structure of the Church, Henry VIII had, however unwittingly, unloosed a host of disruptive forces whose existence was not realised. With the possible exception of that of 1569, these rebellions were in no sense a revival of the baronial strife of the preceding century. Most of them were peasant risings – the Pilgrimage of Grace began as one – and as such constituted a novel phenomenon. And yet not so novel, for they were common enough in Europe, notably the German Peasants' War in 1525, and had occurred in England in earlier times, especially Wat Tyler's revolt in 1381 and Jack Cade's in 1450. To some extent disorder is endemic in agrarian economies: violent, if small-scale, clashes between tenants and their landlords, rick burning, cattle maiming, etc., are commonplace. They can be compared with strikes in the industrial environment, except that, thanks perhaps to the superior discipline of trade unionists, conflict is ritualised within a framework of strict rules. Less frequently, in periods of acute, prolonged economic crisis and social stress, peasant grievances erupt in formidable, well-organised mass movements which challenge the existing social order and the authority of the state which underpins it; rebellion is born. Such a crisis hit England in the sixteenth century, appearing to threaten the traditional way of life of the peasants by breaking up rural institutions and in many cases destroying their livelihood.

There are signs that by the 1540s the peasants were becoming more self-conscious than ever before, and to some extent articulate. It is feasible, though far from certain, that the lingering Lollard tradition, which persecution had failed to eradicate, had become transmuted at the grass roots into a radical questioning of the political order. A century later, in the aftermath of the Great Rebellion, popular religious and social action welled to the surface with remarkable vigour in the shape of the Levellers and numerous kindred movements and sects which fleetingly threatened to turn the world upside down. However, the existence of any continuous tradition of popular dissent connecting events separated by periods as long as 100 years must be regarded as problematical.

The whole question of revolution currently excites keen interest — *The Revolution*, whatever that may be. Popular revolts of long ago, however abortive they might have been in their own day, are eagerly probed for portents of the coming millenium. Whether any form of revolution was brewing in the mid-sixteenth century must depend on how the evidence is interpreted; it is, however, worth remarking that most actual revolutions have commenced more or less by accident, growing out of spontaneous outbursts of frustrated energy. The objectives of these rebels, their means of realising them, and the consequences of their action are, none the less, interesting in themselves. The risings may have been bloodily defeated, but when it was all over the government collapsed, succumbing to a *coup d'état*.

II

The rebellion which Robert Kett organised and led in Norfolk belongs, in a manner of speaking, to every economic historian's folk-lore, marking as it does the climax of peasant discontent, the tragic dénouement of the agrarian problem of the sixteenth century. The coeval Prayer Book Rebellion occupies no comparable niche. A recent authority[1] dismisses it in six lines while devoting a whole page and a half to the 'far more dangerous rebellion' in East Anglia. This is the conventional modern approach. In a materialistic age scholars feel more secure in the relatively mechanical process of analysing and evaluating the multitudinous strands of economic and social phenomena than in accounting for an episode as straightforward as the Western Rising. The present writer was no exception until an investigation of the distribution of wealth as represented in the 'General Proscription', or musters, of 1522 revealed the impressive inventory of armaments in the possession of the Cornish peasants, in contrast with the situation in most other counties. Curiosity prompted a review of the circumstances of the two major risings in which they were involved, from which it emerged that the one in 1549 especially was far removed from a riot by a mob of yokels brandishing scythes and pitchforks, a fundamentally different proposition from the Norfolk affair.

At the time neither was dismissed lightly. The account of each occupies roughly the same space in Holinshed's *Chronicle,* the second edition of which was actually edited by John Vowell, alias Hooker, who was an eye-witness to the western revolt, and whose narrative is the principal source for it. Both were regarded as mortal threats to the state and the social order, and accorded corresponding treatment. Subsequent historians down to and including J. A. Froude (*History of England from the Fall of Wolsey to the Defeat of the Spanish Armada,* 1860) continued the tradition, indeed they mostly followed Holinshed. Recent scholars, from A. F. Pollard onwards, have progressively upstaged the Prayer Book Rebellion, to the extent that the latest, and definitive, history of the Reformation dismisses it briefly and gives equal space to Kett's rebellion in which religious issues played a distinctly minor part.[2]

It appeared that the time was opportune for a re-assessment of the Prayer Book Rebellion, less in the light of its causes, which have never been in dispute (though all too frequently blurred),[3] than of the physical resources at the disposal of the participants and the consequent magnitude of the threat it posed to political stability in the stormy reign of Edward VI. The only exhaustive study was made by Frances Rose-Troup as long ago as 1914 in *The Western Rebellion of 1549* which has long been out of print. It is objective and lavishly documented, but at the same time displays a tendency towards a cloying sentimentality, and in places betrays the influence of the tendentious Catholic interpretation of the Reformation initiated by Cardinal Gasquet. Dr A. L. Rowse's chapter in his *Tudor Cornwall* (1941) is vigorous and authoritative, although lacking appreciation of the psychology of the insurgents. The most recent version, W. K. Jordan, *Edward VI: the Young King* (1968), is not satisfactory.

F. W. Russell's *Kett's Rebellion in Norfolk* (1859), an admirable and exhaustive work, is rare; it certainly deserves a new edition. S. T. Bindoff's *Ket's Rebellion* (1949), although brief, is pithy and authoritative, and unlikely to be bettered. Both he and subsequent scholars owe much to R. J. Hammond's unpublished thesis 'The Economic and Social Background to Ket's Rebellion' (University of London, 1933).

Since the causes of unrest in 1549 have been systematically explored more than once there is little that can be usefully added. A close re-examination of what actually happened is a different matter; in addition to making a good story it reveals a number of facets which have not hitherto received adequate attention. It is also opportune to take into account Dr Bush's recent fundamental reappraisal of government policy in general and the official attitude to social problems in particular.[4]

As previous studies have dealt with just one rebellion in isolation it is well worth considering them together. It is true that there was no connexion of any sort between the risings in East Anglia and the South West; they did not even have one objective in common. Yet in view of the fact that they were in progress at the same time it is difficult to believe that there was not some degree of interaction. The most obvious question is why the mercenaries who eventually crushed Kett so decisively were not sent to deal with him very much sooner. The possibility occurs, which has never before been considered, that they were tied down by the events in the West Country, either because the government was reluctant to commit them until it was certain, that the danger from that quarter was past, or even that these troops (or some of them) were actually engaged in the operations there. Is it, therefore, possible that for some such reason Kett's movement was granted a stay of execution? For it is a matter of fact that numerous other agrarian protests took place in that unhappy year, all of which came to naught because they were promptly and ruthlessly suppressed.

Once these risings were well and truly off the ground the immediate problem was reduced to a purely military one. This has been the weakness of earlier accounts: too many unwarranted assumptions have been made about the action taken. For a long time the military history of England in the sixteenth century was a sadly neglected field, almost completely overshadowed by naval affairs. In recent years much valuable work has been done in this field by C. G. Cruickshank, Lindsay Boynton and, with particular relevance to the structure of national defence in the first half of the century, Jeremy Goring,[5] to whom I am indebted for having first drawn my attention to the musters of 1522, the indispensable starting point for approaching many of the problems of society during the Tudor age. Thanks to these pioneers very much more is known about military matters than was the case a generation ago. It is now possible to deduce with some confidence how the defence system would have operated under any given circumstances. A further problem is the employment of mercenary troops against the rebels. Most existing accounts contrive to convey the impression (a) that large numbers were freely available at the critical time, and (b) that units were even recalled from the army assembling in the North for the invasion of Scotland. By marshalling hitherto untapped sources such as muster rolls, contracts for the employment of mercenaries, and army pay accounts it becomes possible to construct a reasonably convincing picture of the military situation at the time.

The depth of the crisis of 1549 became a function of the military potential of the two sides, the government and the rebels. In practical terms this reduces the mechanics of the business, as nearly as possible to the exact numbers engaged, their efficiency, the weapons employed and their effectiveness, not forgetting that vital factor, the distances involved and the length of time it would have taken bodies of troops to cover them. To reconsider these rebellions as military operations adds a new dimension to them, and in particular prompts us to wonder how close the men of Devon and Cornwall came to reversing the course of the Reformation.

Chapter 1
Agrarian Problems and Others

I

In the month of April 1549 the Privy Council began receiving reports of disturbances among the peasantry in many parts of the country, the Midlands, the West Country, and the South East. The news was not startling in itself. A degree of violence was endemic among all classes in English society in the sixteenth century. Assault, wounding and manslaughter, forcible entry and riotous assembly were daily occurrences. Self-control was not an English virtue, quite the contrary; foreigners saw the English as an emotional, quarrelsome and generally unruly race, who rarely lacked a motive for taking the law into their own hands. As often as not recourse to the courts was the refuge of the man who had been worsted in the direct confrontation.

Agrarian disorder was commonplace and always provided a good proportion of the cases adjudicated by the Star Chamber, the court whose special province was breach of the peace. The inhabitants of Great Dunham, Norfolk, for example, had had a dispute with Sir Thomas Coldyng, the farmer of the demesne of the manor, who had enclosed a piece of the common and thereby deprived them of their rights. They had complained to commissioners appointed to enquire into such abuses, and had obtained an award in their favour. But Coldyng had ignored it, and so at 10 o'clock on the night of 16 May 1544 they had assembled, armed with pitchforks and other weapons, in order to enforce the verdict themselves. Coldyng had then complained to the Star Chamber, arguing that action of this sort 'should much encourage like offenders in time to come if some speedy remedy be not found'.

The history of agrarian disputes in Norfolk has been intensively studied; they had been occurring with some regularity for many years, and not infrequently culminated in violence. But their number could undoubtedly be matched in other counties as well. At about the same time, the tenants of the manor of Ecclesden in West Angmering, Sussex, alleged that the lord, John Palmer, had descended on them with a band of armed servants and ejected them from their farms which he wanted for his own purposes. As it happens there was another side to this story. Nevertheless, we may suspect that Palmer, despite his strenuous denial, did employ some form of intimidation, and that Sir John Rodney's accusations against his tenants at Draycot and Stoke Gifford in Somerset were not without foundation, for all their posturings as the unresisting victims of naked brutality.

The majority of these early stirrings in 1549 were very small affairs which came to nothing, but in the second week of May the duke of Somerset, Lord Protector of the Realm, received a report from his agent, Richard Fulmerston, of a disquieting new development. On the previous Sunday, 5 May, some 200 men, mostly weavers, tinkers and other workmen, had gathered at the small clothmaking town of Frome and set to work tearing down sundry hedges and fences. The next morning the local magnates, Lord Stourton and the bishop of Bath and Wells, with a couple of justices of the peace, had hastened there to confront the lawbreakers. They questioned many of the men who unanimously asserted that what they were doing was entirely lawful, sanctioned by a royal proclamation ordering the destruction of enclosures, which they understood to have been recently published in Somerset.

William Barlow, the bishop, skilfully avoided a collision. He and his colleagues were confident that the trouble was entirely the work of a handful of agitators — 'lewd' or 'light' persons, in contemporary parlance — maliciously stirring up foolish and ignorant people. (Even more than four centuries afterwards this outlook on the part of authority has a tediously familiar ring about it.) To gentlemen and landowners, the natural governors of a predominantly agricultural society, it was inconceivable that anything could be so seriously amiss as to create among those whom they ruled a genuine grievance which stood in such urgent need of redress that the normal processes of law and administration were hopelessly inadequate to satisfy it. In this complacent frame of mind they proceeded to turn a commonplace outburst of irritation into a dangerous confrontation.

Barlow did not attempt to dispute the people's case, contenting himself with pointing out that they were misinformed about the proclamation (which in fact did not go beyond the appointment of a commission of enquiry); he suggested that they should go away quietly to put their complaints in writing and deliver them to Stourton's house. They welcomed his advice. Their assembly had been peaceful; disorder and violence were the last things they intended. Honestly believing that they were doing no more than expedite the due execution of the law, they were more than satisfied with this apparent display of understanding on the part of the county magistrates. Alas, they were speedily undeceived! Not only did the justices have no sympathy whatever for them, they had not the least intention of even trying to understand the nature of the problem. The bishop's ploy was nothing more than a ruse to trap the ringleaders into identifying themselves: the four or five men who presented themselves at Stourhead with the petition were instantly clapped into gaol. But the plan misfired badly. It provoked a menacing wave of unlawful assemblies all over Somerset and Wiltshire. More hedges were uprooted. Subversive opinions were uttered, such as 'why should one man have all and another nothing?', and the rioters boasted that should the magistrates dare arrest one man more, 1,000 at least would come to his rescue.

Now the authorities were forced to resort to sterner measures. Quarter Sessions were due to be held the following Saturday, to which all the gentlemen of the shire were commanded to come at the head of their servants and the 'honest' yeomen and farmers from among their tenants. This, the magistrates were confident, would ensure the mustering of a force ample to deal effectively with the disturbances. Again they underestimated the problem. Disaffection spread rapidly, threatening to engulf both counties. Rioters broke into the parks of Stourton himself and of Sir William Herbert at Washerne, tore down palings and slaughtered his deer. In order to create this park a whole village had been razed to the ground and its inhabitants driven away. The uproar went on for two or three weeks and was only quelled when Herbert marched in Welsh levies from his estates in Glamorgan who 'slew to death divers of the rebels'.

Almost simultaneously came trouble in other shires. By 15 May the Council was warning justices of the peace in the counties bordering Wiltshire to be on their guard, and indeed some sort of assembly took place at Overton, Hampshire, on 20 May. A more violent confrontation had already occurred in Kent which was promptly suppressed by the gentry under the energetic leadership of Sir Thomas Wyatt who hanged two rioters at Ashford on 13 May, and a third at Canterbury a day later. He then borrowed artillery from the government and stationed it at Canterbury where it formed an effective deterrent during the coming months. Soon tremors were felt across the Midlands, in Leicestershire, Rutland and Lincolnshire, although in most places, 'by good policy of the Council and other noblemen of the country', they were pacified. The earl of Shrewsbury was notably successful in maintaining the peace in the north Midlands. In most cases, however, the task was an easy one. The peasants rarely resorted to violence, if at all. Gatherings were on the whole peaceful and businesslike, concentrating on the methodical destruction of offending enclosures. This was what happened at, for example, Attleborough in Norfolk on 10 June when, after they had completed the job, the villagers quietly dispersed to their homes. A disturbance at Bristol in May was largely fortuitous. A band of soldiers *en route* to Ireland had been discharged there without conduct money to get them home, and their captain did not have enough in his own purse to advance it to them. So they had wandered about the city, selling their equipment to buy food, grumbling loudly about the government, and refusing to go home without their pay. A riotous assembly soon formed, although in the end it too fizzled out without serious consequences.

II

The 1540s was a decade of acute crisis which, since four-fifths of the population depended more or less directly on agriculture, was intimately bound up with the land. The agrarian problem comprised several distinct grievances of which the most inflammatory was enclosure, so much so that it had become the omnibus term for the lot.

Strictly defined, enclosure connoted the fencing off for individual use of pieces of common agricultural land over which the whole community of a village exercised rights. On the one hand it might involve individual strips in the open arable fields, which had little practical effect on the other farmers, although the fact that this facilitated more efficient and profitable cultivation could provoke jealously on the part of less progressive men; for as Thomas Tusser, the rhyming advocate of improvement, pointed out,

> Good land that is several crops may have three
> in champion country it may not so be . . . .

But to enclose, on the other hand, a portion of common grazing land clearly diminished the rights of the rest of the community, and if carried far enough could leave some farmers with insufficient pasturage to support their horses and oxen, and so gravely hamper their work. Much enclosure was effected piecemeal by the more enterprising peasants themselves, and probably caused little real damage to their neighbours, but there were occasions when landlords or the farmers of manor demesnes practised it on a large scale, even to the extent of driving the smaller tenants from the land, pulling down their homes and converting the cornfields into sheepwalks. During the fifteenth century scores of villages and hamlets had been depopulated, especially in the Midland counties, in order to take advantage of the rapidly expanding demand of the textile industry for wool. The majority were very small, many having already wasted away with the general decline of population which had commenced early in the fourteenth century, accelerated with the Black Death, and was not reversed until late in the fifteenth century. None the less, there were occasions when thriving communities were deliberately uprooted, as was Pickworth in Rutland in 1489, enough of them to lend substance to the prevalent belief that vast numbers of human beings had been reduced to vagabondage for the sake of sheep and the profits they yielded. Enclosure thus comprehended depopulation and the conversion of arable land to pasture; in reality they were two aspects of a single problem, the destruction of the rural community.

Another grievance, and on the whole the more common experience, was the engrossing of farms, 'gathering of divers men's livings into one man's hand . . .'. In the fifteenth century this had been innocuous enough, when holdings frequently stood vacant for want of takers. But once farms had been thrown together they were apt to stay that way, with the result that the growth of population was creating a new class of landless peasants, and by intensifying demand was also driving up rents. If anything it was this that provoked most of the discontents of the 1540s. Formerly, arable and sheep farming had existed side by side peaceably enough and, with demand restricted, no one had objected when arable land was laid down to grass and farms thrown together. But since about 1520, if not earlier, the situation had begun to be reversed; land came to be in short supply relative to the population, so that there developed an increasingly vociferous condemnation of what had hitherto been tolerated, and insistence that grassland should be ploughed up, enclosures thrown open, and holdings made available for everyone who wished to farm them.

A later generation came to remember the 1530s and 1540s as hard times. In his *Description of England* (1577) William Harrison quotes old men of Radwinter in Essex, who could bear witness to the way in which the standard of living had 'marvellously altered . . . within their sound remembrance'. As anyone who had turned 50 would have been regarded as elderly, these early recollections would have harped back to these very decades when life was perforce Spartan,

> and yet for all this frugality (if it be so justly called) they were scarce able to live and pay their rents at their days without selling of a cow, or an horse, or more, although they paid but four pounds at the uttermost by the year. Such also was their poverty, that if some odd farmer or husbandman had been at the alehouse . . . and there in a bravery to shew what store he had, did cast down his purse, and therein a noble or six shillings show unto them . . . it was very likely that all the rest could not lay down so much against it.

This miserable state of affairs seems to have developed mostly after 1515 when an anonymous writer had asked smugly, 'What common folk in all this world may compare with the commons of England, in riches, freedom, liberty, welfare and all prosperity? What common folk is so mighty, so strong in the field, as the commons of England?'

Simple chauvinism perhaps; the subjects of Henry VIII were a braggart race, like their ruler. Nevertheless, only a few years earlier still an Italian visitor had confirmed the abundance of agricultural land which supplied everything the people could possibly want, and could have yielded an abundance of grain for export had they taken the trouble to grow it. By the time of Edward VI, Englishmen had ceased to boast of their advantages and turned to bewailing their miseries. Had they, one wonders, taken life too easily around the turn of the century, and were they now enduring economic nemesis?

If enclosure as such had ceased to be a factor of importance, the motive behind it remained an active force: sheep farming. Everything was blamed on sheep. A contemporary tract said precisely this in its title:

> Certain causes gathered together, wherein is shewed the decay of England, only by the great multitude of sheep, to the utter decay of household keeping, maintenance of men, dearth of corn, and other notable discommodities, approved by six old proverbs.

These proverbs were employed with disarming simplicity to demonstrate that the increase of sheep made everything else dearer — wool, mutton, beef, corn, white meat and eggs. Despite the obvious contradictions, the writer managed to prove his case to his own, and a great many other people's, satisfaction. One example of his reasoning will suffice to illustrate the way they felt about it:

> the most substance of our feeding was wont to be on beef, and now it is on mutton. And so many mouths goeth to mutton, which causeth mutton to be dear.

Bullocks of course were being crowded off the land by sheep. Before indulging in the luxury of a patronising smile we should remind ourselves that it was through the efforts of successive generations to find an answer to this sort of puzzle that systematic economics gradually evolved.

It remains none the less true that sheep presented a very real problem at this time. The long term buoyancy of the market greatly stimulated the production of wool, and this posed the question where to put the sheep. For the ordinary small farmer it was not a personal concern. His 10, 20, 30 acres were occupied by the crops which fed his family and paid the rent. In those areas where most of the population lived, village custom dictated that individual holdings, scattered round the great fields, should be utilised for this purpose and no other. Most farmers were content to conform and consequently remained small and poor. They had to keep most of their livestock on the common pasture grounds where the number permitted to each man was limited by stint, and since priority had to be given to working animals, few peasants could own more than a handful of sheep. Not that they objected to sheep, quite the reverse. Corn and sheep normally went together, but the prime function of the animal was to manure the land, the fleece was merely a bonus, a sideline like eggs and the butter produced by the farmers' wives.

Even though they possessed but a handful of animals apiece, the many thousands of peasant farmers must have accounted for a considerable volume of wool production, but in order to make the big profits it held out large scale grazing was necessary. For this reason wool growing was the speciality of the big farmer, and was characteristically associated with the exploitation of manorial demesne, whether by the lord in person or by his tenant. In the previous century large flocks had been accommodated without undue strain. An enterprising man experienced little difficulty in renting some grazing land and laying the foundations of a prosperous business. William Spenser of Radbourn, Warwickshire, had emerged from obscurity in this manner, paving the way for his son, John, who built up a large fortune which carried him high into the ranks of the Northamptonshire gentry, with a knighthood to crown it all. (Old families like the Treshams used to refer to him as a shepherd when they felt spiteful.) It is true that most of this took place at the time when peasants were liable to be thrown out of their farms to make way for sheep — Sir John himself earned the distinction of being carpeted by Cardinal Wolsey's commission on depopulation in 1517 — but most of the acres which nurtured the Spenser flocks had been enclosed and depopulated before they moved in, and the general finding is that most land which had been converted to sheepwalk was more or less empty in any case. For all that John Rous, the Warwickshire chronicler, might bitterly catalogue the villages which had vanished in his lifetime, and the Parliament of 1489 pass 'An Act Against the Pulling Down of Towns', there was a large element of shutting the door after the horse had bolted. The fifteenth century was not marked by the widespread agrarian disorder to which a desperate peasantry might have been expected to resort.

By the mid-sixteenth century the battleground had moved to the commons on to which the demesne flocks overflowed as they grew in size. Lords of manors enjoyed substantial residual rights over all unallotted land under their jurisdiction. Legally they might enclose the waste, provided only that they left sufficient of it for the freehold tenants, while their general rights of user were extensive and often ill-defined. Sometimes they or their farmers did indeed enclose it, to the detriment of the small tenants who thereby were put to sore straits to sustain their working beasts, and might perhaps even be driven to the point of being squeezed out. More commonly they simply flooded the commons with sheep, overstocking them, a practice which tended to produce the same result. Where, as not infrequently, they exceeded their legal or customary rights, they often got their way by *force majeure*. Disputes over rights of common were frequent, often protracted and invariably bitter.

The conflict of men versus sheep could be seen at its most acute form in Norfolk. There the East Anglian fold course custom encouraged landlords and their lessees to specialise in sheep on a large scale. The fold course consisted of certain rights of grazing sheep (not cattle) over the fields, meadows and commons of the manor, and since it could be leased a man could feed a large flock without actually holding any land. As long ago as 1520 the villagers of Sculthorpe had complained in the Star Chamber that Sir Henry Fermour pastured 800 sheep on a fold course where he actually owned not more than five acres of land. Since the custom also obliged the tenants to adapt the cultivation of their holdings to the movements of the flock the sheepmaster was tempted to extend the right, to keep his flock on their lands all the year round, thus converting the fold course into permanent pasture. The lord's ill-defined rights over the commons were also capable of abuse. When two gentlemen, John Pygott, the lord of the manor, and John Frencham, overburdened Straddett Common with 1,300 sheep, they put in jeopardy the survival of 12 ploughs, i.e. households; successive farmers of the demesne of Great Dunham kept 800 sheep on the common instead of the 740 to which they were entitled. Small wonder then that Sir Henry Parker's encroachment on Hingham Common had provoked a riot in 1539. Although the feed to be had on commons was generally of poor quality, surplus beasts, perhaps the inferior stock, could be dumped on them in the first instance. The lord might appropriate slices of the common contiguous to his fold course, countering the tenants' protests with the argument that since it was becoming overstocked in its unfenced state they would fare better with the exclusive use of the residue. Whatever the direction taken the outcome was the same: exorbitant demands on both the land itself and the patience of the peasantry whose livelihood depended on the reasonable use of it.

Sheep were inseparable from the arable husbandry of Norfolk, but the balance was a delicate one, easily upset by practices of this type. The light loams needed frequent and regular manuring which was achieved by folding sheep (whose dung was reckoned the best) nightly on each piece of ground in turn. The right to keep sheep belonged exclusively to the lord and his lessees. The custom dated back to the twelfth and thirteenth centuries when the manor had first and foremost been an organisation to support the cultivation of the demesne; not only was the flock kept in order to be folded on the demesne fields, it was also allowed to get a large part of its sustenance from the land of the tenantry. If, moreover, a tenant owned any sheep he was obliged to fold them with the demesne flock, or else pay the lord a composition for the right to pitch a fold of his own. Like many another convention it worked well enough so long as it was respected, but it led to a situation in which the peasant cultivator associated sheep with the land lord's rights and his own liabilities, while unreasonable exploitation of the fold course could cripple his farming, as could encroachment and overstocking on the commons by depriving him of the means of supporting his livestock. With a relatively dense population the demand for land was keen. Average holdings were small, between five and ten acres, enough to provide a living from growing corn, since the soil was highly fertile, but not large enough to feed the animals essential for tilling them. The market was brisk, and holdings were frequently bought on what amounted to hire purchase terms, with the consequence that many small men stood to lose heavily if their activities were disrupted

The agricultural community existed in a state of acute tension arising from the profound changes that were taking place in farming methods. After the relative depression of the preceding century a new vigour was being imparted by the emergence of a new breed of farmer who conducted his operations on a large scale and produced for the market. In this process the multitude of·small cultivators could not avoid a degree of discomfiture, since their primary aim was subsistence only; for this old fashioned methods did indeed suffice, but at the cost of impairing their ability to compete with ruthless, profit-conscious men.

Most peasants held their land by customary tenures. In many districts the custom of the manor gave them a great measure of security, but in others the lord of the manor held very much the upper hand and could force his tenants to adapt to the new order by exacting higher rents. Although the annual rent payable was almost everywhere fixed by custom, he could effectively raise it by demanding an entry fine which was arbitrary, determinable at his will. If he so wished he could force them out of their holdings in order to switch to large scale farming, either by amalgamating tenements to form larger units or by adding them to the demesne over which he exercised complete control. A certain John Bayker of Castle Combe, Wiltshire, who described himself as 'a poor artificer or craftsman', wrote:

> if a poor man come unto one of them [landlords] desiring him to be good unto him in this tenement or farm, that he might have it to inhabit, paying the rent for it as it hath been beforetime, he [the landlord] answers and says,
> 'If that thou wilt have this tenement of me thou must pay me so much money at thy coming in for a fine.'
> So he raiseth that thing which was never at no fine before to a great sum of money, and the rent to be paid yearly besides: the poor

man then seeing there is no remedy but either to have it, or to be destitute of a habitation, sells all that he hath from wife and children to pay the fine thereof. Then the landlord, perceiving the house in decay, will not repair it tenantable although the tenant paid never so much for his fine: so that the tenant cometh to a decayed thing: then the landlord, perceiving that the house is ready to fall down, doth call the tenant into the court, and there commands him to build up his house against a certain day in pain of forfeiting a certain sum of money. Then the poor man, because he paid so great a sum of money for the fine of it, is not able to build it up again so shortly. Then, for the second time he is called in again to the court and there commanded in pain of forfeiting his tenement to build it, so that the poor man, being not able to repair it, doth forfeit it again unto the lord. Then, because it is so far in decay, and the fine so great withal, no man is desirous to take it, so that the house cometh down shortly after.

'Yet,' saith the landlord, 'the lands shall raise me as much rent as they did before when the house was standing.'

And the holding, thrown together with another, is duly let to a richer man.

Except for isolated, usually unavailing outbursts of despairing anger, there was little the peasants could do about this kind of practice. But in some parts of the country a great many of them were small proprietors themselves, even though, as must be appreciated, most such freehold plots were very small and the owners usually augmented them by taking customary tenements in addition. Again in Norfolk this class was numerous, amounting on average to something like one-third of the peasantry; in East Flagg hundred it stood as high as one half. Such men not only had a secure base from which to defend their position, but also stood to suffer a much greater loss if they failed to resist the encroachments of the sheepmen. They knew their rights inside out: popular lore had it that the Norfolk farmer carried his copy of Lyttleton on Tenures with him when he went a-ploughing. The county was famous for the litigiousness of its inhabitants, and there was no accident in the fact that it supported more lawyers than any other in all England, many more than the maximum of eight permitted by a statute of 1455 designed to curb legal racketeering — and with good reason. Men accustomed to fighting stubbornly in the courts might easily take up other weapons in arenas where the law failed to protect them.

III

It might have been possible to assimilate the new ways in agriculture had they been the only problem. But from the third decade of the sixteenth century at least, the situation became bedevilled by two further crises which had infinitely more immediate and universal effects: population growth and price inflation.

Although vital statistics are sporadic and imperfect, one simple fact can be readily established: the population was increasing. The rate of growth was moderate, at most six per 1,000 per year. However, it appeared uncomfortably high for two reasons. It was somewhat above the average of approximately five per 1,000 which has been estimated for the centuries prior to the demographic revolution of the eighteenth century, while even more disturbing was the fact that it was growing at all. Past generations had become accustomed to a very low level of population. Even before the appearance of the Black Death it had begun to fall, and after the plague had reduced it by a third or more the decline had continued. Statistics are non-existent for the fifteenth century, but so far as trends can be deduced they suggest that the total fell below 2,000,000 around 1450 and may have remained near that level for some time. Somewhere around 1500 growth had resumed in earnest, and by 1522 the total population can be computed fairly reliably at very near 2,300,000. By 1549 it must have climbed to something like 2,750,000, perhaps more. The difficulty is that progress was irregular, a spurt followed by a check from some epidemic such as plague, typhus or the sweat. Periodically also the harvest failed, and then there could be famine in some places. It is impossible to estimate the effect of these setbacks. We can be certain that the wave of influenza in 1556—8 temporarily reduced the population by a substantial percentage, possibly 10 or more, but there are no statistics by which to measure the impact of epidemics before 1550. However, those parish registers which survive continously from the starting date in 1538 indicate that nothing comparable occurred in the 1540s at least, and so we may suspect that growth was very fast indeed at that time.

This phenomenon, however, was not recognised by the people to whom it was happening. On the contrary, what they noticed was depopulation, especially in the towns where houses stood unoccupied, either because their trade had fallen away, or they had been devastated by disease, which was mainly an urban scourge. But they also noticed, with mounting concern, one undoubted consequence of population growth, the increase in the numbers of poor and unemployed people. And since they did· not comprehend the demographic problem they placed the blame squarely on the pioneers of change, on landlords who jacked up rents beyond what farmers could afford to pay, on enclosers

nd engrossers of land, on graziers, even on the sheep themselves. Nor,
t should be emphasised, was this attitude merely the poor man's envy
f the rich, it was put forward in all seriousness by educated, well-
nformed observers seeking to expose the roots of the malaise in society
nd devise solutions.

Expanding population not only raised the demand for land and with
t the level of rent, but also, the supply of land being limited, added
onstantly to the numbers of landless labourers whose position worsened
teadily owing to the inability of the economy to expand so as to
reate sufficient employment, not surprisingly when public opinion
ociferously condemned the entrepreneur.

But while population growth amounted to something less than an
xplosion, inflation was accelerating to uncontrollable proportions.
Around the turn of the century the indices of prices and real wages had
tood near the 100 mark. Soon after 1510 the cost of foodstuffs – a
model shopping basket constructed by the researches of E. H. Phelps
Brown and S. V. Hopkins – began to climb noticeably, to 137 in 1520,
nd 169 in 1530, levelling out a little to 148 by 1540, but amounting,
one the less, to a rise of some 50 per cent in the cost of living in less
han half a century. Real wages declined correspondingly, to 73 in 1520
nd 59 in 1530. During the 1540s matters became so confused that it is
ow impossible to reconstruct the movement of wages, although there
re indications that they had begun to readjust themselves and to level
ut at about 60. From 1545 runaway inflation set in. The harvest of
hat year was a disastrous failure; the price of wheat averaged nearly
7s. 6d. per quarter (at Exeter it reached almost 20s.), the highest on
ecord and 42 per cent above the norm for the period. The next three
arvests were abundant, but although wholesale prices dropped the
ost of living index tended upwards, as shown in Table 1. It was not

Table 1

Year	Index
1545	191
1546	248
1547	231
1548	193
1549	214

imply a case of rising costs being passed on to the consumer; most producers were also feeling the pinch. In 1546–8 the average price of grain
ad receded to 7s.–9s. per quarter, pretty much the same as it had been
round 1540 when the consumer price index had been very much lower.

The great majority of producers were small farmers who sent only sma
quantities to market; lacking capital of their own, they were obliged t
exist largely on credit from one harvest to the next, when they had t
dispose of their produce as best they could:

> At Michaelmas time poor men must make money of their grain tha
> they may pay their rents. So long then as the poor man hath to sel
> rich men will bring out none, but rather buy up that which the poo
> bring

and at wretched prices! The poor husbandman had also to purchase hi
seed from the factor on disadvantageous terms.

The rise in consumer prices was paralleled by the upward movemen
of rents. This process is more difficult to view as a whole since i
depended on factors which varied greatly from one area to another
the custom of the district, even of the individual manor, the policy o
the individual estate owner, the relative strength of the positions of lor
and tenants. Very frequently the necessary evidence is inadequate, o
has been lost altogether. In the West of England rents for new tenancie
on the manors of Sir William Herbert were doubled in the decad
1530–9 as compared with 1520–9. In much the same region in th
decade 1540–9 they were 53 per cent up compared with 1510–19 o
the estates of the duke of Somerset. Rents on Crown lands rose mor
slowly; in the 1540s they averaged 17 per cent over the norm fo
1500–29 While it is obvious that there was no uniformity either in the
rate of increase or its timing, some at least of the complaints abou
excessive rents must have had a measure of justification.

In view of the rise in produce prices a rise in rents was inevitable
and by no means unreasonable. Indeed one might easily conclude tha
the farmers ought to have been able to take it in their stride. But this
was not so. Paradoxical as it may seem, the peasants had every reason
to be dissatisfied with the abundant harvests of 1546–8. The reason
was not so much the nominal price they received as the value of the
coin in which they were paid, that is the real price, for the government
had bedevilled the economy by debasing the currency. Debasement was
a device for bridging the gap between state revenue and expenditure by
making the stock of bullion go farther, that is, reducing the fineness of
coin by increasing the proportion of alloy, while of course retaining the
face value. Begun in a small way in 1526, it had been extended in 1542,
and from 1544–7 the Crown had embarked on a veritable orgy of
debasement until the amount of pure silver in the coinage had been
reduced to little more than a third of what it had formerly been. The
result was to drive all the purer coin out of circulation — Sir Thomas
Gresham enunciated his famous 'law' soon after this period — and
threw the price mechanism, and with it all economic activity, into
utter confusion. Inevitably it was the small man who suffered. The

farmer sold his produce for money, but when he came to purchase his necessaries he was informed that the debased coin could not be accepted at its face value and that consequently he must pay more. The labourer received his wages at the old rate, only to find that they would purchase much less than hitherto.

A conclusive explanation of the price revolution of the sixteenth century has yet to be produced. But it does not greatly matter whether it was the outcome of population growth, the influx of American silver, or marginal factors such as tampering with the currency. It is enough that it did occur and was causing acute distress and disruption. What is of greater interest at this point is the attitude adopted by contemporaries to this and other social and economic problems at the time. The point to stress is that what struck them most forcibly was the stark contrast between the bewildering changes they were now experiencing and the comfortable stability which had prevailed until comparatively recently. For something like half a century before 1515 prices and wages had maintained a steady equilibrium. For much the same period or even longer the population had been stabilised near or even below the 2,000,000 mark. Rents had remained unchanged for an even longer period. These conditions extended back not merely to the limits of living memory but well beyond them into times which now could be known only from the fond recollections of long-dead grandparents. From the misery and strife of the England of Edward VI men looked enviously back to a golden age, or at least a tranquil one, and railed against the slings and arrows of outrageous fortune.

IV

The golden age was protrayed by a 65-year-old bishop preaching before the boy King, recalling his own happier childhood.

> My father was a yeoman, and had no lands of his own, only he had a farm of three or four pounds by year at the uttermost, and thereupon he tilled as much as kept half a dozen men. He had walk for a hundred sheep; and my mother milked thirty kine. He was able, and did find the king a harness, with himself and his horse, while he came to the place that he should receive the king's wages. I can remember that I buckled his harness when he went unto Blackheath Field. He kept me to school, or else I had not been able to preach before the king's majesty now. He married my sisters with five pound or twenty nobles apiece: so that he brought them up in godliness and fear of God. He kept hospitality for his poor neighbours, and some alms he gave to the poor. All this he did of the said farm, where he that now hath it payeth sixteen pound by year, or more, and is not able to do anything for his prince, for himself, nor for his children, or give a cup of drink to the poor.

Irresistible as coming from the heart of a sad old man, Hugh Latimer's classic description of an English yeoman is much more than a mere nostalgic recollection; it compresses into a few words of imperishable prose the whole philosophy of his age.

He was one of several preachers and writers who set out to diagnose the sickness which afflicted society. These Commonwealth Men, as their critics somewhat contemptuously called them, did not in any sense form an organised group or party, indeed their only common characteristic was that they were all Protestants, the majority clergymen. If Latimer was the most eminent, Thomas Lever, another brilliant preacher, represented the younger generation, while the literary men included Thomas Becon, Henry Brinkelowe and Robert Crowley who significantly, produced the first printed edition of *The Vision of Piers Plowman,* the medieval *De Profundis* of the peasantry. There was also the minor government official, John Hales, Clerk of the Hanaper, who laboured unremittingly to secure practical reforms.

Vehemently assailing the causes of the malaise in society, they appear as economists and moralists rolled into one: we must remind ourselves that what economic theory there was in those days was a branch of moral theology. Paradoxically, they seemed also to combine radicalism in religion with extreme conservatism, even reactionism, over social questions. Yet in their own minds no conflict existed. The mission of the reformers was to re-establish what they believed to be the purity of faith and simplicity of worship of the primitive church and to hark back to an earlier, more tranquil society was perfectly consistent.

Greed was their *leitmotif,* the selfish pursuit of excessive profit by individuals indifferent to the interests of the community. It took many forms. There was the landlord's exploitation of his tenants by exacting inordinate rents, the engrossment of farms, and the accompanying 'gathering of divers men's livings into one . . . hand' which happened when a man took a second holding other than that on which he had been reared. There was manipulation of the markets by forestallers, engrossers and regrators, dealers who cornered commodities, creating artificial scarcities leading to enhanced prices. And, needless to say, the list was headed by enclosers and graziers.

The main weight of the Commonwealth Men's anger was reserved for the gentry, not indeed all of them but those who conspicuously fell short of the ideal. Never for one moment did they suggest that gentlemen should be liquidated — they preached not class war but social harmony — for the upper class had an essential part to play in the community as governors and magistrates. But the existence of gentlemen was justified by the devotion with which they discharged the duties to which they were born, to protect the weak, succour the nfortunate and punish the wicked; in a word to be fathers to their hildren. Nor was their title to superior wealth questioned; it was llowed that they were exempt from manual labour. But it was precisely his wealth that gave them the power to do good, and unhappily too nany of them neglected their duty in the pursuit of private gain, and he community suffered correspondingly. Worst of all were the ones vho operated on the fringe of the class, the hard-faced men ruthlessly lawing their way up the ladder in this age of unprecedented social nobility, many of them upstart yeomen farmers, ever watchful for a hrewd deal, or lawyers skilled in profiting from other men's adversities, nd petty local officials who corruptly exploited the opportunities onferred by their positions of trust.

Equally reprehensible was the merchant class, the City of London. 'he Commonwealth Men did not call it the Great Wen but they loathed : as passionately as William Cobbett. Here wealth was massed on a cale they regarded as sinful; wealth that sapped the vitality of the rovinces, as witness the decay of once proud cities; wealth too that vas not the righteous fruit of honest toil in field and workshop but the surious profit of commerce, of overseas trade which was doubly bnoxious because it flooded the land with foreign wares, demoralising uxuries which not only put native artisans out of work but also drained he kingdom of silver and so led directly to high prices.

The concentration of inordinate and unprecedented wealth in the ands of the few was contrasted with the unprecedented increase in ardship and poverty. The land abounded with beggars, or so it ppeared; people whose livelihoods had been taken from them when heir homes had been pulled down to make way for sheep, when lready large farmers had outbid them for the tenancies of the small-oldings they might once upon a time have expected to occupy; when armers had taken to weaving, or whatever, and merchants to speculation n land; servants turned adrift when the monasteries had been dissolved, r when country squires shut up their manor houses and migrated to he fleshpots of London in search of favour and fortune at court. All of hem were the victims of covetousness, of the 'greedy gulls and cor-norants' who preyed on the weak and defenceless. And even for those rho had some occupation, times were hard when grasping landlords acked the rents, and forestallers and regrators drove up food prices, rhile wages remained low. It matters not that modern research fails o confirm the truth of much of this. What really matters is what men elieved at the time to be happening — to them. And when they saw he Parliament of landowners and merchants actually make poverty a rime punishable by savage penalties, they could scarcely doubt that he state had been taken over by a breed of men whose policy was to ob the poor for the benefit of the rich.

Unquestionably there was a major redistribution of wealth in pro gress at this time. The rich were certainly getting richer, while the poor necessarily became poorer as their number grew with the increase in population; not only did wages tend to lag far behind prices, but the proportion of the population destined to remain landless labourers also increased rapidly.

Whether or not contemporary observers grasped the true nature of what was going on, the real causes of economic dislocation and social discontent, they were acutely conscious of the results, and desperately afraid of what they might lead to, social strife. And when it came in 1549, Robert Crowley had no hesitation in declaring what brought it about. Asked for his opinion of the causes of sedition, the poor countryman would declare

> that the great farmers, the graziers, the rich butchers, the men of law, the merchants, the gentlemen, the knights, the lords, and I can not tell who; men who have no name because they are doers in all things that any gain hangeth upon. Men without conscience . . utterly devoid of God's fear . . . that live as though there were no God at all . . . are the causes of Sedition! They take our houses over our heads, they levy great (yea unreasonable) fines, they enclose our commons! No custom, law or statute can keep them from oppressing us in such sort, that we know no which way to turn us to live Very need therefore constraineth us to stand up against them.

These greedy cormorants, in their turn, boldly justified themselves

> The peasant knaves to be too wealthy, provender pricketh them They know not themselves, they would know no obedience, they regard no laws, they would have no gentlemen, they would have all men like themselves, they would have all things in common. They would not have us masters of that which is our own: they will appoint us what rent we shall take for our grounds! . . . They will have the law in their own hands . . . . They will compel the King to grant their requests.

Thus simply did they reduce the problem to one of defence of property and in a grim afterthought on the rebellions,

> We will teach them to know their betters. And because they would have all common, we will leave them nothing. And if they once stir again, or do but once cluster together, we will hang them at their own doors! Shall we suffer the villains to disprove our doings? No we will be lords of our own and use it as we shall think good

So the rift in society widened inexorably, each party stubbornly insisting on recognising no interest but its own. As early as 1535–6 an anonymous advocate of agrarian reform had asserted with fine impartiality:

All people in England liveth commonly even as they list with works of sin and mischief to get single riches one from another, having no dread of God, but only dreading the actual pains and punishment of the law, howsoever the wicked people worketh mischief to destroy one another, whereby to destroy the common weal of the whole realm.

t was perhaps this universal wickedness which decreed that the rophets of disaster should remain unhonoured and unheard, relegated o the wilderness of neglect, there to cry out helplessly while the nation arched blindly towards catastrophe. But the common people had no oubts about the justice of their cause, and felt driven to desperation:

No remedy, therefore, we must needs fight it out, or else be brought to the like slavery the French men are in! . . . Better it were, therefore, for us to die like men, than after so great misery in youth to die more miserably in age!

And yet the real tragedy lay in the fact that for all their Christian ompassion for the oppressed, the rigid conservatism of the Common-wealth Men inhibited them from formulating a coherent philosophy on hich a practicable social policy could have been based. With the ossible exception of the author of the *Discourse of the Common Weal*, hey evinced no concern to understand the nature of the changes going n all round them, but were satisfied merely to condemn them out of and. They had nothing new to say. They pinned their faith on a imly remembered past state of affairs, which Latimer idealised in the erson of his father; which they unshakeably believed to have been finitely more commendable than the present. A generation earlier ir Thomas More had gone further and located his vision of an ideal ociety in the imaginary island of Utopia, but while their aspirations ad much in common with his they lacked his comprehensive view and ould only clutch at the visible vestiges of the vanished past.

Of necessity their ideas were rooted in contemporary England. The ation personified in yeoman Latimer of Thurcaston, Leicestershire, as a community of small producers, farmers cultivating a few acres, ufficient to sustain one family apiece, master craftsmen working on heir own assisted by a mere handful of journeymen and apprentices, ach of whom looked forward to the day when he himself would set p as a master. It was the unshakeable belief of many in those days that o man should aspire to own more than was needful to support himself nd his dependents free from want. If no one became inordinately rich, obody could be condemned to poverty. *Utopia* had sketched a rimitive form of communism, but the creed of the Commonwealth Men was really populism, the cult of the little man. In a rough kind of ay society at the beginning of the sixteenth century had conformed to he populist model. Almost exactly half the population of the little

county of Rutland had consisted of medium or small farmers, husband
men as they were described. In the general assessment of 1522 th
median valuation of household goods and farming stock had bee
roughly £5, and there had been comparatively few men worth mor
than £20. It is unlikely that many of them farmed as many as 50 acres
most of them probably had much less, and over and above thei
immediate needs they could hardly have produced for the market mor
than what sufficed to pay the rent and purchase the few articles the
were unable to fabricate for themselves. Since rents in general were no
high, no special effort was necessary. At the turn of the century th
Venetian envoy had stressed that although the English lived well, thei
farmers grew only what was essential and that much of the land was lef
uncultivated. Yeomen formed a minority of more prosperous cultivato
with a more commercial outlook: the milk of Mrs Latimer's 30 cow
must have produced a considerable quantity of Leicestershire cheese
But there were not many yeoman farmers: in several villages in Rutlan
there was not a single inhabitant worth more than about £10 in good
and chattels, and this held good for other counties as well. Scarcel
0.5 per cent were described as craftsmen and tradesmen, but the
Rutland had no rural manufactures, and there were only two in
significant market towns. It is virtually certain that all these craftsme
divided their time between their trade and agriculture, a fact whic
emphasised the complexity of the problem of the period. It meant, o
course, that they engaged in two occupations at once, but since the
served only a minute local market, they could hardly have made a livin
had they done otherwise.

Less than half the population (about 45 per cent) were classed a
labourers and servants, that is, wage earners. Indeed the line betwee
the labouring people and the tenants of very small patches of land wa
much blurred, for the latter usually needed some source of income
such as occasional day labouring, to supplement what they could ek
out of their plots. Conversely, there were casual labourers who relie
greatly on keeping a cow on the commons, as the *Discourse of th
Common Weal* pointed out:

> there be many a thousand cottagers in England which, having n
> lands to live of their own but their handy labours, and some r
> freshing upon the said commons, if they were suddenly thrust ou
> from that commodity might make a great tumult and discord i
> the common wealth.

For some local reason Rutland had become rather a backwater fro
which population tended to drift away, leaving a relatively modes
number of such people. In many other counties the proportion wh
had possessed no goods worth valuation in 1522 or were taxed as wag
earners in 1524 amounted to well over half the total, up to 60 per cen

r more in East Anglia where many worked as weavers and other
peratives in the clothing industry and were vulnerable to the changing
onditions of trade.

No other comparable survey was undertaken during the Tudor
eriod, and so it is impossible to make a precise estimate of the position
s it stood in 1549. But we can be certain that a substantial increase in
opulation in the interim, unmatched by equivalent economic growth,
ad greatly intensified pressure on available resources. The absolute
umber of peasant smallholders and master craftsmen working for
1emselves may have suffered little diminution, but in an increasingly
ompetitive economy, which the majority were ill equipped to cope
/ith, they found both livelihood and status continuously eroded, their
/orld tumbling around their ears.

They didn't ask for much. The case for the common man was stated
y John Bayker. Having 'travelled or gone through the most part of
the] realm to earn and get my living', the evidence of decay and
eglect to be seen everywhere had appalled him:

> Is it not a pitiful case, to come into a little village or town where
> there hath been twenty or thirty houses and now are half of them
> nothing but bare walls standing? Is it not a pitiful case to see one
> man have it in his hands which did suffice two or three men when
> the habitations were standing?

he consequence was vagrancy and crime. Yet all this 'inconvenience'
ould so easily be avoided,

> For if so were that every man might have in towns and villages but
> one little house or cottage to inhabit, and but a little garden ground
> withal they would so order it with labour that they would earn their
> living, so should there no place be untilled nor without inhabiters.

\nd this could be achieved if only the King were to compel the gentle-
1en to whom he had granted estates to 'let them again unto your poor
ubjects to inhabit and till, that they, paying their rent truly to their
andlords, might have a sufficient and complete living by their labours'.

In the final analysis the learned Commonwealth Men could add
1othing to this. They moralised, but ethics are relative and theirs were
iut of date; the very men they exhorted to return to the narrow paths
if righteousness contemptuously brushed their pleadings aside as
rrelevant. The *Discourse of the Common Weal* alone essayed an
ibjective analysis. Cast as a Socratic dialogue between a landlord, a
iusbandman, a merchant and a craftsman, with a learned doctor to act
s moderator, each protagonist describes his plight as a victim of the
conomic whirlwind, and seeks an explanation. There are no villains,
he bogeymen of the clerical polemecists having dissolved into
mpersonal forces. Yet in the end, short of admitting that he can find

no answer, the author is forced back on the old stalking horse
enclosures and sheep.

Everyone was agreed that ultimately the remedy lay in action by th
state. There were good laws on the Statute Book, but they wer
blatantly defied, indeed treated as though they had never been made
Not since 1517, when Cardinal Wolsey had investigated the agraria
question, had any serious attempt been made to enforce them; eve
Wolsey's had come to naught, like so many of his schemes. The *Suppl*
cation of the Poor Commons, composed *c.* 1546, had adjured th
King to 'remember that your office is to defend the innocent an
punish the oppressor'. The unknown author, Protestant and ant
clerical, had formerly been disposed to blame the corrupt an
over-mighty Church for the affliction of the people; but now the clerg
had been tamed, the monasteries suppressed and their lands disperse
and yet he was deeply perplexed that things had not improved, ha
worsened if anything, and he was apprehensive of the future: 'Prince
are punished when the people offend' — a broad hint that revolutio
might not be far away.

Yet there was a faint hope that the worst might be averted. Th
death of Henry VIII had brought to power a man who showed som
interest in the views of the Commonwealth group — Edward Seymou
duke of Somerset. Even so, the auguries were unfavourable, for b
1549 his administration was surviving largely on sufferance, and th
outbreak of disorder could not have come at a worse moment for him

V

Government during a royal minority invariably posed a problem und
a constitution which concentrated all power in the person of th
monarch, and the autocratic Henry VIII's final legacy to his kingdo
had been to make it very much worse. Rather than appoint a regen
he had nominated a body of executors who, in carrying out his last wil
would also act as his son's Council, giving effect to his intention c
virtually ruling England from the grave until the boy came of ag
While he could not give them instructions as such, he could, and di
attempt to create a situation designed to prevent any changes of sul
stance being made in the policies he himself had developed during h
last years. The choice of executors represented a balancing of differer
outlooks which, it was anticipated, would tend to cancel one anoth
out. It was further backed up by the provision of the Act of Successio
1536, which authorised the young Edward VI to repeal all the Acts c
Parliament passed during his minority, on coming of age.

Henry's problem was to ensure the continuation of a policy tha was shot through and through with contradictions. On the one hand he had broken with Rome and the Catholic world, reduced the Church to dependence on the Crown, and destroyed the monasteries. On the other hand, while making use of Protestants to further these innovations, he had vetoed absolutely any dilution of Catholic doctrine and forms of worship, and was keenly aware that this compromise would never satisfy the stronger personalities among the ranks of his advisers. So long as he lived he had been able to control and use them, but once he was dead they would be at liberty to follow their own inclinations. The majority of the regency Council was therefore composed of moderate Protestants and *politiques*, men who were fundamentally Catholic yet uncommitted to any pronounced line of action. Extremists were excluded, in particular those Catholics on whom he had much relied in his later years, including the brilliant Stephen Gardiner, bishop of Winchester, who was perhaps the most formidable politician in the kingdom. Among the conservative lay leaders, the most powerful family in the land, the Howards, had just accomplished their own downfall, the earl of Surrey having been executed for treason, while only Henry's own demise had saved the head of his one-time hatchet man, the duke of Norfolk, although he was destined to remain in confinement until 1553.

Nevertheless, almost before the old King had breathed his last the will had been set aside by the man to whom he had entrusted it for safekeeping, his brother-in-law, Edward Seymour, then earl of Hertford. Through the long hours of waiting for Henry's death, on 28 January 1547, Hertford had concerted other plans with his friend, Sir William Paget, one of the Secretaries of State, who stood high in the old King's confidence. They decided, and other members of the Privy Council concurred, to withold the news of Henry's death for a few days, as well as to suppress that part of the will which purported to lay down the future structure of government. Immediately Henry had expired, the earl proceeded to Hertford Castle to escort the new King, his nephew, to London, while Paget convened the remainder of the Council and secured from them agreement to appoint Hertford Lord Protector, in other words regent. Their assent was readily given, for they did not see how the kingdom could otherwise be governed. Indeed no other course was practicable, since the machinery of state could not function without one man at its head who was competent to take all major decisions, in whom an immense array of powers was concentrated. Ironically, it was Henry's own policy of raising royal despotism to an unprecedented level which had helped to make the appointment inescapable.

There was ample precedent for the election of a Protector, dating from the minorities of Henry VI in 1422 and Edward V in 1483. In 1547, however, the situation was different. Henry had had no younger brother who would have been the obvious candidate for the post. He had a grown-up daughter, the Lady Mary, now aged 32, who could have handled the job perfectly well; but having succeeded in reducing his family affairs to unparalleled chaos, in consequence of which even her legal status was uncertain, he could hardly have entrusted the government to her. It is true that in making his will he had faced up to the fact that so long as Edward remained a minor she would have to be recognised as his successor; but, revering her mother's memory as she did, Mary had remained an uncompromising Catholic who was almost certain to attempt to undo the whole of her father's work, and might conceivably go so far as to imitate Richard III and do away with her young half-brother. Meaningless though the 'ifs' of history must necessarily be, it is tempting to speculate that had Henry adhered more closely to natural law, indeed commonsense, the agonies of the ensuing 11 years might have been avoided. Englishmen in the sixteenth century had a strong sense of legality. Mary, as regent, might have done the job conscientiously — she had certainly inherited enough of her father's, indeed her mother's, strength of character to be able to do it effectively. She might well have conceded that there could be no real question as to her brother's legitimacy, as there was about her sister Elizabeth's, since Henry had married the boy's mother after the death of Catherine of Aragon. And finally, she might have ascended the throne in her own right less obviously a faded, embittered spinster had she been spared a further six years of humiliation made all the worse for being inflicted by low born ministers: as well as being her father, Henry had at least been unchallenged monarch. One cannot help feeling that had power come sooner and more easily she might have proved more than a little reluctant to submit to Rome, save on terms of her own making.

Other considerations militated against the little King's maternal uncle, Hertford. The chief of these was his birth. Although a good family long established in the West Country, the Seymours had ranked no higher than provincial squires until Henry VIII had spotted in Edward a soldier of promise, and chosen Jane for his third wife. There was the clear risk that his authority might not be accepted, either by the old aristocracy or the new military and administrative élite whom Henry himself had raised up, and who might only too readily adopt the attitude that a Seymour was no better than themselves, his relationship to the royal family notwithstanding. Equally material, Hertford was a devout Calvinist who, given the opportunity, was certain to try and lead England into the Protestantism which the old King abhorred. Thus Henry had fallen back on this curious arrangement for collective government.

As things had turned out his colleagues readily accepted Hertford's claim to supreme power. Honours were handed out liberally: Paget, as confidant of the late King, was able to announce — probably quite correctly — that Henry had already planned to bestow them on the men to whom he proposed committing his son and his realm. Seymour's own advancement to be duke of Somerset may, however, have been something additional, hatched up between himself and Paget (who discreetly refrained from awarding himself a peerage) in order to give the Protector precedence over his colleagues: Norfolk, the only other adult duke, lay a prisoner in the Tower.

Yet it may be supposed that the assent of the other executors was basically negative, that they were content to allow Seymour to assume an office which none of them was prepared to undertake. He held it on sufferance, and there would always be the authority of Henry's will in reserve to justify his removal. This document, indeed, came to be the skeleton in the cupboard, for although important parts of it had been withheld from the public, their existence was widely known — or suspected — and their supposed tenor became the pretext for every act of defiance against the government over the next two years, with everyone making out that they contained whatever it suited him to believe. Meanwhile the Protector was free to exercise all the powers of the Crown. He was widely and with satisfaction hailed as the rightful ruler of the kingdom. But at the same time, should his authority wane as a consequence of failure to govern effectively, he could expect no forebearance.

In his own day Somerset acquired the reputation of 'the good duke', deeply concerned with social justice, a reputation which led later historians to represent him as a liberal reformer struggling vainly against a reactionary ruling class. This view has now been convincingly demolished by Dr Bush who has shown him to have been a thoroughly conventional man of his time whose disagreements with his colleagues concerned methods and timing, never principles. So far from possessing a tender social conscience, he was in fact a large scale sheepmaster, encloser and rackrenter. In the building of Somerset House he too openly exploited his great power to enrich himself at public expense; corruption was normal in public life, and was tolerated for much of the time, but as soon as a minister showed signs of failure it was dragged up against him.

It was Somerset's misfortune to lack the politician's arts. He tried to do too much too quickly, and, confident in his own judgment, failed to distinguish between what was practicable and what lay beyond his grasp. Ultimately, with several incompatible projects going ahead simultaneously, he lost control of all of them and became the prisoner of events. The flaw was his lack of ideals; the motive force of all his policy was an obsession with the conquest of Scotland to which all other considerations were subordinated.

From Henry VIII he had inherited a war resulting from a grand design to unite the two crowns by the marriage of Edward to the infant Queen of Scots. In principle the scheme made sense. Throughout the sixteenth century Scotland's independence was becoming ever more precarious. English kings had always laid claim to suzerainty over the northern realm, and periodically attempted to assert it by force. It was virtually inevitable that sooner or later Scotland would drift into dependence on England, and perhaps only Henry's fascination with the illusion of resplendent victories on the continent had preserved its integrity thus far. Pressing eagerly ahead, in the summer of 1547 Somerset marched into Scotland at the head of a large army and won an overwhelming victory at Pinkie. But politically the campaign proved barren. The 'rough wooing' of Mary, Queen of Scots, was self-defeating. She was hurried away to France to be bethrothed to the Dauphin, while a formidable French army was rushed across to Scotland. Having little faith in periodic invasions by large and costly armies which seemed incapable of producing lasting results, Somerset now switched to a policy of establishing garrisons as a means of controlling the country, the chief of which was located at Haddington. However, for the whole of 1548 it was blockaded by Franco-Scottish forces and only held at the cost of great exertions, while shortage of money inhibited resumption of the 'forward policy'. Scotland was fast declining into a French satellite, while England was becoming encircled.

Although the situation in the North did not as such amount to a direct confrontation with France, relations tended inevitably to deteriorate. The bone of contention was Boulogne which Henry VIII had captured in 1544. Although the French had recognised the English occupation for the time being, they could not be expected to tolerate it indefinitely, and there was constant bickering as they applied intermittent pressure against the defences which the English were systematically strengthening in flagrant disregard of the treaty. In the latter months of 1548 war weariness on both sides dictated a degree of détente, but England's position was daily becoming more precarious as Somerset's inept combination of bare-faced aggression and naïve diplomacy brought the country to the brink of complete isolation. The traditional ally, the Emperor Charles V, was wholly absorbed in his efforts to contain Protestantism in Germany. A renewal of hostilities with France was the last thing he wanted at this juncture. At such times as he did go to war with her, English participation was a handy diversion, but the defence of English interests in no way formed a necessary element in his policy. Thus he steadily declined to yield to insistent pressure to guarantee Boulogne, until finally, in 1549, he refused point blank. Pressure on the perimeter of Boulogne was of course one way of distracting attention from Scotland, but by the spring of 1549 the French government, yielding to Scotch demands, had decided to reinforce their army in Scotland — rumours of a projected drive against Berwick were circulating — while Somerset resolved to mount yet another invasion in strength in order to establish further garrisons, and was making strenuous efforts to recruit continental mercenaries.

In pursuing this spectacular foreign policy Somerset enjoyed the full support of his colleagues, despite the heavy financial burden and absence of tangible gains. But preoccupation with it resulted in the mishandling of other and more urgent problems.

The enduring legacy of the Protectorate was the transformation of England into a Protestant country. The moment was opportune. For some 30 years the reformed faith had steadily been gaining adherents. Its numerical strength at this time cannot be estimated but it was already well established in the ranks of the gentry as well as among the merchant class whose members had been exposed to it in their contacts with the continent. It had also claimed the allegiance of many of the clergy, especially those with a keen sense of vocation. Among the common people the persistent strain of Lollardy, which had survived since the beginning of the previous century in numerous pockets, defying fierce persecution, had provided a fertile seedbed in the eastern half of the country. Henry VIII's repression had indeed limited the growth of Protestantism but had been unable to stop it. The main result of his policy had been to reduce Catholics to a condition of numbness. Men such as More and Fisher who had stood up to him out of conviction had been ruthlessly cut down, leaving as leaders of the conservative interest men who were almost exclusively political in their outlook with, on the whole, little in the way of principles, and certainly no vestige of popular appeal.

In reality Catholicism now survived principally as a body of doctrine imposed by law, the Act of Six Articles passed in 1539 — the 'whip with six strings' as it was popularly called — which had defined heresy as denial of the most controversial Catholic dogmas and transferred it from the sphere of canon law to that of criminal law.

As a convinced Calvinist, Somerset might have been expected to speed the changes for which there was now widespread enthusiam. Among the first measures of the Parliament of 1547 were the repeal of the Six Articles and the Act *De Heretico Comburendo* of 1401 which compelled the burning of heretics at the stake. For a brief spell there was an interlude during which Englishmen enjoyed something resembling freedom of belief. In many parts of the country zealous Protestants anticipated the coming changes, taking it upon themselves to remove ornaments from churches and make unauthorised experiments with the liturgy. Independent action of this nature, however, smacked of in-discipline. The government had not the slightest intention of inaugurating an era of toleration, and did not hesitate to take steps to curb these excesses of zeal pending the introduction of planned, orderly change. The Protector himself had to interrupt his victorious return journey from Scotland in the autumn of 1547 to calm down the people of St Neots: the eastern counties were already a stronghold of the Reformation. Early in the following year the Council had to impose restraints on preachers, many of whom were downright inflammatory. The reality was that religion was not the first priority, and in consequence Somerset's policy proved contradictory. Much as he might appear to depart from precedent and permit people to say what they liked, as regent of an absolute monarchy he never showed the slightest sign of letting them do as they liked; indeed the momentary freedom of opinion was unintentional. The form of religion would be what the Crown in Parliament judged beneficial for the nation as a whole; there could be no question of tolerating dissent. The new order would have to be acceptable to the widest possible range of belief; it would also have to be framed so as not to alienate the Emperor. The object was a holding operation designed to avoid any disruption of the Scottish project. The risk was that in seeking to satisfy all he would end by pleasing none.

From the previous reign the government inherited a project to dissolve chantries and gilds and confiscate their property. The surveys had already been executed, and the takeover was effected smoothly. Eleven years earlier the dissolution of the monasteries had provoked a serious rebellion in the North Country. To many people the end of the gilds was a good deal less palatable because it deprived numerous parishes of institutions which formed an intimate part of their existence. Yet there was no resistance, even though the inhabitants of nearly every one of them had pleaded for exemption, for as often as not the chantry priest was the only minister they had. The government was unmoved; it needed extra revenue to finance the conquest of Scotland. The dissolution was speedily followed by the arrival of Crown commissioners to take inventories of the plate and other articles belonging to each parish church, which looked suspiciously like the preliminary to a further round of confiscation. In fact the task had been made necessary by the activities of sundry unscrupulous persons who had seized the opportunity to make off with church goods, and was intended as a safeguard. It did provoke a local riot in the far west of Cornwall in April 1548, during which the archdeacon was murdered. But the affair was largely a matter of personal antipathies in a district notorious for unrest; it had not spread, and indeed other parts of the county had rallied to the side of law and order.

In 1548 a start was made with the reform of ritual. The Council decreed by proclamation that the sacrament should be administered to the laity in both kinds, and abolished ceremonies deemed superfluous, such as candles at Candlemas, ashes on Ash Wednesday, palms on Palm Sunday, and creeping to the Cross on Good Friday. Services, including the Mass, were permitted to be said in English in St Paul's and some other London churches. Many welcomed the innovations, few displayed any hostility.

The greatest innovation of all had still to come, an entirely new ritual in the vernacular. Thomas Cranmer, archbishop of Canterbury, had already been at work on it for some time, and in September 1548 a draft had probably been shown to a meeting of bishops who had apparently given it a general approval, although when it came to be debated in the House of Lords deep differences of opinion among them were revealed. Nevertheless, on 31 March 1549 the royal assent was signified to the Act of Uniformity which made the new liturgy compulsory in every church in the land from Whitsunday onwards.

In its essentials the *Book of Common Prayer* was a compromise, and thus proved a disappointment to many Protestants. It was based on the Sarum Use — the Latin service book most widely used in England — with numerous simplifications, and material drawn from other sources. In a conscious gesture to conservative opinion it maintained a discreet ambiguity on all points involving fundamental doctrine, especially the central one of transubstantiation, and indeed the general form of the order for the Supper of the Lord differed little from the Mass. Even Stephen Gardiner announced from his detention in the Tower that he would be prepared to use the book. The prospects for a favourable reception looked bright, in spite of stray reports of priests attempting to whip up opposition to it, notably in certain Midland counties where there were already agrarian grievances. All that remained to be done was to print and distribute copies to all churches in time for the appointed day.

Most controversial of Somerset's policies was his attempt to promote agrarian reforms. At the very least it marked a break with the recent past. Not for 30 years had government made any attempt to remedy abuses on the land. Wolsey's initiative in 1517 had produced a mass of evidence relating to enclosures and depopulation, followed by a considerable number of prosecutions, but the final result had been negligible. Meanwhile the situation was fast assuming the proportions of a major crisis, and the need for action to enforce the law was becoming urgent.

The Protector himself cared little for social reform as such: the revolutionary character of his policy was one of the allegations framed subsequently to justify his overthrow. The measures adopted generally show no concern for the lower orders; designed mainly to preserve the traditional framework of society, they served equally to protect the 'oppressed' aristocrat. He was, none the less, genuinely worried about the effect of depopulation on the stability of the state, but in the long run his real concern was to eliminate grievances before they could interfere with his cherished Scottish project. Certainly his personal intervention has been greatly overestimated. The private act to give protection to copyholders on his own estates, which he put through in the Parliamentary session of 1548–9, benefited only a very limited class, and was not even unique.

Credit for initiating reform belongs to John Hales. As burgess for Preston he introduced, in the first session of Parliament, bills to restore tillage, to enforce the keeping of cows in addition to sheep, and prevent dealers in victuals manipulating the markets. They got rough handling in a legislature composed almost entirely of landowners, and were all rejected, along with others designed to secure the rights of tenant farmers and provide for the upbringing of poor men's sons. All that emerged was an act to control the growing problem of poverty; but while drawing a distinction between the able-bodied (and by definition idle) and the impotent poor, it emphasised almost exclusively the suppression of 'idleness', prescribing branding and slavery for convicted vagrants.

Not until the middle of 1548 did the government embark on a programme of social reform. In May it set an example by disparking the royal deer chase at Hampton Court which Henry VIII had lately established, to the detriment of the inhabitants of 11 parishes, and which the accession of a child to the throne had rendered superfluous. (The gesture would be more impressive had not Somerset been concurrently engaged in enlarging his private park at Savernake.) On 1 June a proclamation was published which condemned enclosures and depopulation in uncompromising terms.

Effective measures, however, could only be implemented on a basis of incontrovertible evidence, and simultaneously the government appointed commissions with wide powers to investigate the extent of the problem and how far existing laws were being observed. The only one which got down to work was that headed by Hales himself which toured the Midlands. None the less, it unearthed numerous offences. At Cambridge alone these involved at least 16 persons (three of whom could not be identified) as well as Jesus College. The list included two cases of farmhouses which had been severed from their land, and two more which had been allowed to fall down, as well as four almshouses. Six closes had been made out of common land, while in eight cases baulks and pathways had been ploughed or stopped up. A certain Mr Braken was found to be keeping upwards of 600 sheep on the common, and to make a practice of turning large numbers of cattle on to the stubble at Lammastide, crowding out the animals of other tenants. That

Hales went about his work with a will is clear from the fact that in the next session of Parliament he was roundly accused of fomenting trouble, and not without cause, for although he indignantly rebutted the charge, his speeches when empanelling juries were certainly inflammatory. His enquiries led to numerous presentments of offenders, including even the earl of Warwick who, at a Council meeting, blamed him for causing the riots which broke out in Buckinghamshire and Oxfordshire in the wake of the commission. But despite having stirred up a hornets' nest, success was minimal. The juries empanelled to determine the complaints were all too easily intimidated, while landowners coolly claimed that pastures across which they ploughed a single furrow had been restored to tillage, or stuck a single bullock in a field usually occupied by sheep as proof that it was used for fattening cattle.

By the spring of 1549 it began to look as though Hales's detractors were right and that he had stirred up trouble. The root of the problem was that there were already numerous laws designed to combat agrarian abuses, but that nothing was done to enforce them. The gentry did not in the least mind how many there were provided they were allowed to lie dormant. But the government had announced that the law was now to be rigorously enforced, while at the same time the investigations yielded little in the way of tangible results by the time the commissions retired to winter quarters. One reason for suspending their work was Hales's desire to attend the new session of Parliament where he planned to introduce a new and more stringent bill based on his findings in the field. Like his earlier proposals, it was ill-received, thanks, apparently, to the provocative way in which he presented it. To the peasantry, however, it looked very much like one example of the selfishness and hostility of the gentry. This time the people were not content to bow to their inevitable fate. Convinced that they enjoyed the sympathetic approval of 'the good duke', they decided to implement his schemes themselves by enforcing his decrees in spite of the gentlemen, to give the machine the push it needed to get it moving. And so, as spring advanced, they took the law into their own hands and started throwing down enclosures.

A further aggravation was a controversial poll tax on sheep which Somerset had just forced through Parliament. The purpose, as set forth in the lengthy preamble, was to make sheepmen foot the cost of the war — out of what was believed to be their unearned profits. Superficially it appeared to discriminate against large flocks by means of a graduated scale which ranged from 3d. a head for ewes and 2d. for other shearlings kept on enclosed ground, down to 1d. a head on flocks of 11–20 head, and ½d. in the case of flocks of 10 or less. This naturally placed a disproportionate burden on the small man, but it was not, as has often been supposed, intended to tax large scale grazing out of existence, but merely to help finance the Scottish campaign.

The growth of disorder placed Somerset in an intolerable position. Tudor rulers gave orders, men obeyed. When the King's subjects, the lower orders in particular, started to think and act for themselves, it was sedition. To retain the consent of the gentry to his protectorate he had to assert his authority, yet at the same time he had committed himself to curing the ills of society. Somehow order and reform had to be made to proceed hand in hand. In May another proclamation reiterated his determination to restore tillage and arrest depopulation, and at the same time he peremptorily demanded a cessation of disorderly assemblies. Shortly afterwards he directed the commissions to resume their labours, armed now with the power to hear and determine complaints.

So far his colleagues had concurred with the social programme because it sought to maintain traditional interests, but misgivings began to arise as to the methods employed. Already Warwick had taken exception to the commissions when his personal interest was affected, although he was soon reassured and withdrew his opposition. But a majority of the Council objected to the new commissions, which Somerset insisted on issuing on his sole authority, for two pressing reasons — the powers to be given them lacked legal foundation, and the timing was inopportune. Already he had stretched the interpretation of prerogative power in setting up in his own palace a court of poor men's requests. In practice this did no more than sift through lawsuits and direct them to the appropriate tribunal, but it was criticised as unconstitutional, and was no doubt seen as encouraging its prospective clientele to believe that justice was to be weighted in their favour: it probably conferred little real benefit on them.

As a whole the programme of reform looks unimpressive, bearing all the marks of improvisation. The scale of the problem called for patience and persistence, but Somerset needed quick results, and tried to achieve them by questionable methods. The resulting contradictions were beginning to undermine confidence in him on all sides. On the one hand his rule looked weak, an invitation to unruly elements to create disturbances; on the other it appeared ineffective, promising much but achieving little. His motives were not entirely unworthy; he was not unsympathetic towards the victims of injustice, and in spite of all appearances he was genuinely concerned to uphold the law. But it was fast becoming obvious that he was cursed with an inability to take the right decisions, and that his intentions were pursued with an obstinacy born of narrow rectitude and flawed with weakness.

His tragic relations with his brother gravely impaired his reputation. Perhaps he was over indulgent towards his own kin, too ready to overlook the failings of a younger sibling. But Thomas Seymour was a bad lot. Already elevated to the Council before the death of Henry VIII, the

istribution of honours which followed it had brought him a peerage
nd appointment as Lord High Admiral. Almost immediately he had
urtively married his old flame, Catherine Parr, the Queen dowager, on
ne basis of which he had tried to claim a share in the protectorate and
o turn the little King against Somerset, giving him pocket money and
ribing his servants. The brothers quarrelled violently, the flashpoint
eing the Queen's jewels which the Protector asserted were Crown
roperty. When Catherine died in September 1548 Thomas transferred
is attentions to the 15-year-old Princess Elizabeth — he himself was
bout 40, and had had already indecently assaulted her while she was
esiding in his late wife's household. Elizabeth's proximity to the
hrone rendered courtship without the Council's sanction treasonable,
ut this did not deter him since he was gambling for the highest stakes.
imultaneously he was intriguing to marry young Edward to Lady Jane
irey with a view to building himself a nucleus of power based on the
vealth and influence of her father, the marquis of Dorset. Finally, in
anuary 1549, he was detected in a clumsy fraud, inducing Sir William
iharington to milk the Bristol mint, of which he was master, in order to
inance the recruitment of a private army.

The evidence against Seymour was damning, something which was
iot always the case in political trials in those days. It offered an un-
epeatable opportunity to get at the Protector himself, and his rivals on
he Council grasped it eagerly. He could do nothing to save his brother;
o shield him would be construed as connivance, and his enemies were
nexorable, although the problem could have been shelved by the device
of confining the accused indefinitely in the Tower. Yet Somerset had
et matters drift so far that it is difficult to see what else he could have
lone, for he himself had been the target of Thomas's intrigues and had
ncountered nothing but obstruction from him, at one time refusing to
ead the fleet in the operations against Scotland, at others persistently
opposing the government (to which he belonged) in the House of Lords.
Although the Protector was excused from personal participation in the
oroceedings of the Council, and from voting on the bill of attainder in
the Lords, it was impossible to conceal the fact that as head of the
government he was responsible for his brother's execution on Tower
Hill on 20 March. Later on he was to lament his weakness, declaring
that he had been misled by others who momentarily had persuaded him
that his own life was not safe so long as Thomas lived. But the damage
had been done, and not even Bishop Latimer's spirited defence of his
conduct in a sermon delivered on 29 March could still the tongues of
hostile critics.

After two full years of power Somerset still had little to show in
terms of solid achievement, and was impatient for tangible results to
justify his diverse projects — an impatience he was becoming daily more

prone to vent on his colleagues: his personality was anything but congenial. Time was necessary, but the demonstrations in the southern counties were a portent that it was running out. Nevertheless, as May went
by it became possible for him to relax a little. The disturbances had
been contained; other parts of the country remained tranquil. The enclosure commissions were about to resume their work in a relatively
calm atmosphere, and there was the hope that they would speedily
yield concrete results to appease the peasants, which the gentry could
not find grounds to oppose any longer. Simultaneously, plans for the
forthcoming campaign in Scotland were going ahead; after initial setbacks the mercenaries newly recruited on the continent were starting to
arrive.

With the advent of June the first milestone was reached. On 9 June,
to mark the feast of Pentecost, the new order of worship would take
the place of the Latin liturgy. Whitsunday dawned. In churches throughout the land the *Book of Common Prayer* was opened and the new services in English read for the first time. No voice was raised in protest,
although many Protestants experienced keen disappointment at the
numerous concessions to Catholic susceptibilities. And then, within a
day or two, came a bombshell. The people of a remote village in Devonshire had taken up arms and defied the authorities. The magistrates had
temporised, lost control of the situation, and now admitted to the Privy
Council that the flame of revolt was spreading like wildfire, threatening
to engulf the whole county, perhaps all the West Country. And the
most alarming fact was that this was no riot about enclosures purporting to stimulate enforcement of the law, but open defiance of the
government, demanding the withdrawal of the Prayer Book and the
restoration of the Mass.

Chapter 2
A Land Apart

I

'It is apparent and most certain,' wrote John Hooker, the historian of Exeter, 'that this rebellion first was raised at a place in Devon called Sampford Courtenay . . . upon Monday in Whitsun week, being the tenth of June. . . .' He was mistaken.

On the previous Thursday, 6 June, the accumulated tensions of recent years, coupled with a mounting sense of frustration at the erosion of their accustomed way of life by the decisions of a government sitting 300 miles away, had brought the men of Bodmin out onto the street to voice their fears. The central and most important town in Cornwall, Bodmin served as the filter for all the discontents of the county, to add to any peculiar grievances of its own. Small, like all Cornish towns, numbering scarcely 1,000 inhabitants, its economy had undergone a shock when the Augustinian priory there had been dissolved in 1538. And if this had provoked no overt protest at the time — indeed the townsmen had been prompt to exact concessions from Prior Vyvyan once the Church had begun to come under pressure — the accelerating pace of religious innovation had come progressively to dominate the atmosphere of the little community.

Yet Bodmin, indeed the whole county, was experiencing precisely the same changes as the rest of England; in fact the North Country had already staged its own protest while Cornishmen remained passive bystanders. Why, therefore, was it that the South West was the only part of the kingdom to offer armed resistance to the Edwardian reformation? The previous history of Cornwall provides part of the answer.

In 1497 Cornwall had suddenly erupted onto the national scene with two rebellions in quick succession. Up to that year it had lain virtually dormant, living its own separate life at the extremity of the south-western peninsula, remote from the centre of affairs.

It differed radically from the rest of England. Its people were Celts, speaking their own tongue which was akin to Welsh and Breton, many of them having little or no English. The Saxon and Norman conquests had signified little to them save for changes of overlord. Conscious at heart of being a conquered race, they remained down to the end of the sixteenth century and beyond, antipathetic to their English neighbours as John Norden discovered, commenting in his *Description of Cornwall* 'So seem they yet to retain a kind of concealed envy against the English whom they yet affect with a kind of desire for revenge for their fathers sakes, by whom their fathers received the repulse.'

Over the centuries they had retained close links with the rest of the Celtic world, not least Brittany, an autonomous duchy which had not been finally absorbed into the kingdom of France until 1492. Breton sailors and fishermen frequented Cornish havens. In the 1530s John Leland was impressed by the swarm of small craft which had come to Padstow to exchange the commodities of Brittany for fish; he noticed also that the town was full of Irishmen. Many Bretons made their homes in Cornwall, mostly humble folk attracted by wages and conditions better than they could hope to find in their own land. From the taxation records of 1522–4 it is clear that they constituted a very sizeable minority. In Trigg and West hundreds, 79 were registered, some 3.5 per cent of all the men listed there. Over much of the county the proportion was similar, but in Penwith in the far west it reached nearly 10 per cent, 112 out of a total of 1,160 persons. Since the majority had probably come as single men looking for work the ratio to the total population was of course much smaller, probably not much more than 2 per cent, and even less in other districts. But in the coastal towns especially they were very numerous indeed: in East Looe 22 out of 55 men were classed as aliens, and in Polruan 5 out of 13. They were also well represented in the inland market towns, indeed Charles Henderson adumbrated the theory that Cornish towns owed their origins to Breton settlers since the natives refused to give up living in hamlets. Be that as it may, the sheer numbers of immigrants could not but serve to intensify the sense of being different from England, that strange country east of the Tamar.

A Celtic survival not yet assimilated into the English nation, Cornwall also possessed a unique institution which again helped to foster the illusion of autonomy, namely the Duchy, the birthright of the King's eldest son. The administrative structure of the Duchy constituted in effect a miniature government complete with a hierarchy of officials ranging from the top men in London down to a host of local functionaries. Although its lands stretched far beyond the borders of the county, its nucleus was a large group of rich manors in east and mid-Cornwall which formed the largest single estate there. Latterly, indeed, its presence had assumed a new significance when it had absorbed the broad acres of the Courtenay inheritance (its only serious rival) in 1538.

The existence of the Duchy of Cornwall and the consequent concentration of the administration of a large area of the county at its headquarters in Lostwithiel had helped to inhibit the emergence of a strong and influential local gentry. Men of wealth and ambition tended to move away — the poverty of the county and its remoteness from the centre of power also influenced their decision — so that the majority of Cornishmen who made their mark under the Tudors, no small number, usually began by severing personal links with it. In the nature of things these tended to be the descendants of Anglo-Norman families, and they left the county largely to the lesser gentry sprung from native stock. At the beginning of the sixteenth century there were only four houses deserving the title of 'stately home', though more were to go up in Elizabethan times as the local men increased in wealth.

One of the closest links with England, and ironically a major irritant in the connexion, was the tin trade. The streaming of tin was a major occupation of great antiquity. As in all extractive industries the labour was hard and dangerous, and the rewards niggardly, while at the same time the eventual profits were immense. These profits, the veritable surplus value, accrued almost exclusively to the pewterers of the city of London who, virtually monopolising the distribution, obliged the tinners to accept prices which represented a miserable return for their toil. Richard Carew, the Elizabethan antiquary, believed that the appearance of tin working in a district invariably reduced the inhabitants to the depths of poverty: his analysis may be debatable, but his observation of the phenomenon need not seriously be questioned. Cornishmen, as a result, nourished a long standing bitterness against the 'foreigners' who exploited them, and during the sixteenth century matters reached crisis point as the price revolution threw prices out of gear, causing tin to fluctuate wildly.

It was not that the general condition of the people was anything other than poor in the first place. Carew dwells at length on their poverty 'in times not past the remembrance of some yet living . . .'. In those days there had been little corn, and only water to drink, or whey at best, for even the richest farmers did not brew more than twice a year, 'and then God wot such liquor!' For meat they ate what they called 'whitsul', that is, milk, sour milk, cheese, curds, butter 'and such like as come from the cow and ewe'. Clothes were coarse and ill fashioned; people went bare-legged and barefoot — many old folk could not even wear shoes. Houses had earthen walls with low thatched roofs; there were few partitions inside, no planking or window glass. A hole in the roof served for a chimney. Bedding was limited to a heap of straw and a blanket; linen sheets were unknown. 'To conclude, a mazer and a pan or two comprised all their substance.' One should, however, hasten to add that domestic comforts were extremely modest in any part of England in the first half of the sixteenth century, and that thousands of poor labourers fared no better than this; the essential point is that the small farmers who formed the bulk of the population seem to have been measurably worse off than their English counterparts

It was against the background of regional exclusiveness and isolation heightened by poverty and economic injustice, that the rebellions of 1497 broke out.

They were precipitated by taxation. To finance his war with Scotland, Henry VII had obtained a large grant from Parliament, larger than had been customary for half a century or more, and omitting the rebates which had been regularly allowed to impoverished districts. The standardised tax quota for every community had been fixed as far back as 1334 and had remained unaltered until the depression of the second quarter of the fifteenth century had necessitated substantial reductions. It had become established in practice that although quotas could be reduced they could not be increased. Henry, in fact, was trying not so much to increase them as to return to the original position. In the case of Cornwall, however, there was a further complication. Although the final provocation was the oppressive behaviour of one of the principal local assessors, the inhabitants had, or believed they had, a special case, namely that war against Scotland was not their concern, since from time immemorial the defence of the northern Border had been the responsibility of the people who lived there. It was in essence the same argument as John Hampden was to employ in 1635 against the levying of Ship Money on the inland shires: that it was the duty of maritime counties to bear the cost of naval defence. In a word, it was not that Cornwall claimed exemption from national taxation but simply that there was no precedent for this particular levy there.

The first rising was one of the most serious crises of Henry's reign. Led by a blacksmith, Michael Joseph of St Keverne, the movement attracted the support of a number of minor gentry, and in particular Thomas Flamank, an able lawyer, who provided it with the necessary theoretical legal justification. The rebels set out to march to London to lay their case before the King, picking up some recruits in Devon and Somerset, including Lord Audley, a disgruntled peer who felt that his services to Henry's cause had been insufficiently recognised. Although their march was orderly and they scrupulously avoided doing harm to either person or property, it caused consternation in government circles, as well as in the city of London, for they were estimated to number 15,000 men, probably a large exaggeration. Fortunately for Henry, he had the army which was being prepared for the Scotch campaign to oppose them, but the rebels got as far as Blackheath in Kent before their campaign was finally brought to an end only after a sharp fight in which 200 of them were slain.

Apart from executing a handful of the leaders Henry exacted no other retribution, judging it the wiser policy to allow the rank and file to slink back home with their tails between their legs. Perhaps he was too merciful, and in an age when savage retribution was the inevitable consequence of transgressing the law clemency was apt to be interpreted as weakness. At any rate this was the moment that the pretender, Perkin Warbeck, chose to intervene and make his decisive bid for the Crown. Learning of the rebellion, he departed from Scotland and landed with a few men at Whitsand Bay early in September. He hastened to Bodmin where he proclaimed himself King as Richard IV, and within a few days 3,000 Cornishmen, smarting under their recent defeat, had flocked to his standard. Cornwall, incidentally, had traditionally been Lancastrian in sympathy, but at this juncture it readily transferred its allegiance to the Yorkist cause for the sake of hitting back at the now detested Tudor régime.

This time the plan of campaign was less ambitious. As a first step Perkin and advisers decided to attack Exeter, as Sir Francis Bacon put it:

> as well to make his men find the sweetness of rich spoils, and to allure to him all loose and lost people by like hopes of booty, as to be a sure retreat to his forces in case they should have any ill day or unlucky chance in the field.

Since the citizens of Exeter clung stoutly to their allegiance to the Tudor, it was an essential strategic preliminary, but the episode also pinpoints another cleavage in the society of that time. Often there was little love lost between townsman and peasant; the former, as Carew wrote, 'conceived themselves an estranged society from the upland dwellers, and carry . . . an emulation against them, as if one member in a body could continue his well being without a beholdingness to the rest.' An attempt to storm the city by about 6,000 men was held after a limited initial success, and the siege was abandoned after only 24 hours. After a few more days of aimless campaigning in Somerset, the Cornish army broke up and Perkin fled in search of sanctuary. This time they did not get off so lightly. Although very few were actually made to suffer the penalty for treason, a special commission exacted thousands of pounds in fines — many times what would have been paid in tax — which in fact proved a far severer blow to an impoverished community than ever a few score hangings could have done. Having made their first incursion into the national political arena, the Cornish people withdrew into their peninsular isolation for another half century, to be all but forgotten.

Behind the immediate trouble lay a deeper conflict arising from a novel concept of government, ruthlessly applied by the first two Tudor kings, aimed at welding the realm into a new, more rigid unity before which provincial rights and privileges, no matter how ancient and revered, had to yield. Although the existence of the Cornish people as a distinct racial and linguistic entity might appear to suggest an upsurge of nationalism, to make such an assumption would be fundamentally misleading. That an element of separatism was present in the revolts is clear enough, but strictly within the context of medieval ideas. The Cornishmen at Blackheath Field were not fighting for an independent Cornwall. They did not reject the rule of Henry Tudor: they were demanding the removal of what they saw as his evil counsellors, and at bottom what they really wanted was to be left alone. They demanded to be permitted to return to their accustomed obscurity with complete recognition of all their traditional privileges and immunities. Medieval communities set great store on rights which exempted their members from a variety of obligations and burdens, the right of chartered boroughs to regulate their own affairs being perhaps the best known example of this. Not unnaturally immunity from taxation of one kind or another was one of the most valued privileges. Naturally, too, claims were often laid to non-existent, or at any rate dubious ones. All the popular revolts of the Tudor age were in defence of privileges and customs, or what the people involved in them chose to believe their rights to be, and thus the groundwork was laid for conflict between ancient immunities on the one hand, and the claims of modernising government, intent on imposing unity and uniformity, on the other.

Even in a small country like England the problems of the local community held vastly more significance for the majority of people than any national issue. Even as late as the middle of the seventeenth century, the Great Civil War, as it is now recognised, was fought over local grievances rather than the constitutional crisis, and, until the formation of a national army, consisted of several distinct struggles which were localised by the refusal of troops to campaign outside their home districts.

Enough of motives! The state of Cornwall was conducive to disorder. Unlike most other counties it lacked a body of powerful gentlemen capable of taking prompt, effective measures to prevent a threatening situation getting out of hand. The chief landowners, men such as Sir Piers Edgcumbe, could be found serving the Crown anywhere but on their own territory. Too many of the local squires were more concerned to pursue their petty feuds with one another than to do anything effective to maintain public order. Another peculiar local factor was the unusual degree of influence exercised by the parish constables who, according to Carew, were active leaders in all the risings. The hundreds (rural districts) did not have high constables in charge of them, officials who elsewhere were normally men of superior status, often minor gentlemen; and thus another potential check was missing. Society was turbulent. While the gentry bickered among themselves many of the common people took to piracy, whether openly or thinly disguised as privateering. Seafaring, naturally, ranked among their chief occupations. They were ideally located to take toll of shipping entering or leaving the English Channel, and conveniently far away from the bases of the King's handful of warships. The 'Fowey gallants' were notorious for their depredations, although their reputation must have rested largely on the fact that Fowey was much the most flourishing port, with the most ships; the record of the others must doubtless have been proportionate to their size.

More recently the county had flirted with the idea of challenging the government. During the late civil wars it had on the whole backed the Lancastrian cause, although never directly involved in the conflict. When, however, resistance to Richard III's usurpation began to gather momentum in 1483, Cornwall became a focal point. Henry Tudor, earl of Richmond, was waiting in Brittany for an opportunity to make a descent on England, and in anticipation of his arrival he was proclaimed King at Bodmin. But this enterprise aborted, and when Henry did come two years later he landed in Pembrokeshire, with the consequence that Cornishmen remained passive witnesses to the decisive events of 1485.

II

After 1497 Cornwall retreated into quiescence for another 50 years. The protests in the south-eastern counties against the far heavier war taxation of 1522–5 evoked no response there. While the people of Lincolnshire and Yorkshire undertook the Pilgrimage of Grace in 1536, Cornishmen remained apparently indifferent to the dissolution of their own monasteries. More, they furnished a contingent of 364 men for the army concentrated against the northern rebels. Some of these may, none the less, have caught the infection of revolt against religious innovation. It was ascertained shortly afterwards that several had been shown some writing or other of a seditious character. A man named Carpyssack from St Keverne — ominously the birthplace of the rising of 1497 — commissioned a painter to make a banner for the parish church which was to feature a portrait of Christ depicting the Five Wounds, the device of the Pilgrimage. He was also known to have been in communication with disaffected persons in Southampton. Unluckily for him the painter happened to be friendly with no less a person than Sir William Godolphin, the leading justice of the peace of the county. Carpyssack was arrested and very likely hanged; the county, Godolphin reported, remained 'marvellous good quiet'. Nevertheless, as Henry VIII tightened his grip on the Church sundry priests were overheard to drop dark hints of worse to come, while the laity were hardly reassured by the curtailment of wakes and the number of holy days, which robbed them of opportunities for merrymaking. But in the unquiet 1530s rumour wa rife in England; an unguarded remark landed many a person, high o low, in the clutches of the law, and there were no more cases in Corn-wall than anywhere else.

One potential fundamental disturbance of the equilibrium of the South West was the destruction of the marquis of Exeter in 1538. His treason consisted of nothing more sinister than the callous logic of *raison d'état*. It was his misfortune to be descended from King Edward IV, with only a sickly infant, and two girls whom their father was doing his best to repudiate, standing between him and the throne. As well he was by far the most powerful territorial magnate in the West Country, and at best a reluctant supporter of Henry's ecclesiastical policy. In the tense aftermath of the Pilgrimage of Grace, Thomas Cromwell, Henry's chief minister, judged it expedient to eliminate the marquis, and his attainder and execution was a simple judicial murder based on the slenderest of evidence. The great Courtenay estates were confiscated and the territorial influence of this once proud family vanished in a twinkling.

Under the Tudors the nobility occupied an ambiguous position. While the Crown sought to curb their power of independent action which had engendered the intermittent civil strife of the fifteenth century, it needed equally to utilise this power as an agency of govern-ment. At the same time as it forbade, under severe penalties, the keeping of armed retinues, that is, private armies, it had no choice but to tolerate their existence to furnish the nucleus of a national army, a luxury which the royal revenues could not afford. Yet such power and privilege could be entrusted only to men whose loyalty was un-questioned. Loyalty was secured in various ways. In certain cases devoted and able servants of the monarchy, drawn mostly from the ranks of the gentry, were singled out for exceptional advancement, families like the Seymours, the Russells and the Cecils. Dependent on their personal qualities and the King's favour, they rarely posed any threat to the political stability of the realm. The hereditary peerage were kept in line by occasional terrorism: Henry VIII destroyed the Staffords, the Courtenays, and (very nearly) the Howards, as well as manoeuvring the Percys to the brink of financial ruin. An unguarded word, an incautious action could at any moment remind the King and his ruthless advisers of the mighty subject's latent pretensions, his proximity to the throne, leading to a reappraisal of the implications of the network of his family ties and personal influence, until perhaps another noble head tumbled into the sawdust *pour encourager les autres.*

The removal of Exeter provided the opportunity to erect a new, more reliable power structure in the West Country by advancing one of e King's own men. This was Sir John Russell, a member of a respected ut hitherto undistinguished Dorset family, an able diplomat and dministrator who had served the monarchy efficiently and un-btrusively for many years. Prudent, courteous and widely liked, he ad always avoided intrigue, and showed no sign of the grasping political mbition which in those days carried many a man swiftly to the top, nd then abruptly to disgrace and death. Now he was raised to the peer-ge, with an enormous grant of ex-monastic land to support his new ignity, making him at a stroke wealthier than ever the Courtenays had een; he was in fact one of the few men who actually received large gifts f Church property. He was invested also with the late marquis's offices, he stewardship of the Duchy of Cornwall, the wardenship of the tannaries, and others which conferred wide ranging influence and atronage. At the same time he was appointed President of the newly reated Council of the West, a permanent commission, composed hiefly of eminent local gentry, to tighten the government's control ver this distant region and to administer prompt and effective justice. imilar councils already existed for the North and Wales and the Marches, and had been reinforced following the recent rebellion.

There was no discernible resentment of this abrupt change, no wide-pread regret for the marquis, or any sign of sentimental attachment to he memory of the ancient paramount family of the region. Only some ime later did a few embittered adherents show their hand. Lord Russell's gentleness and affability — he was referred to jocularly as father Russell' — together with his deep concern for justice and the rotection of local interests, soon won him ungrudging respect, even ffection. Indeed there was no occasion for him to adopt the role of a epressive proconsul. The government's fears of disaffection in the West proved unfounded. The Council lasted for about three years until y 1544 it was quietly dissolved because there was no need for it. In ny event Russell, now Lord Admiral, was fully occupied administering he Navy at war with France.

III

To borrow Chalmers Johnson's model of the revolutionary process, the 'preconditions' of the Prayer Book Rebellion amount to little more than the existence of an isolated, inward looking society, marked off by linguistic exclusiveness, jealous of encroachment on its privileges, real or imagined, and not unfamiliar with violence.

When we move forward to consider the more immediate causes, or 'precipitants', we have to face up to the fact that there was an entirely new motivation at work in 1549. This, however, need not be magnified.

It will have become clear in the preceding pages that the evidence for
predisposition towards rebellion is flimsy. The county was probably no
significantly more violent than any comparable community at tha
time, indeed its recent record had been unimpeachable. When 50 year
was a good lifetime it can hardly be suggested that rebellion wa
habitual. A revolt does not necessarily have to be long in the making
and certainly change had been so swift and far reaching in the previou
20 years that an entirely new situation had been created. Finally, i
developments in the years 1547–8 are taken as the precipitant, i
becomes extremely difficult to identify, as a separate phenomenon, the
'trigger' which finally set the revolt in motion. In short, to attempt to
fit the ascertainable facts to a theoretical model of revolution is liable
to be highly misleading. Yet all the same a thread of consistency can be
perceived running through all the changing circumstances.

The new spate of religious innovation inaugurated by Protector
Somerset struck at the roots of the beliefs of the ordinary man in the
pew. Henry VIII had, after all, concentrated on intimidating the hierarchy of the Church and despoiling the monasteries – a policy that
appealed to popular anti-clericalism and misgivings about the wealth
and arrogance of the prelates – yet, so far from yielding to the
demands of the Protestant party, had merrily burned heretics, and, in
the Act of Six Articles, 1539, had restated orthodox doctrine
(sanctioned by harsh penalties) in uncompromising terms. The 'whip
with six strings' was undoubtedly popular in the conservative South-
West and must have contributed to the calm prevailing there.

In the long perspective the devotion of Cornishmen to the old religion
is singular when one considers that in 1685 they were to rise again in a
futile attempt to put the Protestant duke of Monmouth on the throne
in place of the Catholic James II, and later still to switch their allegiance
to Nonconformity. Yet there is an odd consistency throughout, a
constant tendency to be out of step with the rest of England, the Celt
rejecting the Saxon in much the same way as the Irish clung fanatically
to Catholicism and the Welsh subsequently embraced Methodism with
fervour.

There was also a practical factor; the clergy may well have exercised
a firmer hold on the people than elsewhere. Nearly every parish represented in the great survey of 1522 enjoyed the ministrations of a
resident priest, often two or more. In Rutland nearly a quarter of all
townships did not. This seems to have been a deplorably common state
of affairs, for although some of the returns, compiled with less care, are
ambiguous on this point, the inference must be that in many areas the
clergy shirked their duties. Non-residence was an ever present blemish
on the Church. It prevailed partly because many parishes belonged to
monasteries which took the profits of the rectories for themselves, and

artly because secular incumbents had other interests (which were
fficially regarded as legitimate) usually in the service of the lay patrons
ho presented them to their livings. An absentee, a duly authorised
ne anyway, was supposed to appoint a chaplain to deputise for him,
ut probably some tried to avoid paying the stipend, while we may
aspect that quite a number of chaplains were inclined to imitate their
mployers and become absentees themselves. It is not difficult, there-
ore, to understand the ease with which Protestantism penetrated the
astern counties, in contrast with Cornwall at least where there were
afficient shepherds to keep the flock tightly penned in the fold.

The first large-scale measure of the new government was the dis-
olution of the chantries, endowments created to maintain priests in
erpetuity to say Masses for the repose of the souls of the founders.
he Act, a complex measure, took into the hands of the Crown not
nerely chantries as such, but also smaller funds such as obits, lights
efore images, and so forth, as well as the property of religious gilds
f lay people which were to be found in many parishes. Not only were
ll such institutions regarded as important adjuncts to the quest for
alvation, but the property involved expressed the conviction even of
iny, poor communities that man did not live by bread alone. Chantries,
eing expensive to found, were naturally the creation of the wealthy,
ut they provided incidentally a valuable service to the community, as
he petitions of nearly all parishes affected for the reprieve of their own
hantries clearly demonstrate. Frequently the cantarist was the only
riest living in the parish, while many of them supplemented a small
tipend by acting as village schoolmasters.

Commissions were appointed in every county to survey the
oundations. They were also instructed to take inventories of all bells,
late and other valuables belonging to churches; a wise provision, since
he wave of righteous iconoclasm sweeping many parts of the country
ould easily be, and probably was, made a cover for the fraudulent
onversion of many such items.

The Cornish commission, consisting of three respected justices,
ir William Godolphin, John Grenville and Henry Chiverton, set to
vork late in 1547. In accordance with their instructions they visited
ach parish in turn, preparing a complete survey and inventory. At first
he work proceeded smoothly enough, even though before they got
oing Godolphin had had to send a 'lewd priest' to be examined by the
rivy Council, presumably for having attempted to incite resistance.
Then, towards the end of November, William Body arrived in Penryn
nd in effect set up a rival enquiry.

Body was well known in Cornwall. A disreputable character, he
ad emerged from the twilight world which had supplied Thomas
Cromwell with many of his agents. In 1537, although a layman, he had

purchased a lease of the archdeaconry of Cornwall from the incumben
Possibly pressure from his patron had been instrumental in obtaining
for the newly appointed archdeacon was Thomas Winter, the illegitima
(and third-rate) son of Cardinal Wolsey, who was deep in debt and r
doubt quite amenable to doing a deal. To be blunt, Body's business w.
graft; the situation was a disgrace to the Church, which the bishop
Exeter, John Veysey, determined to end if he could. At the end of th
term of three years, during which time one supposes that the lessee ha
neglected the real business of the archdeaconry and merely collecte
the revenues, the bishop had him cited before the chancellor of th
diocese for misconduct, while Archdeacon Winter appointed th
bishop's commissary, John Harris, prebendary of Glasney, to act
his deputy. Harris proceeded to Launceston to commence a visitatio
Body, despite his lay status, decided to attempt to exercise the righ
of the office personally. He arrived in the town, strode into St Stephen
church where Harris was in the middle of examining the representativ
of the rural deanery, and announced that he had come to take ove
Armed with his commission, Harris ordered Body out, and urged th
assembled clergy not to pay their procurations to him. Unabashe
Body attempted to take charge; Harris made to restrain him, and Bod
began to draw his dagger, at which point the remainder of the assembl
closed in, hustled him outside and locked the door in his face. Afte
this unseemly episode he successfully defended his position in th
courts, in fact the bishop and his officers got much the worst of th
business, and Body remained in unshakeable control of the archdeaconry

Now in 1548 he was again asserting his right to hold any visitatio
that took place in Cornwall, despite his obvious unpopularity. Ignorin
the prescribed procedure, he summoned all the incumbents and church
wardens of Penwith deanery to Glasney College, Penryn, where he se
up his headquarters. This provoked a hostile demonstration, for hi
manner was insolent, and the local population assumed (probabl
correctly) that his intention was to confiscate church goods — som
malicious source had already started the rumour that this was th
purpose of the commission anyway.

Either on their own initiative, or possibly in response to Body's ple
for protection, the local justices of the peace — Godolphin, Joh
Militon and Thomas St Aubyn — made an urgent report to the Counci
who, in reply, made it quite clear that in their view Body had mad
unnecessary trouble, that he

> further handled himself after such a manner as thereby the peopl
> were persuaded that the ensearch to be taken tended only to th
> effect as if thereupon a confiscation should have ensued to th
> King's Majesty's behalf, much contrary to the Council's intent wh
> meant but only to see the same preserved entirely to the churches
> without embezzling or private sales.

o put the record straight the justices were to make Body countersign is letter, and then to show it to the substantial inhabitants of every arish so that they could see how mistaken they had been. Finally, as o disturbance could be allowed to go wholly unpunished, no matter ie provocation, Body was to be held in custody for a week and then ailed on a large sum to appear before the Council to explain himself. wo or three troublemakers were also to be sent to cool off in prison or a short time.

The authorities had handled this awkward incident with admirable ict, but unfortunately the Council allowed themselves to be persuaded y Body — assuming that they examined him — that he wanted only to e helpful and had muddled up the instructions out of an excess of eal, and a desire to save time and trouble. Orders had just been pro-ulgated for the discontinuation of useless ceremonies, Candlemas, Ash 'ednesday, and so on. In February 1548 the Council ordered the emoval of images from churches, and commissioned Body to see this arried out in the archdeaconry of Cornwall.

Working his way across the county he arrived on 5 April at Helston here none other than his old adversary John Harris owned the Priory f St John and enjoyed considerable influence. In the same district also as situated the parish of St Keverne. The parish priest there, Martin effrey, led an angry crowd of his parishioners to Helston where they ere joined by men from Constantine — in which parish the principal indowners were Harris and William Winslade — led by the Kylter rothers, and from Gwennap and at least half a dozen other places. lany of the men were armed.

Alarmed, Body shut himself up in a house near the church. Led by /illiam Kylter, closely followed by Geffrey, the mob forced their way 1 and dragged Body outside where he was stabbed – by a priest it was aid later — and Kylter and Pascoe Trevian finished him off. No one else as hurt.

Uncertain what to do next the crowd withdrew to the old cemetery nd waited for the law to make the next move. A justice of the peace ccompanied by a few armed retainers soon appeared and called on them o hand over the assassins. The mob was sullen; John Pyers, a sailor rom St Keverne, refused, and the magistrate, helpless in the face of umbers, rode away. When he had gone the people came out of the emetery and gathered in the market place where John Resseigh, eoman of Helston, addressed them, concluding by declaring flatly

that they would have all such laws as was made by the late King Henry VIII and none other until the King's Majesty that now is accomplished the age of xxiv years, and that who would defend Body or follow such new fashions as he did, they would punish him likewise.

The meaning was clear. It was the line taken by the Catholic part
based on the Act of 1536 which had empowered Henry VIII's he
should he succeed as a minor, to repudiate all Acts of the regency o
attaining the age of 24. Although the Parliament of 1547 had repeale
it, there were pundits ready to argue that this too could be set asid
But the real trouble lay not in the finer points of law, but in the dece
on which Somerset's government was founded, in consequence of h
suppression of Henry's will. Since no one knew precisely what it co
tained there was ample scope for invention, and no great degree o
shrewdness was required to draw the inference that it was designed t
inhibit any radical change being made in the interim.

Next day, 6 April, the justices of the peace returned in great
strength but still not sufficient to overcome the people's resistance t
the arrest of the murderers. By 7 April the crowd had swollen to 3,00
and was talking openly of rebellion. The magistrates, powerless t
control the situation, could do little but make appeals and utter threa
which only provoked the people to proclaim that 'on Tuesday next a
the general sessions to be holden at Helston we will be there with
greater number to see if any man will be avenged therein'. In the face o
this defiance the justices dared not hold the sessions. They handed th
few men they had managed to arrest to the sheriff, and Sir Willia
Godolphin scribbled a note to the Privy Council requesting immediat
assistance and the appointment of a special commission of oyer an
terminer to sit at Launceston. This was dispatched by the hand o
William Welche who was ordered to raise the alarm as he rode acro
country. The response of the parishes further to the east showed tha
the western men were very much on their own. The churchwardens o
St Winnow recorded payment to William Lowry 'their captain whe
they went westwards in the King's Majesty's affairs against th
rebellers . . .'. Lanteglos and Polruan paid the wages of 26 men wit
horses, and Boconnoc for 18, borrowing £4 for the purpose; othe
parishes did the same, selling their church goods in some case
Assistance also came from Devonshire, from Plymouth among othe
places, where the Black Book says: 'the Commons were pacified by th
gentlemen of the country with small trouble'. For all their wil
speeches the Helston rioters seem to have been irresolute, while th
authorities acted swiftly to assemble the militia in such strength tha
the would-be rebels could only surrender, and 28 of their ringleade
were placed under arrest to await trial.

It was not the government's policy to act vindictively. On 19 May
general pardon was proclaimed at Launceston, and on 21 May th
special commission convened. The grand jury, which included two o
the leaders of the rebellion of the following year, namely Humphr
Arundell and Robert Smyth, sat on 22 indictments, bringing in a tru

ill in every case. They threw out a bill against Hugh Mason of Grade. He had been in Helston on 5 April but had got cold feet and left. Threatened with hanging, he had fled to Pendennis and then crossed the Carrick Roads to St Mawes whence he had made for Exeter where he was arrested on suspicion of complicity in the riot. Trevian and Kylter made no bones about their part in the affair and pleaded guilty. The others were tried and convicted, with the exception of two men from the more distant parishes of Illogan and Peranuthnoe who may perhaps have become involved only by accident. Because of a technicality there was a delay in the executions. The gallows on Castle Green belonged to the Duchy, but St Stephen's Priory had had the right of gallows also, and this, in consequence of the dissolution, had fallen to the Crown, and treason was an offence against the Crown. While this puzzle was sorted out the Council had second thoughts. Although some members considered the number of pending executions excessive, the sentences had been confirmed on 3 June; yet on 16 June payments were made to Serjeant John Harris, a member of the special commission, Henry Chiverton and John Roscarrock for riding to Cornwall on the King's business, very possibly carrying stay of execution for the six men who were in due course pardoned. Kylter and Trevian were hanged, drawn and quartered, the remainder hanged, some at Launceston, others at Plymouth and elsewhere.

Martin Geffrey and five other men had been taken to London on 5 May. On 11 June they went on trial in Westminster Hall and were convicted. Geffrey was taken to Smithfield on 3 July where he was hanged, drawn and quartered, his head being exhibited on London Bridge, the quarters at the city gates. Four others, including John Pyers, were pardoned. The fate of the sixth man is unknown; perhaps he died in prison. John Resseigh, who had acted as a spokesman, disappeared — killed possibly in some unrecorded scuffle; his brother Martin was executed in Cornwall.

The Helston riot of 1548 was over. The participants had turned out to be an isolated group from west Cornwall, who, once they had murdered Body, discovered that they did not really want to go any further; moreover, so far from gaining wider support, they found that men from adjacent districts willingly rallied to the side of the authorities. By contemporary standards they were dealt with leniently, especially since both government and local officials had been thoroughly alarmed. Unhappily the authorities gravely misjudged public opinion in Cornwall. Convinced that the commons had been led like sheep by a handful of evilly disposed agitators, they made the mistake of believing that the execution of the ringleaders would obviate the risk of any further trouble. They compounded their error by executing, on the one hand, too few to terrorise the countryside into submissiveness, and on

the other, too many. Uncertain of the precise identity of the leader
officials probably selected a number of men at random or on extremel
slender evidence: this seems clear from the number of pardons, especiall
in respect of the men tried at Westminster. The 15 local execution
seem in the event to have accomplished nothing more than th
antagonisation of the hitherto loyal people of east Cornwall.

Although to all appearences the county had been pacified,
seemingly trivial incident recalled by Richard Carew reflects the mount
ing tension. Hard on the heels of the Helston riot, feelings becam
inflamed among the boys of the free school at Bodmin. Like schoo
boys of all ages they 'accustomably divided themselves for bette
exploiting their pastimes', and in this uneasy summer of 1548 the
temporarily abandoned the sixteenth-century equivalent of cowboy
and Indians for the more topical and exciting Catholics and Protestants
the old religion versus the new. They threw themselves into this nev
game with zest, not to say roughness, 'each party knowing and stil
keeping the same companions and system'. Eventually one boy wa
carried away by it; perhaps he was emotionally disturbed. He converte
an old candlestick into a gun, got hold of some gunpowder, and foun
a pebble of the right size and shape for a bullet. He then proceeded t
show off in front of his admiring and envious chums. Alas! Either b
accident or in response to a dare, he aimed this lethal toy at a calf an
killed it. The boys no doubt dispersed hurriedly to their homes, lookin
unnaturally innocent, but the owner of the beast was not deceived, an
he complained to the schoolmaster who proceed to hand out thrashing
all round. At this point the miniature war of religion was summaril
terminated, very likely with the whole-hearted co-operation of th
parents. But in clamping down on their high-spirited offspring th
burgesses of Bodmin seem almost as if seeking to repress their ow
guilty impulses.

IV

It was against this background that on the morning of 6 June 1549 th
feeling of crisis mounted to a climax among the townsmen of Bodmin
In just three days' time the *Book of Common Prayer* would be opene
for the first time in the church of St Petrock, and they would hav
willy-nilly to join in celebrating the Supper of the Lord in Englisl
instead of hearing the traditional Latin Mass. A copy was already in th
vicar's hands. We may surmise that he had lost no time in acquaintin
his prinicpal parishioners with its contents, and, with the instinctiv
reaction of the conservative, had picked out and emphasised some o
the more radical and disturbing passages.

At a first cursory glance laymen are likely to have been most dismayed by the rubric prefacing the public baptism of infants: 'the
people are to be admonished that it is most convenient that baptism
should not be administered but upon Sundays and other holy days . . .'.
In an age when infant life was cheap, when at least one baby in 10 died
in its first year of life — perhaps a fifth of these the day they were born
and as many more within the week — the effect of such a restriction
could only be to exclude so many souls from salvation; the proviso,
nevertheless (if necessity so require) children ought at all times to be
baptised, either at the church or else at home', seemed a grudging
concession. The subtleties of dogma may have escaped their notice,
but this appeared to undermine the very basis of religious belief and
practice. Their manner of rejecting the new order for the Eucharist
sounds superficial, and in likening it to a 'Christmas game' they could
easily have been contriving an excuse; not so the contrary assertion:
but we will have our old service of Mattins, Mass, Evensong and
Procession in Latin as it was before. And so we the Cornish men
wherof certain of us understand no English) utterly refuse this new
English'. At this distance of time it is impossible to estimate what
proportion of the Cornish people had no English in the middle of the
sixteenth century, perhaps not as many as they tried to make out
since the Protector subsequently retorted that they were many times
more ignorant of Latin. However, as they saw it, Latin was the sacred
tongue, English merely an alien one, and its imposition for public
worship was rejected as a flagrant attempt to destroy their identity
as a people: the Catholic Church had tolerantly permitted the Lord's
Prayer, Creed and Commandments to be recited in Cornish. Like all
Edward VI's subjects, they were jealous of their ancient rights and
ever prompt to spring to their defence when threatened. Time and
again in the sixteenth century communities applied to the courts to
confirm their customs, not always unsuccessfully. It was the misfortune of Cornishmen as a whole that they were laying claim to
traditional privileges which had been overridden by statute. They
believed both that their local custom took precedence and that they
were strong enough to defy the remainder of England and extort
concessions. Religion, particularism and antipathy to the English
language all became fused in a single grievance.

For Henry Bray, mayor of Bodmin, there was no crisis of conscience arising from divided loyalty. His clear duty was the defence of
the borough's privileges rather than preservation of the King's peace,
or rather, as he would have seen it, the latter depended absolutely on
the former. One thing that was conspicuously absent in Bodmin that
day was any sense of conflict between rich and poor, for there was
scarcely one man in the town who could be accounted wealthy: in

1524 the two richest burgesses had been assessed at £40 apiece, an
there was nothing to suggest the existence of an exclusive merchan
class. The absence of the extremes of wealth and poverty that could b
found in other counties was a noticeable feature of Cornish society a
this period. In contrast with most of England there were few labourers
in the various fiscal returns of 1522–5 they did not amount to mor
than 15 per cent. Where, as in some parishes of Kerrier hundred, th
proportion was higher, it was partly accounted for by the presence o
poor immigrants from Brittany. Conversely only 2 per cent of th
people were rated as high as £40 and fewer still above it. In Devonshir
about 36 per cent of taxpayers were assessed on wages in 1524, an
since a good many of the poorer people were left out they probabl
amounted to well over 40 per cent altogether.

There was no disorder in Bodmin that June morning. As he figure
as one of the principal leaders of the rebels from first to last, it is fair t
assume that Mayor Bray had convened a town meeting in due form; i
the day had begun with a spontaneous demonstration the protest wa
very soon turned into a properly constituted assembly under th
presidency of the chief magistrate. The business can only be con
jectured, but it may be inferred that Bray and his closest colleague
framed and put to the meeting resolutions which contained the gis
of the rebels' eventual list of demands. Having settled on thei
programme they proceeded directly to concert steps to enforce it
summoning the able-bodied manhood of the shire to muster in defenc
of their liberties. The lesson of the last disturbance had not been lost
they must strike first and not wait to be crushed.

The procedure for holding musters was familar. Periodically (an
with increasing frequency in recent years) able-bodied men age
between 16 and 60 were assembled, and lists of available arms an
armour compiled. Bodmin was the assembly point for the men o
Trigg hundred. But on an occasion such as this, one necessary elemen
failed to appear – the officers. The captains and petty captains of eac
band were drawn from the ranks of the local gentry, for the squire
who ruled the countryside in peacetime also led its fighting men i
war, and it was still taken for granted that military expertise was th
prerogative of this class. It is noticeable how in the autumn of 1536 th
insurgent peasants of Lincolnshire had gone the rounds of the mano
houses obliging as many gentlemen as they could find to turn out wit
them. The need was two-fold. Not only were gentlemen wanted t
provide leadership – and, one suspects, to bear the brunt of any
fighting at the head of their household servants – but also to provid
the rank and file with defensive armour. In many areas of England mos
of what little harness there was belonged to them: the musters fo
Rutland in 1522 listed 82 complete outfits of which no fewer than 5

ere owned by gentlemen, and several more by their personal retainers.
ne reason for the speedy collapse of the Lincolnshire rising is un-
oubtedly the fact that many gentry were unwilling conscripts who
ade off and took refuge with the King's forces as soon as they
ppeared on the scene. When, immediately afterwards, the trouble
read to Yorkshire, the gentry, and indeed one nobleman, took the
ad in organising it, with the result that the government experienced an
neasy moment, for with only a small force under his command the
ing's Lieutenant was obliged to negotiate with the rebels. When he
ad talked the gentlemen into going home the Pilgrimage of Grace came
o an abrupt end.

In Cornwall there was one fundamental difference. The extremely
modest means of most of the gentry prevented all but a few keeping
nything resembling an arsenal. In contrast, an exceptionally high
roportion of the common people fulfilled their statutory obligation
nd equipped themselves with harness in accordance with their purses.
onically, it was their compliance with the law, intended to secure the
efence of the realm, that enabled them to mount a serious challenge to
ne government of the day. Without having to rely on the gentry at all
ney could field a couple of thousand well armed men at the very least.

Taken completely by surprise, the response of the majority of the
ornish gentry was confused and hesitant. Like their Yorkshire counter-
arts in 1536, some may have sympathised with the aims of the
nsurgents. But circumstances had changed; the propaganda of the
ommonwealth Men gave the gentry ample cause to fear that the rising
ould turn into a *Jacquerie* directed as much against themselves and
neir property as against any policies of government. Besides, they were
esponsible for law and order, and by a tacit agreement with the Crown
ere left to maintain it as they saw fit; since they usually interpreted
nis as the protection of their own interests it was a system which they
ad little incentive to upset. If now they made any attempt to recall the
ommons to their allegiance, the response was nil. Many gentlemen
etired with their families to the sanctuary of St Michael's Mount,
thers to Sir Richard Grenville's castle of Trematon. Moreover, some of
ne chief magistrates, such as Sir William Godolphin, lived in the far
est, and for the moment were cut off from the outside world by the
aring up of revolt at Bodmin. A few, however, had made up their
minds.

A day or two earlier Humphry Arundell, who commanded the tiny
arrison of St Michael's Mount, had received an urgent message from his
wife Elizabeth summoning him home to Helland where she was
reparing for her confinement. Now this was but an hour's brisk walk
om Bodmin, and no sooner was he home than news arrived of the
ommotion there and the appeal of the common folk to the gentry to

join them. Two other local gentlemen called on him — possibly the
brought the news — and all three decided to go into hiding in a nearb
wood, hoping that the storm would soon blow itself out. Two day
went by, and then, on Saturday or Sunday, Mrs Arundell sent a messag
to her husband imploring him to come home, if only briefly. (On
imagines that she was experiencing a difficult labour and was now i
some fear of death.) While Humphry was at her side a man from
Bodmin called at Helland seeking to recruit him. When he declined t
go he was overpowered and carried off by force; the visitor, presumabl
was not alone. The next morning the rebels permitted him to writ
a letter to Sir Hugh Trevanion, who had lately completed his year a
High Sheriff, to ask what he ought to do. Trevanion in reply advise
him to act circumspectly, 'to tarry with the rebels and to be in the
favour to the intent to "admittigate" their outrageous doings'. Arundel
therefore, took his seat on the committee which drew up the manifest
hoping to persuade them to keep it as moderate as possible. But try a
he might he could not talk them out of the next step they proposed, t
arm themselves in order to enforce their demands on King an
Parliament. Pretending to have been taken suddenly ill, he mounted h
horse and rode off to Helland, but a band of insurgents followed an
dragged him back to Bodmin. Closely watched from this time onward
he had no choice but to remain with the rebel host until, 10 week
later, he was able to effect his escape from the defeated and demoralise
remnant at Launceston, and give himself up to Sir Richard Grenville

This is what he told the Attorney General and Serjeant Molyneu
when they interrogated him, but, both at the time and subsequentl
no one seriously doubted that he had been the willing leader of th
revolt from the very outset.

The facts of his life are against him; he was a turbulent spirit, neve
unduly troubled by moral scruples. Born about 1513, he was a grand
son of Thomas Arundell of Lanherne, the most influential branch o
one of the foremost county families, and was thus cousin to Sir John
Arundell, its present head. He had been named after his matern
grandfather, Humphry Calwoodley of Calwoodleigh, Devon, who
whilst residing at Helland in 1497, had joined Perkin Warbeck
rebellion and had in consequence been attainted. The attainder ha
been reversed in 1507 and his lands restored to his daughter, Joan, from
whom Humphry Arundell had inherited them in 1537 togethe
perhaps, with a family leaning towards rebellion. Endowed with ampl
estates in Devon and Cornwall, Joan and her husband, Roger Arundel
had enjoyed a position of esteem in local society. In the 1520s Roger
income from land was assessed at £40 a year, and his personal propert
at £60; Humphry's income was calculated at £55 8s. 10d. in 1549
Although this did not place him in the first rank of the gentry it wa

good by Cornish standards, enough to give him security together with what limited degree of comfort there was to be found in the smaller manor houses of the day.

Humphry was bred to the profession of arms in which he earned a good reputation, and led a band of foot soldiers to the siege of Boulogne in 1544. But there was another and less attractive side to his character. He was frequently involved in lawsuits, charged several times with forcible entry on the lands of other men, accused by his younger brothers of withholding money due to them under their mother's will, and was once sued by his servant and tenant, Thomas a Leigh, for unpaid expenses incurred on four journeys to London on his behalf. His marriage to Elizabeth, daughter of Sir John Fulford, a prominent Devonshire squire, must have brought him an augmented income, though evidently it had not made him more respectful of the property of others.

Arundell's return to Helland at the beginning of June may have been fortuitous, but so much attention came to be given to the events at Sampford Courtenay on Whit Monday that much of what took place at Bodmin has never been fully elucidated. However, whereas the outbreak at the former place was completely spontaneous, the same cannot be asserted in the latter case. Although it is true that Arundell had ample reason for wishing to be at his wife's side at that moment, it could have been a highly convenient cover for an arrangement that had already been made with the Bodmin men. The chief reason for doubting his story is that it is identical in its main features with the explanation given by everyone else of his class who became involved. Presumably he would have stuck as closely to the truth as was safe, departing from it only where it became necessary to avoid incrimination. Whether he did go into hiding in the first instance cannot be verified; he could equally well have temporised for a few days, long enough to cover both the alleged sojourn in the wood and the consultation with Sir Hugh Trevanion. What can be inferred with some confidence is the fact that the arrival of the latter gentleman's advice — which he denied ever having given — must have coincided with the news from Devonshire which provided good evidence that the rebellion would find strong support outside Cornwall. On the assumption that his dissatisfied ego thirsted for a short cut to power and prestige, we may well conclude that this determined him to place his social prestige and professional expertise at the service of the insurgents. As far as we know he was not tortured to extract a confession. The mere fact that he went with the rebels (plus the ambivalent attitude of his kinsman, Sir John Arundell) was sufficient to convict him.

The other Cornish gentleman who joined was John Winslade of Tregarick, a fairly rich man whose income from his Cornish estates topped £40, with a further £74 from lands in Devonshire. He claimed that a gang of rebels had threatened to burn down his house, and so he had consented to accompany them to Bodmin where he stayed four or five weeks, avoiding the fighting. He, too, through his wife, had disaffected connexions: one William Kendall of Plelynt who had been executed for complicity in the Exeter 'conspiracy', as well as others more distantly related. He was well liked, generous, and noted for his great hospitality. He was also impulsive and perhaps easily aroused. Not long since he had conveyed all his estates in Cornwall to his second wife by way of jointure, already maybe contemplating the possibility of what he now found himself engaged in. With him came his son William a very young man who followed his father unquestioningly. The government did not consider him to have been deeply committed to the rebel cause and subsequently pardoned hin.

Winslade excepted, the leadership was strongly centred on Arundell. Another (and minor) gentleman named Coffin was his servant; he may have come from Porthledge and have been related to a certain John Kestell who acted as Arundell's unwilling secretary, turning King's evidence against him afterwards. Thomas Holmes, a yeoman of Blisland hard by Bodmin and Helland, was another servant; also at Blisland, his wife's home, dwelt another substantial yeoman, Robert Smyth, who had come originally from Tregonack in St Germans.

The professional touch of Arundell the soldier rapidly asserted itself in the rebels' councils. As general of the host he directed the men who were soon flocking by the hundred into Bodmin from all over the county to Castle Kynoch, an ancient earthwork half a mile away, where a camp was formed and the work of organisation commenced. Coffin, Smyth and Holmes, along with Mayor Bray, were certainly his right-hand men, acting as captains of bands. The names of the other leaders indicate the source of many of the recruits. The Winslades hailed from near Looe on the south coast, John and James Rosogan from St Colomb Major in Pydar hundred; there were John Payne, the port reeve of St Ives, John Bochym of Gulvall, and Robert his brother who was one of several priests among whom were included the parsons of St Cleer, St Veep, St Neot, Lelant and Poundstock.

While training went briskly ahead at Kynoch measures were taken to forestall the possible rallying of loyalists to the gentry who had gone to ground in various strong places. To St Michael's Mount, Arundell dispatched a column of picked horse and foot, including men who had served under his command and were familiar with the castle. They crossed the causeway at ebb tide and occupied the flat ground at the foot of the Mount. The path to the fort on the summit was steep and exposed, but the assailants collected trusses of hay which they carried in front of them to deaden the defenders' arrows and musket balls, and

hus protected they forced their way to the top. Here they formed up
or the assault, and while their bowmen maintained a steady fire to
ake the garrison keep their heads down, the billmen scaled the outer
vall, encountering only slight resistance. Short of food and ammunition,
nd disheartened by the terrified wailing of their women and children,
he gentlemen surrendered. Carew's account must have been founded
n local memories, but unsympathetic as he was to the rebels and their
ause, he presented it in such a way as to show them in the worst
ossible light. The garrison yielded 'to those rakehells' mercy, who,
othing guilty of that effeminate virtue, spoiled their goods, imprisoned
heir bodies, and were rather by God's gracious providence than by
ny want of will, purpose or attempt, restrained from murdering the
rincipal persons'. Their objective achieved, the victors marched back
o Kynoch carrying their prisoners with them.

All over the county gentlemen were rounded up and imprisoned at
Bodmin, later to be removed to the county gaol at Launceston. Mean-
vhile, hundreds of peasants and craftsmen, tinners and fishermen
oured into Kynoch, many of them doubtless fired with enthusiasm,
lthough inevitably it was later to be alleged that many were intimidated
nto joining. The rounding up of gentry and the easy success at
st Michael's Mount won over many waverers, so that the fighting
trength was in all probability mustered within a few days.

As for the sheriff, John Militon, 'with all the power of his bailiwick
he] durst not encounter' the insurgents. To be rather more accurate,
is power failed to materialise. If he attempted to call out the shire
evies the result could only have demonstrated the blunt truth that
nost of the officers were on the run or in custody, while the rank and
ile were holding musters of their own in defiance of his authority. To
nake matters worse, his home, Pengerick Castle, was isolated in the far
vest of the county, and for some days at least he was completely out of
ommunication with the government.

Chapter 3
Protest and Provocation

I

If news of the tumult at Bodmin had travelled the 45 miles to Sampford Courtenay in Devonshire before the week-end it had made no immediate impression on this secluded village which lies up a by-road three or four miles from Okehampton. Except for its air of quiet prosperity, it cannot at the present time look very different from how it did at Whitsuntide 1549. W. G. Hoskins's affectionate description cannot be bettered:

> The village is cheerful, neat and clean with much whitewashed cob and good thatching. The church of St Andrew is exceedingly attractive both inside and out: granite building at its most elegant. The lofty pinnacles of the west tower are stained by an orange lichen, so that they glow perpetually with colour.

It was a large parish with a population of about 500, nearly as many as nowadays, if we ignore Honeychurch which it absorbed in 1894. Strolling down the charming main street, you wonder why it has not been 'discovered', for it is such a picture postcard village. A less likely birthplace for a bloody civil war could hardly be imagined. Perhaps it was this very isolation from the mainstream of national affairs which helped to sow the seeds of dissent; this and the accident that a tiny community could throw up a handful of articulate leaders.

Unlike Bodmin people, the parishioners of Sampford had shown no signs of anticipating developments. On Whit Sunday morning they had gone to church to hear their parson, William Harper, read the new services, and on this first occasion at least they 'could not in any respect find fault or justly reprehend the same'. Later in the day, however, they began to compare notes, and gradually opinions hardened, influenced perhaps by rumours from Bodmin. They at least had waited to find out what the new order of worship was like., Respect for Mr Harper's grey hairs may have restrained them at first, for he was 70 years of age and had, moreover, been instituted as recently as the previous October on the presentation of Queen Catherine in whose service he had been Clerk of the Closet. Later on the rumour got round that he was a chaplain to the Princess Mary — he must of course ave had some contact with her in the Queen's household — and the rivy Council actually complained to her, alleging that he was a ring-ader of the rebellion, which she vehemently disclaimed.

After some discussion a number of villagers decided to voice their bjections, and on Monday morning, led by William Underhill, a tailor, nd William Segar, described as a labourer, they entered the vestry where Harper was preparing for Morning Prayer, and asked what form f service he proposed to conduct. His answer was that he would omply with the law and use the Prayer Book as he had done the day efore: priests were liable to penalties for failure to do so, although aymen were not. The men forbade him to use it, informed him of their esolution to keep to the ancient faith of their forefathers, and claimed hat Henry VIII's will had lain it down that there was to be no alteration 1 religion before his son came of age. Eventually most of the village rrived and unanimously insisted that the rector should get out his nissal and say the Mass to which they had been accustomed all their ves. Perhaps he shared their sentiments; if not, he was an old man and weary, while they were many and importunate. He put on 'his old opish attire' and celebrated Mass as they desired.

Here, as elsewhere, although antipathy to the Prayer Book and fear f worse to follow were the dominant motives, there was probably a ackground of contributory irritants. Besides having formerly belonged o the Courtenays, Sampford had lost the chantry at Sticklepath a ouple of years earlier, and with it a major part of the religious structure round which so much of their lives revolved. It had been one of the nost valuable chantries attached to a rural parish in Devonshire, worth 9 10s. 8d. per annum; the chapel, which stood a mile away, contained rnaments and vessels worth £6 9s. To make matters worse, it had been ranted to Sir Anthony Auches while, further, other lands in the parish elonging to the chantry in Okehampton had been granted to another mbitious gentleman, John Prideaux, who was actually one of the ommissioners for the disposal of chantries. Here as elsewhere the lement of class conflict loomed large, deepened by the fact that many f the gentry had warmly embraced Protestantism and were active in preading it. That odd, and seemingly inexplicable, demand in the ebels' manifesto that the number of servants permitted to gentlemen hould be restricted seems to imply a desire to curb their pretensions nd power; only in this way can it be reconciled with the more usual omplaint about gentlemen who failed in their duty to keep adequate ouseholds, and so created unemployment.

In the course of the next day or two the local justices of the peace earnt of the disorderly happenings at Sampford and the unwonted lefiance of the law by the common people; also the disquieting fact

that men from other parishes were beginning to gather there, giving
every indication of being intent on persisting in their mutinous
behaviour. The gravity of the situation did not escape the authorities
who immediately realised the urgency of dispersing the assembly
before any greater mischief could occur. Therefore Sir Hugh Pollard of
King's Nympton rode over to Sampford Courtenay to find out exactly
what was going on, hoping that, having learnt the nature of the people's
grievance, it would be possible to devise some means of pacifying them
and to persuade them to return to their homes. He took with him
Anthony Harvey of Columb John and Alexander Wood of North Tawton
who was accompanied by his son-in-law, Mark Slader from Bath.

Now Underhill and Segar knew well enough that it would not be
long before the magistrates appeared on the scene and tried to talk
them out of going on with their protest. Contrary to the impression
given by John Hooker, they were by no means mere yokels but men of
some standing in the parish. Sampford was a homogeneous community
composed almost entirely of farmers and labourers with a handful of
tradesmen. Segar was certainly no labourer in the accepted sense. For
the subsidy of 1544 he had been assessed at £8, one of the highest
amounts in the parish: labourers did not pay tax. The Underhills were a
fairly prominent family; William's assessment was £4, and three others
were taxed on smaller amounts, while a fifth, Gilbert, had an assessment of £6 in 1545. They had also been well represented in 1524,
mostly in the middle rank of the community. They had a fair inkling of
what to expect from Pollard: an appeal to remain calm and avoid doing
anything foolish; to trust the gentlemen and the government which in
its wisdom had ordained a form of service better suited to the spirit of
the times than the old Latin rites, and which, as reasonable men, they
would come to accept if only they would give it a fair trial. Finally
they would be reminded of their allegiance to the King and the dire
consequences of rebellion. But the villagers had already made up their
minds and were determined not to be put off by fair words.

So far not a great many people had gathered at Sampford. It was
probably Tuesday, Wednesday at the latest, when Pollard and his
colleagues rode up to the village followed by a company of servants
and retainers, all of course armed. The entrance to the street was
perhaps already barricaded. Underhill and Segar refused bluntly to talk
unless the justices consented to leave their men at a distance, and
accompany them to a nearby croft where they could confer in safety.
Although Pollard, had he cared to, might very well have been able to
scatter the small number who had so far assembled, he agreed. What
his thoughts and those of his colleagues were no one ever knew
whether, as Hooker surmised,

it were because they thought in such a cause to use all the best and quietest ways for the pacifying of them or whether some of them being like affected as they were did not like the alteration as it was greatly suspected.

After discussions lasting much of the day the justices departed having achieved nothing. Not surprisingly their conduct was branded as cowardice, even treachery. Perhaps Pollard was just too clever by half, but whatever it was, his failure to damp down the embers of revolt allowed it to become 'such a fire as they had not been able to quench'. In one afternoon the authorities had lost all control of the situation.

The news of this successful stand on the part of the Sampford folk spread across Devon like wildfire,

> as a cloud carried with a violent wind and as a thunder clap sounding through the whole county is carried and noised abroad throughout the whole country: and the common people so well allowed and liked thereof that they clapped their hands for joy and agreed in one mind to have the same in every one of their several parishes.

There was, however, one man in the district who took a different view, a franklin or minor gentleman named William Hellyons, who took it into his head that he could succeed where his betters had failed, and quell the riot single-handed.

A day or two later Hellyons made his way to Sampford. Arrested as he approached the village, he was conducted to the church house where the rebels had made their headquarters in the upper chamber. It still stands there, half-way up the village street; the exterior is unpromisingly Victorian, but once you have mounted the external staircase, walking through the door is like taking a step back in time into the sixteenth century. At the far side of the room stands a long table, rough-hewn out of oak and bolted to the floor; along the nearer side there is an oak bench, and at one end a similar stool, about as comfortable as a misericord, for the chairman. Here the rebel leaders sat in council. They let Hellyons have his say, but he was an opinionated man and gave free rein to his tongue. He 'earnestly reproved them' and 'sharply threatened them of an evil success', provoking them into a rage. His was the type the peasants detested most. In origin he can have been little better than they – some said he was of foreign birth – but one who aped the manners of the true gentleman, a man on the make who aspired to higher status by coolly exploiting every avenue of profit, and taking every opportunity of asserting his superiority over his less successful neighbours. Uninhibited by any feeling of deference, they abused him roundly. The atmosphere in the chamber grew ugly and he slunk out. But as he hurried down the steps a man named Lithibridge dashed after him brandishing a bill, and felled him with a blow on the neck.

The wretched man rolled down the steps screaming for mercy, but other villagers gathered round and hacked him to pieces. When it was all over they began an unseemly argument over the bleeding corpse. Some heatedly insisted that since he was a heretic the body should be cast into the nearest ditch, but cooler heads prevailed, and the rector was permitted to give him a Christian burial in the churchyard. It was a nasty incident, but it stands alone as the only authenticated atrocity committed by the common people during the whole of the commotion.

The revolt gathered momentum in the absence of effective steps to arrest its course. Having committed themselves, the country folk began to believe that nothing could stop them; in the picturesque metaphor of the time, 'they had wound the garland before they had run the race, nothing forecasting what might ensue nor yet accounting what folly it is to triumph before the victory'. In his narrative Hooker allowed his pen to get the better of his reason, and all subsequent accounts have followed him in giving a rather misleading impression of the next few days, suggesting that the whole of Devon and Cornwall flew to arms and went storming up the road to London: 'wherefore they assemble and confederate themselves throughout the whole shire in great troops and companies and do associate the flock unto them the Cornish people minding to join together & foolishly to maintain what rashly they had begun'. The implication is that all this developed in less than 10 days, where in fact close attention to the details leaves little room for doubt that the build-up was somewhat slower and that there were further incidents still to come to add fuel to the fire.

How soon other villages got wind of the doings at Sampford Courtenay must remain a matter of speculation, but for the time being the trouble was largely confined to the north-west quarter of Devonshire. Certainly within a few days a sizeable band of malcontents had collected at Sampford. Another concentration may have formed simultaneously at Torrington, for Henry Lee, the mayor, was one of the chiefs. But the best part of 10 days were to pass before the Council far away in London realised that it had a major uprising on its hands. The point at which the insurgents joined forces with the Cornishmen must remain a matter for conjecture, but there are good grounds for supposing that the main Cornish force did not move until almost the end of June. However, an advance party may already have joined the Devonshire rebels, who were assembled at Crediton, by 20 June at the latest.

II

Dissatisfaction with the Prayer Book was by no means entirely confined to the South West. As early as 11 June the duke of Somerset wrote to the marquis of Dorset and the earl of Huntingdon in the Midlands warning them that malcontents had assembled in many places; earlier on, such people had been protesting against enclosures, but more recently, incited by seditious priests and other evilly disposed men, they had begun to demand the restoration of 'thold bloody laws', meaning the Six Articles and so forth. At this stage it is clear that the Protector was thinking in terms of prevention. As proof of the government's solicitude for the common weal he enclosed a proclamation condemning enclosures, to be published by the sheriffs, and advised that the gentlemen of Leicestershire should make discreet preparations to resist any open disturbances. Nevertheless, for the present the accent was to be on the avoidance of provocation: the gentry were to hold themselves in readiness in the seclusion of their homes lest the people should be alarmed by any fear that they were about to be 'overrun'. This precaution, he added, should save his correspondents unnecessary expense, a gentle hint, it may be, that the government's financial straits were such that it was not prepared to defray the cost to landowners of guarding their own property. A further proclamation dated 13 June commanded agrarian rioters in general to keep the peace, threatening dire consequences should they persist; it made no mention of religious dissent.

The precise date on which the Protector heard of the revolt at Sampford Courtenay is not clear. It may be inferred that the first definite report arrived in the middle of Whit week, intimating that Sir Hugh Pollard had bungled the business, followed in quick succession by news of further incidents, and of the Devonshire magistrates' admission that they were incapable of containing them.

Somerset's thoughts may well be imagined. An armed uprising was bad enough at any time, but the present one could not have come at a worse moment, jeopardising the Scottish project to which all other considerations had been subordinated. Further, it implied that recent measures of reform had failed in their prime object of preserving the traditional order. The overriding need was the maintenance of public confidence, or rather regaining it, for it was fast ebbing away. The people were losing hope of redress for their grievances, and so were being driven to take the law into their own hands. The gentry of Devon were at their wits' end, faced with a situation for which they were unprepared, and as a result did nothing. He himself as well as his policies were on trial. If rebellion actually broke out he would have to crush it decisively, but that would be a pyrrhic victory because he was still liable to be held responsible for having opened the way to it. Moreover, the idea of slaughtering large numbers of peasants conflicted with his aim of checking depopulation. The essential thing was that there should be no rebellion at all.

The government's first responses indicate muddle and indecision.

Not only was it unwelcome, the news arrived incomplete and contra
dictory. By 20 June the Protector realised that there was serious
trouble afoot, while remaining ignorant of, or possibly shutting his eyes
to, its true dimensions. A directive under the Signet to the Sheriff and
justices of Devon expressed the conviction that it was localised in one
quarter of the county and comparable in scale with the disturbances
which had already flared up briefly and died down. Clinging to the
belief that it was actuated by ignorance rather than malice, instigated
by a handful of agitators, he recommended, 'at the suit of divers
gentlemen', an initial policy of holding out the olive branch as a means
of minimising the trouble. The rioters, therefore, were to be offered a
free pardon for their activities to date on condition of their future
good behaviour and obedience to the law, while it was hoped that the
threat of severe sanctions would deter possible future transgressors. Did
he, one wonders, permit himself to be misled by malicious reports
designed to induce a sense of false security and gain time for the
rebellion to develop?

One certain fact emerges from the confusion of these tense days:
while everyone's attention was focused on Sampford Courtenay everything else was overlooked. In this sense Hooker was right in saying
that the affair started there. This commotion effectively masked the
far more dangerous movement gathering force west of the Tamar,
while the prompt action already taken by Humphry Arundell to round
up the Cornish gentry guaranteed that for a few cruicial days that
county was insulated from prying eyes; indeed it was not until 11 July
that official recognition was given to the fact that Cornwall was in a
state of rebellion. Moreover, so long as it was believed that the trouble
was restricted to the Sampford district there was no great reason to fear
that it might escalate into civil war since the muster returns proved that
the local population had access to very few arms. The possibility of the
trouble speading to Cornwall could have passed through the minds of
some Privy Councillors, but no news was good news, and the punishments meted out to terrorists there scarcely 12 months since had
evidently frightened it into submission.

However, the failure of the local authorities to retrieve the consequences of Pollard's paltry conduct made intervention imperative.
They needed the stiffening of men who combined strong local
connexions with the full weight of the Council's authority. For the long
term tasks of allaying discontent and re-establishing administration the
obvious choice was the experienced Lord Russell, the Lord Privy Seal,
who had been created principal magnate of the region for precisely this
purpose. But to deal with the immediate crisis a trouble-shooter was
needed, a man of action and military background who would be able to
seize control of the situation, as well as give expert advice as to the

measures it demanded. With all his other commitments, as well as the overriding need to avoid any interruption of the build-up of the army being assembled for the invasion of Scotland, Somerset relied on such a man to succeed in quelling the commotion by the force of his own personality. The choice fell on Sir Peter Carew: it was to prove less than fortunate.

III

The decision to send Carew must have been taken towards the end of Whit week, but a few days' delay was imposed by the necessity of summoning him from Lincolnshire where he was enjoying a protracted honeymoon, an interval of repose in the middle of a stormy and colourful career.

He was born at Mohuns Ottery in 1514, the youngest son of Sir William Carew, and grandson of Sir Edmund who had been killed by a French cannon ball at the siege of Thérouanne the previous year.

The chronology of his earlier years, as recounted by John Hooker, his biographer, is somewhat confused, but the story is unquestionably colourful. At the age of 12 he was sent to the grammar school in Exeter, lodging with the draper, Alderman Thomas Hunt, whose misfortune it was to waste much valuable time searching the city for him. The truth is that his education was nothing more than a record of persistent truancy. Either the boy was quite uninterested in learning or he was terrorised by the ferocious Mr Freer who 'was counted to be a very hard and cruel master'. For Hunt the last straw came one day when he discovered Peter loitering about the city wall. The lad promptly climbed to the top of a turret and threatened to hurl himself to the ground if the alderman came after him. Nonplussed, the worthy citizen tipped a bystander to keep an eye on Peter, and hurried away to scribble a hasty report of his son's misdeeds to Sir William. Carew senior came storming into Exeter to deal with the delinquent, 'tied him up in a line, and delivered him to one of his servants to be carried about town as one of his hounds, and they led him home to Mohuns Ottery like a dog', and kept him actually tethered to one of the hounds for the next few days.

After this Peter was placed in Dean Colet's new and renowned foundation at St Paul's in London, but since he was 'more desirous of liberty than of learning . . . do the schoolmaster what he could, he in no wise could frame the young Peter to smell to a book, or to like of any learning'. After he had to all intents been expelled, his father jumped at the offer of a gentleman of his acquaintance to take him to France as a page, to continue his education at the French court. This new master, however, neglected him shamefully and consigned him to the stables from which he was fortunately rescued by a kinsman who happened to notice him, and who took in hand his courtly upbringing.

Peter next attracted the attention of the marquis of Saluzzo who invited him to join his retinue for the invasion of Italy which ended in disaster at Naples in 1528 and Landriano in June 1529.[1] Following the death of the marquis he showed remarkably mature judgment in changing sides and entering the service of the Prince of Orange, the victor in this campaign. In this household he served happily until he reached the age of 18 (1532–3) when he felt the call to return home, and was dispatched on his journey with much honour and furnished by the Princess of Orange with letters of recommendation to his father and the King of England.

When this richly apparelled, well set up young man walked into the parlour at Mohuns Ottery his parents must have suspected him of being an impostor — or a ghost — for, having heard no tidings of him for six years, they believed him dead. Sir William was decidedly reserved — until he had read and digested the Princess's fulsome letter. More to the point Peter's wit and skill in knightly exercises, horsemanship especially, won him the immediate favour of Henry VIII·who soon appointed him a gentleman of the privy chamber and frequently employed him on confidential errands. His spirit of adventure took him, in company with other young gentlemen, on a trip to eastern Europe in the course of which he visited Constantinople, a perilous undertaking for a Christian.

In 1543 he served in France in command of 100 foot, his elder brother, Sir George, being the Lieutenant of Horse; in the following year he was himself a captain of horse at the siege of Boulogne. In 1545 he was appointed captain of a warship, while George commanded the great *Mary Rose*. It was Peter who first sighted the French fleet, the approach of which brought the English out of Portsmouth in a manoeuvre in which the *Mary Rose* capsized and sank with the loss of hundreds of lives, including her captain's and again Peter who led the subsequent attack on the French fleet at Freyport which earned him his knighthood.

Owner now of the family estates, he could begin to think of marriage, and duly fell in love with a lady of the court. The King approved and promised to settle £100 a year in lands on them. The marriage was solemnised shortly after the coronation of Edward VI, and for the next two years Carew busied himself about his bride's estates in Lincolnshire, completely cut off from the court.

As a man of wealth and power, and high standing in his own county — he had served as sheriff in 1546 — he seemed the obvious choice to deal with the crisis at Sampford Courtenay. But his talents lay in the direction of vigorous, decisive action; his skill in diplomacy amounted

o no more than the arts of the courtier, and his career showed that he
was not a man who could abide being thwarted.

Sir Peter was briefed in London on 20 June, 10 days after the outbreak at Sampford Courtenay. To accompany him the Council selected
his uncle, Sir Gawen Carew; his role throughout the business, as a
spectator, would appear to have been no new experience, since on that
fatal day four years earlier it had fallen to him to stand helplessly on
his own quarterdeck and watch his elder nephew drown.

The Carews' instructions, drafted by the duke of Somerset and
issued under the Signet, were clearly aimed at conciliation. They were
to proclaim that the government, preferring to believe the disorders 'to
have been done rather of ignorance than of malice, and the motion of
some light and naughty persons than of any evil will', and, influenced
by 'the suit of divers gentlemen', was prepared to pardon offenders on
the understanding that they would keep the peace in future. At the
same time the Carews were empowered to arrest anyone else who
assembled to protest against the Prayer Book, 'and to see our laws duly
and severely executed against all such offenders as appertaineth'. It is
impossible to determine how far these orders were enlarged and clarified
verbally. Certainly it is not improbable that Sir Peter, as an experienced
soldier, took them as orders to be obeyed and did not raise the question
of interpretation. It may well be inferred that the harassed Protector,
conscious by this time that he was really out of his depth, angrily
brushed aside any question which could have implied that his directions
were in any way ambiguous. There was nothing in writing to indicate
how much patience Carew was expected to show should the rioters
decline to listen to him; but the hard-liners on the Council urged him
to act toughly, and later he was to tell Hooker that he had been
authorised to employ 'by the advice of the [local] justices all the best
means and ways that they might for the appeasing of the rebellion,
quieting of the people, and pacifying of the country . . .'.

IV

Having probably received their orders early in the morning, the two
knights rode hard through the long summer day and into the night,
making only brief halts for rest and refreshment, and to pick up new
mounts. Thus rapidly covering the 170 miles they could have reached
Exeter by noon on the 21 June.

As soon as they had dismounted they summoned the sheriff, Sir
Piers Courtenay, and the justices of the peace, to an immediate conference in order to exhibit the King's commission entrusting them with
plenary powers to pacify the rebels, and the proclamation which

commanded the commons to return forthwith to the paths of obedience.

The up-to-date situation outlined by the magistrates was more than sufficient to raise the irascible Sir Peter's wrath to flashpoint. While they had tarried irresolutely in Exeter, a numerous band of insurgents, the Sampford men well to the fore, had seized Crediton, not eight miles away, where all too obviously they were gathering strength for an advance on the city among whose inhabitants were a great many who sympathised with them. Nor can the sympathisers have been confined to the lower classes; the meeting must have included a leavening of those 'divers gentlemen' who had been prompt to urge conciliation, not least the influential but ineffectual Sir Hugh Pollard. They can have had little in the way of practical suggestions to offer, and it is probable that, having complied with his instructions to the extent of going through the form of consulting with his colleagues, Sir Peter curtly terminated proceedings with the announcement that he and his uncle proposed setting out immediately to confront the rebels, and got them to agree to ride to Crediton with him. He could at least hope that his masterful personality, backed by the full weight of the Privy Council's authority, would reduce an undisciplined throng of poor peasants to a state of sheepish confusion, no matter how keen their sense of grievance. And so the county notables, with their servants, armed and harnessed, 'a competent company' amounting perhaps to a couple of hundred men all told, took horse and rode out of Exeter, through Cowley and Newton St Cyres, to the little town of Crediton, 'there to have conference and speeches with the said commons . . . they then supposing and being persuaded that by good speeches and gentle conferences they should have been able to have compassed and persuaded the said commons'.

It took long enough for this troop to muster and buckle on their harness for 'some secret intelligence' to precede them and give warning of their approach. The rebels for their part were fully determined to stand their ground. They armed themselves with whatever weapons they could lay hands on, mostly bills and bows eked out with scythes and pitchforks, the more fortunate ones being also clad in jacks and sallets, and proceeded to put the township in a state of defence, digging trenches across all the ways leading into it. The road from Exeter entered Crediton between two very large barns inside which archers took up position, piercing the walls with loopholes. Between the barns and across the highway a stout rampart was thrown up and strongly manned with billmen and archers.

Thus it was that when Carew rode up with his troop he found the way into the town barred against him. They halted a little distance outside, dismounted, and started to walk towards the breastwork, expecting

be permitted to cross it and hold a parley inside. To their amazement
they were greeted with cries warning them to keep back. Carew called
out that he carried the King's commission to negotiate, but the rebels
blankly refused to listen or to heed his warnings of the consequences of
prolonging their resistance. For some minutes the two sides shouted at
each other down the length of the street, but to no purpose, because
the peasants were deeply mistrustful of this large band of armed men
and would not be talked into relaxing their guard:

> for the sun being in Cancer & the Midsummer moon at full, their
> minds were imbrewed in such follies and their heads carried with
> such vanities that, as the man of Athens, they would hear no man
> speak but themselves, and thought nothing well said but what came
> out of their own mouths.

More prosaically, they had no leader of quality to act as their spokesman, and, as simple rustics, they mistrusted their ability to match the
polished vocabulary of experienced men of the world. Moreover, there
was a complete absence of common ground. The gentry evidently
assumed that they had to contend merely with a negative, if belligerent,
protest against the new liturgy, whereas the rebels were determined to
enforce the unqualified restoration of the old, and were not going to
disperse until they had gained their point. To make matters worse,
Carew's manner was far from conciliatory. A Protestant of advanced
views, he was incapable of appreciating the depth of their attachment
to the popish faith, and they mere unlettered yokels! The longer he
was thwarted the more he hectored. At the best of times gentlemen
were not disposed to mince their words when dealing with awkward
peasants. It was only a few years since John Palmer was said to have
told his Angmering tenants as he forcibly evicted them from their
homes: 'Now is the time come that we gentlemen will pull down the
houses of such poor knaves as ye be!'

Deeply mortified and infuriated by the insolence of their rebuff,
the gentlemen unanimously resolved to rush the barricade and disperse
the rebels without further ado. The loose phrasing of the Carews'
commission gave no guidance as to the precise point at which negotiations might be abandoned as unproductive, or what degree of force
should be employed. No doubt a further attempt to talk might have
been indicated, after an interval for tempers to cool; in view of their
earlier conduct some of the gentlemen must have inclined to this course.
But Carew was impetuous. Tired and edgy after galloping many miles
with little or no rest, it seemed to him that there had already been too
much talking to no purpose. Evening was drawing in and he was concerned only to finish the job he had been sent to do without further
delay. And so he arrayed his band in fighting order and, pausing only to

limber their sword arms, they began to advance up the narrow stree
between the barns, towards the rampart.

For a veteran campaigner he showed a remarkable ignorance (
tactics in flinging his men headlong into a frontal assault. But apa
from the fact that he despised the low-bred clowns manning the breas
work, without men of quality to infuse them with fighting spirit, the
was no other course to him since the town consisted of little mo
than a single street and the only other openings were narrow gap
between the houses. His real blunder was to attack without recol
noitring, for he had failed to notice anything menacing about the barr
between which he had to lead his men, and from the loopholes in whic
there now poured a hail of arrows which drove them back in confusior
with the loss of several killed and many wounded, before they could ge
to 'push of pike'. Since up to this point the affair had been merely
riot and not open war, it is doubtful whether even the gentlemen wer
encased in full armour, if indeed many of them owned it.

The situation was retrieved by a man named Foxe, one of Sir Hug
Pollard's servants, who, on his own initiative, set fire to the thatch (
the barns — 'unawares of the gentlemen', says Hooker, though since h
contrived to blame Pollard for everything that went wrong his mai
concern may well have been to acquit Carew of any stigma of error. A
it is this laboured explanation may have been superfluous since Carev
did not trouble to disclaim responsibility; not only would it have bee
in character for him to order the use of fire, it was regular stree
fighting tactics. At all events it settled the affray. At the cry of 'fire
the defenders took fright and came streaming out of the barns; thei
panic spread to the men behind the rampart, and one and all fled dow
the street and out of the town, carrying most of the inhabitants wit
them. The gentlemen advanced again, passed the barricade withou
opposition, only to find themselves in possession of a town that wa
now empty save for a handful of poor and aged persons.

The fight had been won, but since there was no one left to talk wit
there was nothing for it but to return to Exeter 'without anythin
done . . . leaving all things, as they thought, in some quietness'. N
pursuit was undertaken, partly because night was about to close in
partly because it was assumed that the commoners would slink off t
their homes and not dare to face the gentlemen again.

Carew could not have made a greater miscalculation. Although th
insurgents had been scattered they had been neither pacified no
punished. The flames of Crediton set the whole shire ablaze. The repor
of it 'was in post haste, and as it were in a moment, carried and blaste
throughout the whole country'; and as it travelled so it grew i
enormity until it was widely believed that the gentry were about to fal
on the commoners, to despoil and destroy them. Everywhere th

people gathered together, enraged by the barns of Crediton, 'and in this rage, as it were a swarm of wasps, they cluster themselves in great troops and multitudes' to defend themselves, fortifying their villages and barring the approaches to them with trenches across the roads.

V

The inhabitants of Clyst St Mary, near Topsham, may not at first have attached great importance to the rumours, but an incident which took place there the following day was to bring the crisis home to them in no uncertain manner.

That Saturday morning, a holy day, Walter Ralegh, esquire, set out from his home at Hayes Barton in the parish of East Budleigh to ride into Exeter. Approaching Clyst he overtook an old woman walking to church, her rosary in her hands. Irritated by the sight of this popish gewgaw, he accosted her and testily enquired what she was doing with it. Presumably she replied that she was about to use the beads for the obvious purpose of meditating on the mysteries of the Blessed Virgin Mary. The chronicler does not say whether her mien was defiant or becomingly humble, but the mere fact of her stubborn persistence in outmoded superstition outraged the Protestant sensibility of Mr Ralegh and led him to make the mistake of starting an argument about religion. No doubt he attempted to explain that services were now conducted in English so that lay folk could readily understand them and join in the responses, and need no longer tell beads while the priest mumbled away in unintelligible Latin. He certainly pointed out that the Act of Uniformity had come into force the previous Sunday to reform and purify religion; he exhorted her to act like a good Christian woman and obedient subject of the King, and threatened her with the rigours of the law — quite erroneously, as it happens, since the Act prescribed no penalties against the laity. All he succeeded in doing was to frighten and confuse the old woman who took to her heels, burst into the church where all the parishioners were gathered for the service, and poured out a confused torrent of words — 'very hard and seemly speeches concerning religion' — from which they gathered that a strange gentleman had threatened that if she did not throw away her rosary there and then and renounce Holy Bread and Holy Water, he and his friends would come back, burn down the village and plunder their homes. The terrified old woman added, says Hooker, much else that was 'very false and untrue & whereof no talk at all had passed between her and the gentleman'.

The effect on her neighbours was electrifying. So it was no less than the appalling truth that a band of gentlemen had burned down Crediton and driven out its inhabitants; that they were roaming the countryside harrying the people with fire and sword; that these outrages were being perpetrated on no less an authority than the King and his Council who had sent an official down to Devonshire to direct operations. Down the years strange tales had filtered into the West Country of townships stripped and laid waste, of humble folk driven from their homes, weeping bitterly, to wander the roads as homeless beggars. Once it had been vague gossip retailed by tinkers about doings in far off shires; now it was actually happening in Devonshire itself, and their own village was next on the list for destruction.

Pouring out of the church and down the half mile to the village, they began hastily to dig trenches and erect ramparts across all the approaches. Messengers were sent out to all the surrounding hamlets and farms to spread word of what was afoot and beg assistance for the defence of Clyst.

Someone suggested that guns could be fetched from ships moored at Topsham, and a party of men was sent to get them. Before they had gone far they overtook Ralegh who presumably had turned off the Exeter road in order to pay a call in Topsham. The villagers would have attacked, and perhaps killed him on the spot, had he not taken to his heels and found refuge in the chapel where he was rescued by some sailors from Exmouth who happened to come along. Historians have professed to detect a manifestation of the militant Protestantism of Devon seamen in this incident; but it was equally likely, if not more so, that they happened to be full of beer and were roaming around looking for the chance of a punch-up. They did not look after him very well for a day or two later he fell into the hands of another lot of rebels who imprisoned him in the church of St Sidwell's, outside Exeter, as long as the commotion lasted, during which time he was frequently threatened with execution.

Meanwhile guns were taken from a ship and hauled to Clyst where they were placed in position to cover the bridge which carried the Exeter road over the Clyst stream; the roadway was also blocked with the trunks of felled trees. Behind these makeshift fortifications the parishioners settled down for the night.

Not many hours passed before Sir Peter Carew was informed. Once again he called the justices of the peace and other gentlemen together to concert measures to contain this new and unexpected disturbance. After a lengthy discussion it was agreed that he and his uncle, together with Sir Thomas Denys of Bicton, Pollard and several others, should ride out to Clyst and endeavour to persuade the rioters to disperse quietly.

The next morning, Sunday, 23 June, therefore found them in the saddle and on the road to Clyst St Mary. As they approached the

ridge they could see that it was blocked and guarded, just as the
entrance to Crediton had been. Carew, none the less, dismounted and
began confidently to walk towards it, unware, it would seem, of the
hatred with which he was now regarded on account both of his religious
views and the burning of the barns, for which he was being exclusively
blamed. The guns were ready loaded, in the charge of John Hammon, a
blacksmith and an alien ́ (probably a Breton) who lived at the nearby
village of Woodbury. Urged on by his comrades he aimed one of the
pieces at Carew and was about to apply the match to the touch hole
when Hugh Osborne (servant to Serjeant Prideaux) grabbed his arm and
stopped him. Careless though he was to danger, Carew saw clearly that
to go on would be to tempt providence, and he retired to consult his
colleagues.

After a brief discussion they sent a servant across the bridge with a
message to the effect that their errand was peaceful, and that they
wished merely to hold a friendly conference with the villagers in order
to ascertain the nature of their grievances and whether they had been
misused by anyone.

The people were dubious. They feared Carew and suspected a ruse
to get them to drop their guard. At the same time they could not
remain mewed up in Clyst indefinitely; sooner or later they would have
to negotiate with someone in authority to try and reach some sort of
settlement. After a short delay they sent their reply: they would permit
Denys, Pollard and Thomas Yarde, esquire, of Bradley to enter the village
alone, while the remainder of the party, the Carews especially, waited
on the far side of the bridge, on the heath, on the understanding that
they would not attempt to cross the river or make any other move
against the village while the conference was in progress. On these conditions the three gentlemen were permitted to enter the town at about
10 o'clock in the forenoon, and spent most of the rest of the day 'in
much talk & to no purpose'. Although they must have spelt out the
government's promise of unconditional pardon many times over, they
were unable to reassure the people; in particular they were obliged to
insist that they had no authority to make concessions over the question
of the Prayer Book, and that the law had to be obeyed. They had no
copy of the Act of Uniformity with them: indeed since Acts were not
printed at that time it is probable that long periods used to elapse
before anything better than brief summaries of them were transmitted
to the provinces. Thus it was impossible to convince the villagers that
they, as laymen, were not liable to punishment for infringement of it,
while the latter could have readily consulted their priest who must have
known that he himself risked 6 months' imprisonment for a first
offence, 12 for the second, and life for the third, but would most
probably not have been clear about the position of laymen. In short,

the people's fears about Carew's presence in the district could not
allayed.

Across the river on Clyst Heath the day dragged on interminably f
Carew and his companions. Although the village was quiet, no messag
had come from the delegation, and as the shadows began to length
their unease increased. As they speculated about what might be goi
on, some advocated continued patience, others voiced their fears
treachery, while Sir Peter stood on one side, moody and uncommunic
tive. At length one group bluntly announced their intention of going
look for a ford and to cross into the town to learn for themselves wh
was going on. But the friends and servants of the three envoys becan
alarmed lest this breach of faith might endanger their lives, and pr
tested vigorously. A heated argument ensued which ended in t
proposal being dropped. None the less, one or two men slipped quiet
down to the river and started sounding the depth of the water wi
their staves: the river was tidal and the level varied greatly from hour
hour. They were spotted by watchers on the opposite bank who calle
out to their comrades to stand to arms. Some of the peasants became
angry that Pollard and his companions feared that their lives were
imminent peril. The conference was abruptly terminated, and they le
the village thankful to have got away in one piece.

As soon as they had rejoined the rest of the party Carew demande
what they had been doing all day and what they had achieved. No
committally they answered, 'well enough', but refused to elaborat
until they got back to Exeter. Not only were they tired and hungr
they wanted the moral support of the rest of their colleagues befor
admitting to the intimidating Sir Peter that they had failed to accomplis
anything. In the gathering gloom the little cavalcade rode silently bac
to the city.

VI

That evening the county justices supped together at the Mermaid Inr
waiting until they had finished the meal and dismissed the serving me
before getting down to business.

Carew opened the proceedings, asking the three emissaries for a
account of their negotiations and what had been agreed with the rebel
They replied that the commoners had given an undertaking to remai
peaceful and orderly on condition that the King and his Council woul
suspend the innovations in religion and maintain the situation a
Henry VIII had left it until Edward himself came of age. The delegate
had not, of course, concluded any agreement but had merely promise
to notify these terms to their colleagues.

This report was received coldly, indeed incredulously, for it fell short of expectation. The magistrates sat 'for the time in a great dump or study' considering its disquieting implications. At no time was it any part of their duties as justices of the peace to strike bargains with mutinous peasants; their clear obligation was to disarm and disperse them. Not only had Pollard and Denys manifestly failed to do this, they seemed to have agreed to act as intermediaries, and hence virtually to condone the rebellion. The others began to attack them for 'both the matter and the manner of their dealings', and a bitter quarrel developed.

Sir Peter Carew, supported by Sir Piers Courtenay, the sheriff, came straight to the point; he 'openly, sharply and in plain terms inveighed against them for their slender or rather sinister dealings in so weighty a cause'. The facts spoke for themselves and could not be disguised. It was Pollard who had failed to suppress the original demonstration at Sampford and allowed it to spread all over the county, now he had proved equally ineffective at Clyst St Mary. He had wasted many hours in fruitless talking when he should simply have employed all available means to put down these outrages. To all intents he, along with Denys and Yarde, had given tacit encouragement to the rebels; who could say that they had not openly sympathised with the complaints? (Hooker's earlier comment on this may well have retailed Carew's opinion.) They and they alone were to blame for this rising, if only because they hadn't the guts to stand up to the people.

Although their chief concern was to justify their actions and protest their sincerity, Pollard, Denys and Yarde could, and very probably did, rejoin tartly that Carew's strong arm methods had provoked even more trouble than their more tactful approach. But by this hour the tensions which had been mounting steadily for the past week could no longer be restrained; every word spoken was taken up and flung back until the meeting broke up in noisy confusion.

Carew snatched a few hours' sleep at the 'Mermaid', and very early next morning took horse and slipped out of the city to go in search of Lord Russell who was now on his way to take over. Behind him he left an atmosphere of fear and suspicion. The night's stormy meeting had brought to the surface personal antipathies and mutual distrust. The magistracy of the county had ceased to exist as a coherent body. No one knew whom he could trust. Some already believed Pollard to be in league with the peasants; how many more of the gentry were secretly abetting them? The whole countryside was sliding into anarchy; their homes might even be being sacked at this moment, and their families massacred while they wasted time in Exeter concocting irrelevant plans to deal with a situation about which they knew virtually nothing. Thus every man shifted for himself, some one way & some another', and made for home with all speed. Many of them never made it.

The country people soon knew what was afoot from their many sympathisers in Exeter. They dug deep trenches and felled trees across the roads to block them, and manned roadblocks. Many a homeward bound gentleman rode unsuspectingly into an ambush, and was captured and locked up for the duration of the rebellion; but although Hooker asserted that many of them suffered great hardship and lived in daily fear of outrage and death, there is no evidence that the peasants ever attempted to injure them. Some gentlemen gave themselves up, thinking to make a favourable impression. Others deserted their homes for the safety of woods and other hiding places. Six or seven only remained in Exeter — apart from one or two who may have gone into hiding there — and did good service both in counselling the municipal authorities and in organising the defence.

Chapter 4
Half Measures

The roads were still open in the early morning of 24 June, and Sir Peter Carew was able to journey unhindered to Hinton St George, Somerset, where he reported to Lord Russell who had just arrived from London and was resting at the house of Sir Hugh Paulet. When he had rendered an account of the events of the previous two days, Russell ordered him to proceed to London to brief the Council on the situation.

Carew made his report formally to the 12-year-old King and the full Privy Council. Greatly affronted at the disloyalty of his Devonshire subjects, Edward formally charged his advisors to devise a speedy remedy. Then the business began in earnest. Somerset, whose policies were being challenged, was deeply disturbed, for not only did this add to tumults in other parts of the country, it complicated his problem by introducing the element of religious strife. Moreover, if the commotion in the West was as serious as the report indicated there was the depressing possibility that it would necessitate military measures which might delay the start of his cherished campaign in Scotland and, even worse, dissipate the costly force of mercenaries which had been assembled for it. The deadliest danger of all was the latent threat to his own position, and he resolved, therefore, to make an attempt to fix the blame for the disaster in Devonshire squarely on Carew's shoulders. He had already consulted Richard Rich, the Lord Chancellor, and together they confronted their trouble-shooter.

The Protector opened proceedings by charging Carew with having exceeded his commission which had been one of pacification, not violent action. In firing the barns at Crediton he had not only failed in this but had provoked a reaction on a far greater scale. Responsibility for the consequences, therefore, must rest on him and him alone. Carew retorted that as the man on the spot he had taken the measures demanded by the situation, the fact being that so far from dispersing peaceably, the rioters had refused even to listen to him. It is to his credit that he did not seek to evade responsibility for the burning of the barns; secure in the knowledge that many of those who sat facing him

across the Council board heartily approved of summary measures, h
brandished his commission, signed by the King and sealed with th
Signet, under Somerset's nose and claimed, with justice, that it gav
him complete discretion.

Here Rich the lawyer came in. He did not attempt to dispute th
wording of the commission, which could not be gainsaid, but adopte
a subtler line of attack. The authority of the letters could not cove
Carew's action because they had been issued under the Signet, wherea
the Great Seal alone could confer the power which he had arrogated t
himself. He had, Rich continued, effectively taken the law into his ow
hands, committed a felony, and now stood liable to be hanged for i
Sir Peter's reaction was precisely what might have been expected fror
him:

> These words being very sharp and touching the quick he asket
> pardon, and that he may have leave to answer thereunto, which bein
> granted, he did in such order and pithy manner, and not without
> reasonable stoutness, so answer the Duke and the Lord Chancellor
> and also both satisfy the King and Council, that he was well allowe
> and commended for the same.

Somewhat mollified, he pleaded that the·Council rather than berat
him should forward both men and money with all speed to the Lor
Privy Seal, and begged to be permitted to hasten back to Devon t
place his services at Russell's disposal. His request was granted and h
departed bearing fresh instructions.

He found that Russell had moved from Hinton St George to Honiton
20 miles short of Exeter, where he had set up his headquarters. There
apart from intervals spent at Carew's house at Mohuns Ottery, h
awaited the arrival of the men and munitions he had been promised
though for precious weeks he was to wait in vain.

II

It had been the task of the Carews to deal with the immediate trouble
at Sampford Courtenay, but for the general pacification of the region
man of greater authority was required. John Lord Russell had already
in 1540 presided over the short-lived Council of the West. A native o
the region, he had served as sheriff of Dorset and Somerset in 1528 an
had been High Steward of the Duchy of Cornwall since 1539. Now age
63, he had given a lifetime of service to the Crown, and in addition t
his accomplishments in the arts of the courtier he was also highly
valued as a man of affairs. His military experience was, however, some
what limited, and most of it lay far in the past, although it had include

ommand of the vanguard in the invasion of France in 1544. Much of
is service had been as a diplomat. He seems to have been widely liked
ad respected for his good qualities: the soubriquet 'Father Russell' is
oquent. In the course of his duties he had written in a kindly manner
o Cardinal Wolsey after the latter's disgrace. When he had served as a
ommissioner for punishing the rebels in Lincolnshire in 1536 one of
ae prisoners had been overheard observing: 'as for Sir John Russell and
ir Francis Bryan, God never died for a better couple'. His independence
f character is further borne out by the friendly relations he maintained
ith the Lady Mary and the support he gave her in her conflict with
ae Council during the latter part of her brother's reign. He himself held
o pronounced religious views, though he was believed to lean towards
ae reformed faith. Essentially he was a *politique*. This and one further
ality amply justified his selection to deal with the emergency: his
mple, unswerving loyalty to the Crown and belief in the necessity of
stable government. It was this that three years later was to induce him
o add his signature to the Letters Patent which limited the succession
o the throne to Lady Jane Grey. On the collapse of this project,
esigned as he saw it in the best interests of the realm, he unhesitatingly
ansferred his whole allegiance to Mary. Continuing as Lord Privy Seal,
e helped to negotiate her marriage with Philip of Spain, and took an
ctive part in resisting Sir Thomas Wyatt's rebellion.

It had been decided that Russell should go to Devonshire at the same
me as the Carews. On 20 June he was advanced £300 for expenses; on
3 June a further warrant was issued for coat and conduct money for
oldiers levied in London for his service. He must have departed with
ae least possible delay, though his journey was made slower by a con-
derable retinue. By 25 June he had reached Salisbury where he halted
o take stock of the situation and send a preliminary report to his
olleagues giving such particulars as he had been able to gather thus far,
ad enclosing the additional report of a man named Stowell. Here too
e received his first instructions. He travelled on into Somerset where,
Hinton St George, he met Sir Peter Carew and learned the alarming
ews from Exeter. A day or two later he reached Honiton where he was
orced to halt as the road to Exeter was blocked and the countryside
varming with rebels. Here the reply to his letter from Salisbury
ached him containing fresh orders drawn up in the light of Carew's
ccount of the situation and reports from the Devonshire justices of
ae peace. But these, although reflecting the Council's growing aware-
ess of the gravity of the crisis, were already out of date.

The sluggishness of the government's reaction indicates that the
telligence reaching it not only underestimated the revolt, but was also
afficiently ambiguous to justify a policy of minimising the danger. For
omerset, too, there was the further consideration of denying his critics

the opportunity to brand his policies as failures, and dangerous ones a
that. The simplest solution would have been to adopt the tough line h
friend Paget advocated, writing from Brussels, where he was engaged o
a diplomatic mission, to urge him to take the field at the head c
mercenary soldiers and beat the rebels to the ground. To do so woul
be to concede that his social and religious reforms were at fault. T
justify his policy he had to prove that conciliation could work, bu
this necessitated striking a delicate balance between the demands of th
law and the grievances of the lower orders, an impossibility if hothead
like Carew aggravated the situation and destroyed the people
confidence in his good faith.

Relying on the fact that none of the recent manifestations of unre
had proved particularly menacing, and had all been put down quickl
and quietly by local officials, seconded in some cases by members c
the government who had landed interests in the districts affected, th
Protector could afford to hope that the apparent scale of the Devonshi
outbreak was a function of the distance the reports of it had travelle
At this early stage there was no reason to suppose that it involved mor
than a handful of villages. Without reliable intelligence he could ignor
vague rumours of a really formidable build-up beyond the Tamar, an
hope to hear no more of it. This air of optimism is implicit in th
earlier proclamations and instructions to the Carews and the Devonshi
authorities. With the burning of the barns at Crediton it wa
momentarily shaken. Alarmed by the ominous turn of events, he ha
rounded on Carew, casting him in the role of whipping boy — wit
ample justification if it was no accident that the latter appeared to hav
bungled the affair and so precipitated the crisis it was so desperatel
necessary to avoid. Doing his best to discredit Carew, he perseverec
with habitual obstinacy, in his original course. Nor was he necessaril
deceiving himself or misleading the public. Organised rebellion, a
distinct from more or less aimless rioting, was extremely rare, an
although the Pilgrimage of Grace had been a peasant revolt, it had bee
directed by dissident nobility and gentry, as indeed had the Cornis
rising in 1497.

The low key approach pervades Lord Russell's original brief whic
reflects the knowledge of the dispersal of the insurgents at Crediton, bu
not the reaction provoked by the incident. It directed him to ascertai
from the justices and other influential men — from any available sourc
in fact — the state of the four western shires, and if he found ther
tranquil to take appropriate steps to ensure that they remained so. T
this end he was to exhort masters to rule their servants firmly, father
their children. Clothworkers and other artificers should be kept full
employed so that the Devil might not make work for idle hand
Opportunities for unlawful assemblies were to be avoided as far a

ssible. He should seek out and detain originators of scares and
mours, punishing them as necessary, and make a special example of
y disturbers of the peace. His chief task, nevertheless, was to use his
st endeavours to investigate the causes of any disturbances, and in the
ght of them strive to pacify the people with fair words and gentle
rsuasion. Only if this failed did his commission empower him to levy
ldiers and crush rebellion by force. To complicate matters he was
rther charged with organising the defence of the district against an
ticipated invasion should the war with France, now threatening,
aterialise.

It is to be noted that in this initial phase Russell was not provided
ith troops — Somerset was reluctant to break up the army he was
ping to send to Scotland — but with preachers. A Mr Gregory and a
r Reynolds were licensed to propagate the reformed word of God as
d where he might direct, although at the last moment they seem to
ve been discarded in favour of Dr Miles Coverdale, the translator of the
ble, who had already been preaching in the West. While the Protector
as prepared to deal with the economic grievances on their merits there
ere to be no concessions in the matter of religion, for this was a
atter of state and as such wholly within the prerogative of the Crown,
cked up by Act of Parliament, as opposed to other popular dis-
ntents which were matters of commonwealth and thus negotiable.

Two days later, 26 June, apprised of the re-assembly of the people
a greatly increased scale and the fiasco at Clyst St Mary, the govern-
ent persisted in blaming the usual handful of agitators from whose
fluence it was merely necessary to wean the simple commoners. The
stices of the peace were urged to continue talking with the people, to
ead with them even, to point out how unkind it was of them to take a
ean advantage of the King's youthfulness, stressing the consequent
shonour and insecurity to the whole kingdom, and the encouragement
ey must surely be giving to the French and other foes. If they felt
grieved they should petition the King for redress, not resort to arms,
rticularly since the laws they complained of had been made by
rliament in the name of the whole nation. Even if this conciliatory
proach failed to appease the people it should at least suffice to
ollify their wrath. The great thing was to try by every means to pre-
nt any more of them coming out in rebellion, and to persuade those
ho had already done so to return quietly to their homes. Only as a
ecaution was it recommended that the gentry, together with trust-
orthy servants and tenants, should hold themselves secretly in
adiness to carry out the justices' orders.

Finally, as late as 29 June, when at length becoming resigned to the
ed to employ force, the Council still showed no sign of awareness of
velopments in Cornwall: their gaze remained riveted on the gathering

of rebels around Sampford Courtenay at a time when much, if no
most, of Cornwall was in revolt. Yet even now there persisted som
residue of the belief that the rebels could still be persuaded by th
promise of clemency or cajoled by the threat of the dreadful penalti
for treason. Some inkling of the nature of the specific complaints w
beginning to dawn on the authorities. The Council advised Russell
reassure the people that their fear that henceforth babies could b
baptised on Sundays only was unfounded, as also was the rumo
(which would have come as news to the Devonshire men!) that th
subsidy on sheep was to be extended to pigs, cheese, etc. And whi
Russell attended to the business of fixing the blame for such maliciou
allegations squarely on the shoulders of popish priests, Mr Blakisto
the ecclesiastical commissary, would spur on the clergy to preac
obedience to the law, and counteract the misrepresentation of th
changes in religion.

Somerset could well have been forgiven his reluctance to comm
himself to any irrevocable decision during these early weeks. Tremo
were again running the length of the land, and until each could b
separately evaluated it was impossible to decide whether any was likel
to constitute a real threat. Most were in counties much nearer Londo
and therefore more immediately worrying. Even where there was n
overt trouble reports were far from reassuring. On 29 June the earl o
Arundel wrote from Guildford to inform Secretary Sir William Petr
that 'these parts remain as may be in a quavering quiet', and urge th
need for prompt, effective measures: 'the honest promise faithfully t
serve the King, the rest will follow', if there was no delay. But ci
cumspection was essential. The appointment of Sir William George t
the commission of oyer and terminer was disquieting because 'h
fame soundeth not among the people for the administration of Justice
Petre was requested to approach the judge in confidence with a vie
to getting him to withdraw tactfully. Incidents did occur in Surre
including a fairly serious riot at Witley Park over the enclosure of th
former common, and in Sussex where several small camps were forme
Arundel was fully occupied all summer keeping both counties und
control, and succeeded remarkably well. In the last ever example of th
exercise of purely feudal authority, owing nothing to central gover
ment, he summoned all who had grievances to Arundel Castle, din
them well, adjudicated complaints and ordered gentlemen and othe
to reform any enclosures they had made, which they willingly did;
also arrested agitators. The ample armed force at his command he ke
in the background. According to the musters of 1539 he had 123 full
armed servants and could call on double that number from the hous
holds of Lords La Warr and Southampton, in addition to which sever
leading Sussex gentlemen could furnish 10 or 20 men apiece.

At one time or another during the spring and summer almost every ounty in the east Midlands and south of England was affected in some ay. The majority of such disturbances were minor in character and olated from each other. Although little or nothing is known of the etails they clearly amounted to little more than demonstrations against enclosures, and were brought under control by the local magnates and gentry in nearly all cases. But in the atmosphere of crisis their mere number seemed to threaten imminent general insurrection, nd so contributed to the government's hesitation over committing its ender forces to any single district, more especially a distant one from hich they could not be quickly recalled should danger threaten the apital.

In the instructions he sent to Russell on 29 June, Somerset was early growing pessimistic about the prospects for reconciliation, and signed to the need for some form of military action. Now the seasoned ampaigner and victor of Pinkie was beginning to entertain doubts out the elderly Lord Privy Seal's fitness to exercise an independent ommand for the first time, and tendered detailed advice on the conduct f operations.

Two or three days before he began his march against the rebels ussell ought to infiltrate two or three men into Sampford Courtenay, the capacity of *agents provocateurs,* to gain the confidence of the surgents by a conspicuous display of zeal for their cause. Concurrently eps should be taken to deprive the rebels of supplies by arranging for e whole district to be stripped of victuals in nightly forays and by the nposition of a blockade on their camp. As the army approached the llage the cavalry should hover about the field making periodic feints, hile mounted arquebusiers seized points of vantage and harassed the bels with their fire to provoke them into sallying out from behind the ains with which they had closed off all entrances to the village. Once ut in the open they would be pounded by cannon at a range of 10 or 2 score paces until either mounting casualties forced them to surrender they were provoked into charging the gun line, when the cavalry ould close in and cut them to pieces. Economical and envisaging a latively small but highly trained force, this was in essence the strategy timately employed later in Norfolk. For the present, however, such a rce existed only in the Protector's mind.

The victory gained, the persons of the ringleaders were to be secured:

We desire especially those six men which do solicit the causes of their complying unto one especial man Steple[1] of the said town, and the same man also may be apprehended to be punished above the others for example's sake.

ould they refuse to confess except under torture they were to be sent to London together with any others Russell might think worth exami ing: racks and thumbscrews, presumably, were not widely available the provinces, at any rate they were the only amenities he was assum to lack.

The flaw in this recipe for victory was that it envisaged Russ taking the offensive at a moment when he was at his wits' end to blo the rebels' advance into Somerset and Dorset, and was actually co templating the necessity of retreating. He had brought only a handf of men with him, and knew only too well that there was no time recruit locally (as he was expected to do), for the full weight of t enemy's offensive was about to engulf him. It was probably as late 30 June or 1 July that the Council learnt definitively from him that t insurgents were everywhere on the move and were on the point laying siege to Exeter. And thus it turned out that three precious wee had been squandered, and what had begun as isolated disturbances in few widely scattered places had grown into a civil war of serio dimensions.

III

In the crisis of 1549 the determining factor was ultimately the resourc in men and munitions available to each side. Engrossed in analysis the causes of revolt, historians have uniformly neglected this cruc aspect, assuming that the rebels were a sketchily armed mob witho the least notion of military science, while the state had at its disposal ample force of foreign professional soldiers. Nothing is further from t truth; had it been so none of the rebellions could ever have got off t ground.

In the ordinary way the only permanent land forces of the Crow consisted of the garrisons of Berwick-on-Tweed and Calais, which we of some size but not available for general service, and handfuls of m stationed in various fortresses, including the recently erected coa defence forts, which amounted to nothing more than maintenan details. The Yeomen of the Guard and Gentlemen Pensioners, totalli about 100 men each, had mainly ceremonial duties; they were n tactical formations, and in wartime their members often served officers on land and sea.

In 1549 there was, unusually, a substantial number of forei mercenaries in the country who had been recruited for the war Scotland. Accurate information about them is scarce, and hence it easy to exaggerate their numbers, as many historians have tended to d falling into the error of assuming that they were readily available f any purpose.

At the beginning of the year not very many can have been left over
om the campaigning season of 1548. In January Sir Philip Hoby,
mbassador in Brussels, informed the Emperor that the majority of
em had been lost, and sought leave to recruit 2,000 men in Friesland.
he level of wastage may be judged from the report in March that
onrad Pfeyning's command of 2,000 German infantry had dwindled
to 600 from sickness and other causes. Other corps had no doubt
ffered correspondingly, and so the first half of 1549 was occupied in
cruiting fresh troops for the summer campaign. It is probable that
e numbers reached their peak this year, exceeding the total employed
the Pinkie campaign of 1547, in order to match the large French
xpeditionary force which was now in Scotland.

On 24 May, on the eve of the rebellion, the return of the strength of
e army on the northern Border commanded by the earl of Rutland
sted bands of Italians, Germans and Spaniards totalling 200 horse
d 2,200 foot. Further drafts and new companies were at various
ages on their way north, but some units were still on the continent
waiting shipment, even still in process of formation there.

John Dymock, the recruiting agent, had great difficulty in getting
en to enlist. Many were reluctant to sign on because of tales about
e extreme hostility of the English towards strangers. The pay offered
as poor, Somerset's meanness in this respect, the result of straitened
rcumstances, compared badly with Henry VIII's generosity. There was
en competition for men in Germany and the Netherlands, and other
lers offered better terms. One wonders whether England ended up
ith second rate troops; if this was so the rebels stood that much better
ance of success. Permission was obtained to recruit 2,000 foot in
ower Saxony for Pfeyning, but, thanks to his reputation for cheating
d ill-treating his soldiers, men were loath to enlist under him, and
any who did so soon deserted. The intricacies of international politics
so conspired to cause delays. On 5 May Dymock reported difficulty
ver getting passports at Hamburg. On 11 May Hoby in Brussels had
btained clearance for 500 men under Wilhelm von Walderden, though
opeful that the authorities would wink at the embarkation of the
mainder. By the end of the month Dymock's efforts had produced
least 1,100 recruits for Pfeyning on the Border, when his corps
talled 1,700 including presumably the 600 left over from the previous
ear.

Heavy cavalry were raised in the Netherlands by Henry Hakfort and
arlos de Guevara. Ready to embark on 15 June, they were detained by
e Emperor's command. Hakfort was soon cleared, but Guevara did
ot reach London until mid-July, bringing 108 troopers.

As regards deployment, it is to be assumed that since mercenaries
ere enlisted specifically for the campaign in Scotland every effort was

made to concentrate them on the Border. Some of the Saxon recruit
may have been shipped direct to northern ports, but there was also
constant stream of men travelling from Dover, either in ones and tw
or complete bands. Some at least of Guevara's men must have proceede
straight to Northumberland where they were stationed by mid-Augus
However, the imperial ambassador stated that the band served
Norfolk at the beginning of that month, and although M. A. S. Hume
his study of Spanish mercenaries in England has denied this, tl
probable explanation is that the company was divided: two contrac
exist, for 108 and 200 men respectively, while Guevara was paid f
130 men up to 29 August, a date which implies service in Norfolk t
that number. Meanwhile, an advance detachment had already gone t
far north to be recalled; there is little doubt that Somerset was r
inforcing the northern army while the emergency was in progress in tl
South, hoping, despite everything, that the campaign could go ahe
as planned. Conversely, there is no evidence that troops were transferre
from it to either Norfolk or Devonshire, indeed it was a question eith
of matching the supposed French build-up in Scotland or abandoni
Haddington to its fate and imperilling the Border counties into tl
bargain. Although there is no extant order of battle during the cruci
period, all units which had been in Rutland's command in May we
still there in October with the addition of Guevara and three other ne
bands. Not until 11 October is there any evidence of troops being wit
drawn, when units formerly on the Border had joined the garrison
Boulogne following the abandonment of the Scotch war and the shif
ing of the main operations to France.

The forces available in the South can be approximately reconstructe
as in Table 2. There may possibly have been one or two other ban
which cannot be traced; Malatesta's, for example, was a scrat
formation improvised out of men who were trickling through Londc
on their way north, and was disbanded as soon as the emergency w
over. But it would be unwise to try to invent any more than the 2,96
which can be more or less counted. Mercenaries were expensive ar
were hired chiefly to stiffen the native levies which were alread
numerous and also had to be paid and fed − 3,000 in Rutland's arm
not to mention others based on Carlisle and more still to be raise
Irish kerns were also recruited.

During July and August there were at most about 7,500 foreig
troops in England of which not more than about 3,000 can have bee
available near London for counter-insurgency measures. And not on
was Somerset reluctant to divert them from Scotland, some objecte
to becoming embroiled in a civil war. In addition, the German infant
were so universally hated that there were cogent political objections
using them, although in the end this consideration had to go by tl
board.

Table 2

Captain	Formation	Strength*
Hakfort	Clevois (German) heavy horse	420
Guevara	Spanish heavy horse	130
Hermigny	Burgundian, or German and Italian heavy horse	259
Sanga	Albanian, or 'Hault Burgundy at the least', light horse	141
		950
von Walderden	German landsknechts, 4 ensigns, say†	1,600
Spinola	Italian arquebusiers	216
Malatesta	Italian foot, say	200
		2,016

*As far as possible strengths are taken from pay accounts which consistently show that more men were enlisted, exclusive of allowances for 'dead pays', than were contracted for.
†The contract strength of the ensign was 400 men; two of them had 464 on the payroll. Other references speak of total of 1,000—1,200.

Mobility is a further factor to which due weight must be given. Ten or 12 miles was a normal day's march in the sixteenth century; 15 was good. The only troops which could have taken part in any action were those who would have had time to get to it after the appropriate initiating decisions had been taken. In every case operations were initiated so belatedly that there was never enough time to get troops from the North (where other disturbances also occurred). In particular this applies to the formation of Warwick's army in East Anglia in August. The plan was not adopted until 2 August at the very earliest. Assuming that prompt decisions were taken and orders issued it seems unlikely that troops near Berwick could have received them and commenced their march until at least 6 August. The distance to Norwich was about 350 miles, and it would have taken them until the first week in September to get there, by which time the rebellion was all over. It seems impossible to reach any conclusion other than that the government never had more than 2,500 professional troops to deal with all the commotions in the south of England, and that not all of them were willing to take part.

Henry VIII, who had considerably enlarged the Royal Navy, had entertained ambitions of creating a permanent professional army like those of France and Spain, but was constantly thwarted by lack of financial resources. For the supply of troops he relied principally on the nobility. Peers, and some of the richer gentry, were accustomed to keep large numbers of servants, usually much in excess of what the needed to attend to their wants. The real function of these retinues in which members of the inferior gentry were prominent, was to dis play their lords' liveries and accompany them when they rode abroad thus advertising their eminence. Additionally, the nobility retained other men, usually gentlemen, whom they could call on to attend whenever they wished, whether to put on a special display of pomp o to answer the King's call to raise a company for war. In theory this practice breached Henry VII's Acts against livery and maintenance which had been passed to prevent the formation of private armies. In practice, however, it was winked at and magnates were granted licences to retain men, naturally those whom the Crown could trust In 1518 there had been a move to extend the system. Gentlemen o known loyalty had been invited to take up appointments as captain with licences to retain men who were to be kept in readiness for service and equipped with harness and horse. The licences stipulated the captain's own tenants, men living on lands under his jurisdiction, a well as anyone willing to serve under him who was not already someone else's man. The advantages of this system were two-fold: when soldier were required the Crown could be certain that a limited number a least could be produced at short notice; at the same time the risks o internal disorder were limited, and if trouble did break out the main military potential was under the control of reliable men.

This quasi-feudal establishment existed side by side with the county militia; indeed, since gentlemen and their retainers were also listed in shire musters, the two were not clearly distinguished. The fact has an important bearing on the interpretation of mere total figures of men and equipment. By the Statute of Winchester, 1285, every free man was obliged to equip himself in accordance with his wealth and status and be available for home defence. From 1522 onwards this obligation was much revived. Frequent musters of the able-bodied men, aged 16–60 were taken in every county and surveys made of the arms and armou available. Members of the gentry were formally appointed as captain and petty captains of local bands.

Although no complete set of muster rolls for any one year survive the substantial number of extant partial returns reveal a wide gap between the ideal and the actual. In many counties the bulk of the equipment, arms and armour, was in the hands of the gentry and their followers. Repeatedly one notices that gentlemen owned two or more complete outfits, where the ordinary farmer never had more than one and if he had any fighting gear at all it was likely to be just a weapon or odd piece of armour. Moreover, the greater the man the larger his armoury, some even employing armourers to look after it. The earl o Rutland certainly did, and so must nobles who were active militarily

ke the earl of Shrewsbury and the duke of Norfolk. So did a rising
entleman like Sir William Petre: as Secretary of State he was a member
f the government, and so had added reason for it. In the little county
f Rutland in 1522 there were 732 able-bodied men, but there were
nly 87 complete harnesses, 59 of which belonged to gentlemen and
ine more to clients of theirs. It is true that a good many men owned a
veapon — a bow or a bill — while others had miscellaneous pieces of
rmour — a sallet, a jack or some minor item — but the preponderance
n favour of the gentry in terms of fully armed men is obvious. The pro-
ortions were not the same everywhere, but in nearly every county
here was nowhere enough equipment for all the able men — indeed for
ess than one third overall — and where the situation can be studied in
etail the bulk of it was controlled by the gentry.

In the emergency of 1549 the government made little use of local
evies, except from Wales. Disaffection was so widespread in the southern
alf of England that they would have been thoroughly unreliable.
nstead it concentrated on rallying the gentry with their servants and
etainers, while the army commanders recruited such men as were
villing to volunteer, and no doubt equipped them very largely from the
esources of the royal armouries.

The rebels, on the other hand, were wholly dependent on local
esources, and these need to be examined in detail.

At the height of the rebellion the duke of Somerset estimated the
ombined fighting strength of Devon and Cornwall at not above 7,000,
tag and rag' included, and that since 1,000 were defending Exeter and
thers would have been left behind to guard their homes the effective
trength of Arundell's army could not have exceeded 4,000, 'and the
nore part unarmed'. This he must have based on muster returns: those
or 1544 reported 4,000 men in Devon and 1,117 in Cornwall, and he
robably added a couple of thousand to cover a considerable body of
nen who had not been counted. In reality the total should have stood
ery much higher. It was 11,720 for Devonshire alone in 1524, and
ormally around 10,000 in the Elizabethan period. Cornwall could
robably have produced at least 4,000 on its own, for its population
nust have been a good 50,000, and the very full Rutland figures of
522 show that nearly 10 per cent of the population were able-bodied
nales. So far as can be judged nearly the whole of Cornwall was
nvolved in the rising, so that a good 3,000 or more men may have
aken the field. In Devonshire the position is less clear. Not all the
ounty participated: Exeter and Plymouth stood out, and one may
uess that the South was less affected than the North. Perhaps a minimum
f 5,000 were actively involved; a few may have joined in from
Somerset which remained restive throughout the summer. Holinshed
ut the total rebel force at 10,000 which may be an exaggeration,

although the relevant section was actually revised by John Hooke
who was an eye-witness.

But mere numbers signified little, the important thing is to determin
the number of men who were properly armed and accoutred. Almos
all were infantry. The full harness of a foot soldier consisted of
sallet (helmet), a gorget protecting the throat, a jack or brigandine —
coat of leather or canvas with small metal plates sewn into it — an
splints protecting the forearms. Archers frequently dispensed with thes
last, wearing a bracer on the left wrist. About one in three were bow
men, the remainder were armed with the bill, a multi-purpose weapor
6 feet long, the head of which combined a spear point and an ax
blade backed by a spike. In the mêlée it was a most effectiv
weapon, although unable to stop a cavalry charge like the 16-foot Swis
pike. Both archer and billman often carried a short sword. Som
Cornishmen were armed with slings. Firearms were rare. In 1551 th
Venetian ambassador noted that the English had very few arquebuse
and little campaign experience with them, while the pike was only jus
being adopted from the continent. The Devonshire men were poorl
equipped in general. In 1544 only 1,000 complete harnesses wer
counted, to go round 4,000 men; the superior return of 1524 indicate
that there was a harness for just one man in three, but a considerabl
number were kept in the towns, Exeter especially, leaving some of th
rural districts very poorly off. In 1539 the hundreds of Liston
Rodborough and Tavistock (in the heart of the disaffected area) ther
were only 29 full suits for 776 men, plus enough bits to make uj
perhaps 40 more. There could very well have been more armou
around which was not inventorised, but altogether the total canno
have been anywhere near what was needed. Some was probably obtaine
from the homes of various gentlemen who were arrested. Altogethe
there may not have been more than a few hundred fully armed men

The Cornishmen, in contrast, were very well armed: in 1544 ther
were said to be 1,069 harnesses available for 1,117 men; in 1524 a
many as 1,710 for only 1,247 men. Detailed returns for four of th
nine hundreds in 1522 listed 804 harnesses, from which it may be con
cluded that the total shown two years later was more or less correct. I
addition something like half that number of men had a weapon witl
various pieces of armour, and many more had a bow or a bill. But th
crucial factor was that in this county almost all military equipmen
belonged to the common people; there was no need to go looking for i
in the homes of the gentry. On the assumption that the situation ha
not changed materially over the years, it is possible to state with som
certainty that Cornwall was able to put some 2,000 fully equipped me
into the field in 1549, possibly more if there were substantial reserv
stocks to be raided in the royal forts such as St Michael's Mount an

St Mawes, and if the rising was in fact planned well in advance, Arundell could have used his influence as Captain of St Michael's Mount to stockpile harness there. These could be backed up by perhaps 1,000 half-armoured men, and 1,000 light troops who carried weapons only. But it was the fully armed men who counted for most. When battle was joined morale necessarily hinged largely on wearing the standard protective gear. Whatever its exact strength — and the numbers we have mentioned may be somewhat exaggerated — the army assembling at Bodmin was anything but a rabble of country bumpkins waving pitchforks and scythes, but a well armed, well equipped fighting force, similar indeed both in size and armament to the one which had routed the flower of French chivalry at Agincourt. In fact it was better armed because it was able to provide itself with a useful artillery train, obtained from ships and coastal batteries.

The total strength of the rebels may thus be reckoned as anything up to 3,000 first line troops with perhaps twice as many light armed men in support. The actual number who took part in the campaign was very possibly smaller. But their main strength almost certainly lay in the well armed Cornish contingent welded together by the bond of language and sense of fighting for their survival as a people.

Chapter 5
The Siege of Exeter

I

The disturbances so far had appeared to involve a comparatively small number of people from north-west Devon only; the Cornishmen had yet to appear on the scene. The reasons for their holding back are partly a matter of record, partly of surmise. In their camp at Kynoch they were holding lengthy discussions about their aims. It was alleged by John Foxe, the martyrologist, and others that some proposed the abolition of justices of the peace, because they were too ignorant to construe Latin, lawyers on account of their high fees and sharp practices, and manorial courts because of the expense they caused. But what really concerned them was religion, and the articles they drafted to present to the King dealt with little else. Simultaneously, it may be taken for granted that under Arundell's experienced leadership their forces were being systematically mobilised, organised into companies, and trained for the combats which they had to expect.

It was not long before the camp became restless for action. Some of the men began threatening the prisoners with violence. The eventual indictment was to allege that they paraded tumultuously through Bodmin crying: 'Kill the gentlemen! and we will have the Six Articles and ceremonies as they were in King Henry VIII's time.' There was also the problem of feeding them, the obvious solution to which was to avail themselves of the lands and goods of other men. Now that the list of demands was settled the Council of War resolved to open its campaign to enforce them.

First they secured their flanks. A strong detachment, very probably led by Robert Smyth of St Germans, was dispatched in the direction of Plymouth to raise the country thereabouts. Probably at the crossing of the river Lynher near Landrake, Sir Richard Grenville attempted to oppose them with a hastily assembled band of gentlemen and their retainers. These the rebels thrust aside and forced to take refuge, with their families, in Grenville's castle of Trematon, to which they laid siege. But it was a poor stronghold: in 1538 John Leland the antiquary had noted its ruinous condition, and even though the rebels had no

rtillery, some of the defenders lost heart, slipped over the walls and
nade off during the night. In the morning Grenville went out through
. postern to negotiate. A party of insurgents slipped smartly behind
im barring his retreat, while others laid hands on his 'aged unwieldy
)ody' and threatened to kill him on the spot unless the garrison
urrendered. It promptly did. The rebels sacked the castle; ladies, says
`arew, were ill-treated, stripped to their smocks, and in some cases
uffered broken fingers when their rings were snatched roughly from
hem. The prisoners were carted away and shut up in Launceston castle
o which by now it would seem that the main body of rebels had
noved.

Fear spread throughout the district. Many of the gentry shut them-
elves up for safety on St Nicholas' Island in Cawsand Bay and in
imilar refuges elsewhere. Plymouth offered little resistance, although
he steeple of the church and the corporation's records got burnt: the
`rivy Council subsequently hinted at treachery. But the stubborn
lefence of the castle must have been frustrating since the rebels would
:ertainly have counted on laying hands on a good supply of arms
here, including guns. It seems that a small company was detached to
nask it, while the remainder marched off to rejoin Arundell.

In the course of the next few days Arundell completed the work of
nustering and organisation, and led his men out of Cornwall. Their
)bjective is not known for certain. The precedent of 1497 indicates a
;eneral intention of marching on London to challenge Protector and
`ouncil; at the very least there must have been some expectation of
ittracting general support in the southern counties.

The column made a colourful and menacing sight, a mingling of the
nartial with the devotional. Flanked by crosses, candlesticks, banners,
uoly bread and holy water, it was headed by a procession of priests
)earing the consecrated Host in a pyx beneath a canopy. For the
;tandard they had a banner depicting the Five Wounds of Christ, the
;ame as had been borne in the Pilgrimage of Grace 13 years earlier. The
uearts of all were elated: 'Christian soldiers, marching as to war, with
:he Cross of Jesus going on before.' Could that antiquarian-minded
west countryman Sabine Baring-Gould have had this episode in mind
when composing his famous verses? The date cannot have been earlier
:han 25 June, nor much later. Progress was probably slow as they
)aused along the road to rally supporters, and hence it must have taken
:he best part of a week to cover the 68 miles to Exeter.

Having driven the gentlemen into flight or concealment, many of
:he common people of Devon now declared for the rebels, gathering
n many places and electing captains to lead them. Foremost among
:hese were the men of Sampford Courtenay: Underhill, a tailor, Segar, a
abourer, Maunder, a shoemaker and Asheridge, a fish driver,

with sundry others such like the worst men & the refuse of all others thought most meet in this service. Howbeit, it was not long before that certain gentlemen and yeomen of good countenance and credit . . . were contented not only to be associated of this rebellion, but also to carry the cross before this procession and be captains & guides of this wicked enterprise.

However much Hooker despised the rebels he could not help admitting that they succeeded in attracting the support of men of some consequence. From Berry Pomeroy near Totnes came Sir Thomas Pomeroy, a hare-brained fellow who probably had little understanding of what it was all about and joined up for a lark. More formidable was John Bury of Silverton in the Exe Valley who was 'the chief captain of all saving one', inferring that he was the effective leader of the Devon men. He claimed to wear the livery of Sir Thomas Denys, and at one time had certainly been the marquis of Exeter's man. His principal, perhaps his sole, motive was the reinstatement of Cardinal Pole (for many years the Catholic leader in exile) and was presumably responsible for the insertion of an article to this effect in the final version of the manifesto. Another gentleman, Coffin by name, was a retainer of Sir John Arundell.

II

The city of Exeter, strongly fortified and commanding the route to the east, had to be the first objective. Rich, populous and well stocked with the arms so urgently needed by many of the peasants, its support would give an incalculable accession of strength to the cause. In advance of his coming Arundell sent messengers to John Blackaller, the mayor, praying him to open the gates and throw in his lot with the rebels. The response was disappointing. As early as 22 June, on receipt of news of the disturbance at Clyst St Mary, the city council had debated the situation and decided to convert the forthcoming Midsummer Watch from the customary pageant to a serious precaution against disorder. They directed each of the four gilds of craftsmen — tailors, weavers and tuckers, shoemakers, and bakers and brewers — to furnish 10 men in full harness who were householders and honest, discreet inhabitants, to act as a guard, and further empowered the mayor to appoint one or more constables in every quarter of the city.

Blackaller was no Protestant. There were indeed some to be found among the leading citizens, but they were not numerous. The city as a whole was Catholic. The cathedral was regarded as a hotbed of disaffection, from Bishop Veysey (who lived in Sutton Coldfield) downwards. The chapter had resisted the appointment of the reformer,

Simon Heyne, to the deanery in 1537, and in 1543 had attempted to frame him on a charge of treason. There were many in the city who would willingly have thrown in their lot with the insurgents, having already vigorously expressed their hostility to new ideas. It was only possible for Dean Heyne to preach because he enjoyed the active protection of men of the stature of the Carews, while another reformer, William Alley, 'being an earnest preacher and much inveighing against false doctrine', had got such a hot reception when he attempted to preach, that he dared not go into the pulpit again except when the Carews stood guard over him, defying the hostile congregation. But the council, although several aldermen 'were well affected to the Romish religion', gave first place to their duty to God, obedience to the King, and loyalty to their country — not to mention the safety of their own skins — and resolutely declined to side with the insurgents or aid them in any way.

On receiving this rebuff, the rebel leaders sent back a second, peremptory demand that the council should demonstrate its unqualified adherence to the ancient faith by coming over to their side without further prevarication, failing which they threatened to lay siege to the city. The corporation reiterated their previous answer, adding for good measure the opinion that the Cornishmen were wicked men, whom they regarded as their enemies, and rebels against God, King and country, on account of which they would have nothing to do with them. This the Cornish captains could not and would not accept. Possession of the city was the cornerstone of their strategy. To the need to lay hands on the abundance of munitions and hundreds of potential recruits they believed to be inside the walls, there were added, now that their overtures had been rejected, the lively danger that the inhabitants were less well disposed than had been assumed. They could not take the risk of bypassing so formidable a fortress, while at the same time the army was too small to be divided, leaving a detachment to mask the city while the remainder pressed on towards London. Arundell, therefore, had no choice but to undertake a siege, although both he and his council of war hoped and believed that the presence of numbers of sympathisers inside the walls would make it a short one. And so on 2 July, he commenced, with some 2,000 men (on Hooker's reckoning), the investment of a city whose population was upwards of 8,000. A fateful, yet inescapable decision. The siege proved to be the turning point of the campaign and the ruination of his plans, for it meant surrendering the initiative and granting the government a desperately needed breathing space during which to mobilise and take the measures necessary to confine operations to the south-western peninsula.

John Hooker was present during the whole of the siege and has left a vivid account of it. Exeter had a fine record of loyalty to the Crown, having stubbornly resisted Perkins Warbeck's assault in 1497. In addition, as Hooker records, Mayor Blackaller entertained the lively fear that if he opened the gates the city could be given to the sack, and there must have been a majority among the population who shared his view, believing that the Cornishmen

> brought their wives, horses and panniers, persuading themselves and promising them[selves] by such a day & upon such a day to enter into the city, and then to measure velvets & silk by the bow and to lade their horses home again with plate, money and other great riches.

The notion of looters preparing to measure out fine cloth by the bow's length — double the normal yard — looks like a highly effective piece of propaganda, an atrocity story designed to instil hatred and fear in the citizens, for there is no evidence that any depredations were committed by the rebels in respect of either persons or property. Almost certainly a good many women and other hangers on accompanied the army; it was still a common practice in the nineteenth century, indeed it was essential before the days of ancillary corps.

In anticipation of the attack the mayor and aldermen had made preparations both to defend the walls and to harass the enemy. The city was viewed for armour, able-bodied men were mustered and the best of them enrolled as soldiers, making a garrison of some 1,000 men, as the Privy Council subsequently estimated. Captains were appointed for every ward, and they in turn assigned warders for the day and watch-men for the nights. Guns were positioned to cover each gate; others were mounted at strategic points on the walls. Emplacements were erected at various points for guns as well as for sentries and snipers. At the end of St Edmund's bridge a *chevaux de frise* of sharpened stakes was set up. In short, every possible measure was taken to repel the expected assault.

III

Determined to lose no time, Arundell commenced a close investment of the city. Roads leading into it were blocked with trenches and felled trees, and bridges were broken down. Constant patrols effectively severed all communication with the outside world. The besiegers boasted that they had penned up Exeter as if in a chicken coop or a mew — a cage in which a hawk was confined while moulting. The water pipes and conduits were broken up and melted down to make shot, depriving the inhabitants of their regular water supply, although in fact, thanks to the situation of the city on a low hill, which was full of

rings, they suffered no real deprivation. In view of the smallness of
1e rebel army there was probably no attempt to construct a continuous
ne of entrenchments, the investment being based rather on a series of
rongpoints or camps, eight in all, in which the men were disposed.
he governors of these camps included Henry Bray, mayor of Bodmin,
lenry Lee, mayor of Torrington, and Roger Baret and John Thompson
ho were priests. The original 2,000 or so Cornishmen were joined by
1any others from Devonshire and perhaps Somerset too. Holinshed
ut their total strength at 10,000 'stout and valiant persons', but it
ounds a bit of an exaggeration, and may have included camp followers.
looker estimated that 6,000 were engaged on the second day of the
attle of Clyst St Mary, apparently exclusive of those who were still
eeping the siege. The high command was Arundell's council of war
n which Cornwall was represented by John Winslade and Thomas
lolmes, Devonshire by Pomeroy, Bury and Coffin, and the commoners
y Underhill, Sloman and Segar, all of Sampford Courtenay. John Bury
ppears to have acted as second in command; Thomas Smyth was
lmost certainly absent at first, occupied in the vain attempt to capture
lymouth castle.

The rebel army was hopelessly under-equipped for the task it had set
tself. Not only was it nowhere near large enough to mount an effective
peration against a city the size of Exeter, while at the same time
roviding an adequate covering force, it had no siege train to breach
he walls. Guns had been obtained from coastal forts like Pendennis
astle, but since they would have been mounted on trucks, not field
arriages, it would have been impossible to transport any but the lighter
ieces which could make no impression on well built fortifications. The
est that could be done was to position batteries on the high ground
orth of the city from which they could sweep on the streets, or else
pposite the gates.

The one real asset the besiegers possessed were the tinners, men
killed in sapping and mining, who began to dig their way under the
valls in order to blow them up. They drove a gallery under one side of
he West Gate, filled it with barrels of gunpowder, pitch and other
nflammables, and made preparations to detonate it during the hours of
arkness while a storming party stood by to go in immediately after-
vards. Unfortunately for their plans, there happened also to be a miner
1 the city, a Teignmouth man named John Newcombe, who had heard
he sound of digging underfoot, and immediately realised what was
oing on. He hurried away and sought out Alderman William Hurst, to
vhom he had some obligation, and warned him of the danger. At first
he alderman, who was 66 years old and had been mayor four times
vas inclined to scoff: how could anyone divine what was going on in
he bowels of the earth? But Newcombe was so insistent that he agreed

to walk as far as the gate with him. Before they went out Newcombe requested the loan of a pan. When they reached the gate he filled it with water, placed it on the ground and bade Hurst observe the surface. The latter saw that instead of settling down the water went on moving and Newcombe explained that this was caused by tremors in the ground on which it rested, caused undoubtedly by picks striking the earth underneath. Moving the pan around he located the exact spot below which the miners were working.

Much impressed by this demonstration, Hurst, who as a lad had perhaps settled in Exeter in time to experience the siege of 1497 hurried away to inform the mayor. Recognising the danger, Blackaller instantly accepted Newcombe's proposal that countermining should be commenced without delay, since the mine was more or less ready and might be exploded at any time. Newcombe's team speedily penetrated the chamber and was able to see clearly the charge ready to be detonated. His experience provided a simple solution to the problem of dealing with it. Taking advantage of the fact that the town was sited on a hill which sloped downwards towards the West Gate, he got every one living in the streets on this side to fill a large tub with water and place it outside his front door. At a given signal they all emptied their tubs simultaneously; the water cascaded down towards the gate, down Newcombe's shaft and into the mine itself, drowning it. A violent thunderstorm is said to have broken providentially at the same moment, adding to the torrent. Disheartened, the rebels abandoned their mining; powder may not have been plentiful and the gunners may have objected to wasting it in this way.

Had they so chosen the rebels could have inflicted terrible damage. Their most skilful gunner, a Breton, fired many deadly shots from his emplacement on St David's Hill, killing among others a man named Smyth while he was standing in the doorway of his house in Northgate Street. The gunner came forward with a plan to lay down a barrage of incendiary shot which he calculated would burn the whole city to the ground in four hours. Arundell was enthusiastic, and the council of war fixed the date and hour for the bombardment to commence. The day arrived, the ammunition had been brought up, and the guns were on the point of opening fire when Robert Welsh, the vicar of St Thomas Exe Island, heard about the plan. Appalled, he collected as many men as he could find and ran to the battery where he appealed earnestly to the gunners not to fire.

'Do what you can by policy, force, or dint of sword to take the city,' he cried, 'I will join with you and do my best, but to burn a city which shall be hurtful to all men and good to no man, I will never consent thereunto, but will stand here with all my power against you.'

A Cornishman from Penryn and renowned for his prowess in all manly sports, he was highly respected in the army and so got his way. In fact he held a position of some authority among the rebels, not as a captain but as a sort of magistrate. His devotion to the cause was unquestioned, as his way of dealing with spies showed. There was the case of a certain Kyngeswell, a tin miner of Chagford and a servant of Mr John Charles of Tavistock, who was apprehended carrying letters between his master and Lord Russell. Even before the rebellion he had become widely known as an enthusiastic Protestant, and the eagerness with which he seized every opportunity to advocate the reformed creed and decry Catholicism had made him thoroughly disliked. It seems that he was allowed a wide measure of liberty, although kept under fairly close surveillance and never able to escape from the camp. Many of the insurgents tried to change his opinions, sometimes by disputation, sometimes using threats, occasionally imprisoning him. Eventually they lost patience and haled him in front of Welsh who condemned him to death. He was hanged on an elm tree outside the house of Nicholas Cove on Exe Island, opposite the West Gate of the city.

Although too weak seriously to contemplate any attempt to carry the walls by storm, the besiegers tried their hardest to wear down the spirits of the garrison by keeping them constantly on the alert. Sometimes they formed up in front of the walls carrying ladders as if about to make an assault. At other times they tried out various ploys to approach the gates and burn them. They made one such attempt on the South Gate, pushing a cart laden with old, dry hay up to it and setting it alight. But although they kept well behind it they did not escape casualties.

Here and at the West Gate there were 'great port pieces' mounted on beds of logs: these were guns constructed of flat iron bars strongly bound together with iron hoops, 12 feet in length with a bore of 12 inches at the muzzle. They had last been used in the siege of 1497. Now they were loaded with bags of flints and hail shot. As the cart came near, the gate was suddenly flung open and the guns discharged point blank doing great execution. After this the gates were left permanently open, but the insurgents did not dare confront these murderous, if antique, weapons again. The defenders threw up earthen ramparts which made far stronger barriers, and at night kept fires burning in front of them to prevent surprise attacks under cover of darkness.

The main form of harassment was sniping, and there was very little the inhabitants could do except try and avoid it. Here the lie of the ground, which otherwise was so beneficial, was a positive disadvantage, for the streets, clinging to the side of the hill, were not masked by the walls. Marksmen posted in houses in the suburbs kept up a galling fire on both the guards on the walls and anyone who showed his head at an upstairs window, killing and injuring a considerable number. In retaliation the garrison made sorties in the course of which they demolished some houses and tried to burn others down. More serious were the cannons which swept certain streets with their fire, making it hazardous for anyone to venture into them until some sort of screens were devised – 'certain mounts to shadow the streets from the same' – which prevented the gunners from seeing their targets. Other methods of harassment proved more of an irritation than a danger.

IV

Against a garrison of nearly 1,000 starvation was the most effective weapon in the besiegers' armoury. From the outset the city was closely invested to deprive it of victuals. Famine, Hooker observed,

> of all other turmoils and perils is most dangerous: and no other plague to it to be compared: for no force is feared, no laws observed no magistrate obeyed, nor common society esteemed where famine ruleth: for as the Poet saith: *Nescit plebs iuena timere.*

In the absence of forewarning no emergency stocks of food had been laid in; the disturbed state of the countryside had rendered any attempts at last minute provisioning impossible. What there was could not be expected to last long. Lord Russell's information was variously that supplies in hand were sufficient for two days or eight. There was a good store of dried fish, rice, prunes, raisins and wine in the merchants' warehouses at reasonable prices, but bread and flour were extremely scarce. Bakers and housewives were driven to retrieve 'puffins', or stale pastry and bran which in normal circumstances were made into feed for horses, swine and poultry; now the mixture was moulded in cloths to hold it together, and baked. Hooker recalled how Plutarch had written that 'hunger maketh all things sweet, and the hungry belly shunneth nothing'. In time even this wretched fare was all consumed, and the common people 'being not acquainted with so hard a diet as famine doth prescribe, were very impatient to endure the continual barking of their hungry bellies'. Morale declined rapidly. Soon it became easy for defeatists to persuade them – if they had not already persuaded themselves – that it would be better to surrender for the sake of getting at the stolen food which was believed to be plentiful in the enemy's camp, rather than hold out a little longer in the hope of deliverance. Nor was the atmosphere improved by the activities of a brewer named Reve who did his best to persuade his brother tradesmen to combine to enhance the price of beer. Even a small war breeds its own species of petty profiteers.

In a time of acute crisis behaviour of this sort could easily bring latent antagonisms to the surface. Half the wealth of the community was held by some 30 merchant families, an oligarchy which ruled the city; indeed the 100 or so merchant families owned a good three-quarters of its wealth. Magistrates and aldermen, although (according to their apologist, Hooker) putting the public weal before their private interests, thus met with numerous insults in return for their efforts to ensure equality of sacrifice and sustain the spirit of resistance. Nevertheless, they strove hard to care for the welfare of the poorer citizens — the greater their want the greater the concern for their needs, for it was keenly recognised that the faintest hearts were likely to go with the emptiest bellies. A poor rate was assessed and weekly collections made which enabled distress to be 'liberally' (or at least adequately) relieved. This possibly included the commandeering of all supplies of food, for certainly some form of rationing was imposed, as a result of which the poor were able to get food free or at a very low price. With equitable sharing out of what there was, and everyone getting enough to keep body and soul together, morale was preserved. Even the prisoners languishing in irons in the town gaol got their share of whatever was going. In the end they had to be fed on horseflesh, but happily they found it palatable and there were no complaints. As ever, Hooker found the appropriate proverb: 'hunger findeth no faults but all things are sweet'.

From time to time cattle were observed wandering close to the walls, and sorties were organised to round them up. Some skirmishes which developed in the course of these forays helped to sustain morale. A taste of action came as a welcome relief to the endless monotonous watching and waiting for the appearance of some relief force, and a few casualties were a price well worth paying for a little additional food. Besides, each was a little victory in itself. Not merely did every bullock or sheep driven through the gates mean another meal, it also gave the comforting feeling of having scored a point off the enemy, and to this extent checked the growing feeling of utter helplessness. Save for maintaining a vigilant guard and endeavouring to intercept and destroy them, there was little the rebels could do about these raiding parties. Arundell had too few men to seal off the whole long perimeter of Exeter; the effectiveness of the blockade relied on the close alliance of the countryside around with the insurgents.

The state of siege was in no way allowed to become the pretext for any lowering of standards. The mayor continued to hold his court as usual and dealt promptly and effectively with any offences against public order or disputes between citizens. Forbearance was the keynote. Sensibly it was recognised that the tensions arising from the state of close and prolonged confinement within the walls could easily rise to unbearable levels, more especially since there were deep fissures within the community.

There was one day when the mayor held a review of the citizen arrayed in their armour, in the High Street outside the Guildhall Quarrelling broke out between Protestants and the conservatives who formed the larger number. Hooker insists that the latter, loosely styled 'papists', were intent on bringing about a tumult in the course of which they planned to down the Protestants and wrest control of the city from the mayor. The prime mover was a clothier called Richard Taylor who bent his bow and loosed an arrow at one of the opposite party. In his excitement he released the shaft jerkily; it flew wild and struck his best friend, John Petre, though luckily the point glanced off a rib and he was not seriously hurt. 'A gentleman of good countenance and credit', Customer of the Port of Exeter also, he was the brother of Sir William Petre, the Secretary of State, and perhaps like him, as well as the majority of Exeter men, a Catholic. We are not told where he was standing, but it had probably not occurred to him to keep clear of the loyalists. Horrified at the possible fatal consequences of his error, Taylor forgot his original intention. What could have developed into a very nasty incident did not go beyond a 'great muttering', and in the end calm was restored. Years afterwards he was to die in a debtors prison, and not a few people who remembered this day regarded it as a judgment.

Throughout the tense middle decades of this century opinions in Exeter were often sharply divided, but as a rule citizens respected each others' views. Disorderly behaviour, of which this was the most flagrant example, was dealt with tolerantly during the siege. The magistrates would earnestly entreat men who reacted violently under the strain to exercise patience, to be of good heart and trust in the good God to send His deliverance.

> And thus, and by these means, in hope almost against hope, they continued dutiful and obedient, from the second day of July 1549 until the sixth day of August then following, the same being five whole weeks, upon which day they were delivered.

It was to become an experience graven on their very souls, and which afterwards they resolved never to forget. For 200 years the ending of the siege 'in memorial for ever to endure is kept for a high and holy feast . . . yearly upon the sixth day of August'.

Lacking the strength to mount a full scale assault, the rebels let pass no opportunity to exploit their certain knowledge that given the choice the people of Exeter would have voted in favour of retaining the ancient forms of worship. Frequent truces were arranged and discussions held to try and reach some form of agreement. Each time the rebels stipulated for an exchange of hostages as surety for the safety of those who were engaged in the parley. In Hooker's slanted view it was an unequal bargain, for while the besiegers insisted that the city should produce its most eminent and respected men, they would send only 'the refuse, the scum and the rascals of the whole country'. He did, however, concede that these were leaders: 'the worse the man the greater his authority among them, which was good enough for so wicked a matter'.

So far as Arundell and his associates were concerned these negotiations had only one end in view, to persuade the citizens to renounce their allegiance and join the rebellion, and although the matters discussed ranged far and wide, everyone being free to raise whatever he wished, they always came back to this basic proposition. Blackaller himself, William Hurst, John Buller, John Britnall and William Periam were the chief spokesmen for the city. Nurtured in the Catholic faith, in their hearts they still clung to it. Yet despite their convictions they could not bring themselves to commit treason; ever loyal to their King and anxious for the safety of the commonwealth, they asserted time and again that they would never yield so long as they lived and were able to man the ramparts. The rebel chiefs employed every variety of argument to enlist them to the cause, but to each they returned with one voice the same flat refusal. They had been reared in the city and owed all they had to it; there they had sworn allegiance to their King and there they would resist to the death.

A few did waver. There was a member of the common council, John Wolcot, merchant, a man of unblemished character, who was disturbed by the rebel propaganda. One morning when it was his turn to act as captain of the watch, he and two friends went to the West Gate where they stood talking for a while. Suddenly they strode to the wicket gate, which Wolcot unlocked, and went outside carrying the keys: at this time the inner rampart had not yet been erected. As he was a councillor and in command of the guard no one thought to stop him. They walked on and into the rebel lines where Wolcot spent some hours in earnest conference with the leaders. Whatever offer he may have made to them it was more than he was capable of fulfilling. Perhaps he said he had left the gate unlocked, and invited them to use it; perhaps too they reconnoitred it and their findings led them to suspect him of trying to lure them into an ambush. Anyway, in the end they lost their tempers with him and he only just managed to escape and race back to the gate, leaving his friends behind as prisoners. When he got in he was severely reprimanded for deserting his post, but apparently nothing more drastic followed. Hooker omitted to say what became of the keys.

Men who actively sympathised with the insurgents were careful not to do so too openly, but kept up a fairly regular communication with them in a variety of ways. Sometimes it was possible to hold a conversation over the walls undetected. Letters were frequently carried by messengers who slipped unobtrusively through the shadows, while a common dodge was to wrap notes around arrows which were shot to and fro. Open conversations were sometimes held during a truce. There were always people plotting to open the gates and admit the rebel troops, mainly at night, but either they were very incompetent or a close watch was kept on their doings, because nothing untoward ever took place.

The worst that happened was a conspiracy involving the soldiers who guarded the castle. Some unnamed persons bribed them to admit a party of rebels through a postern. The day and hour had been agreed, but just before the operation was about to start an official party arrived to inspect the castle and its garrison, realised what was afoot and put a stop to it. Either the council had been quietly tipped off or something had happened to arouse their suspicions. Pure coincidence cannot be ruled out or, as devout Protestants said: 'it pleased God to move the hearts of certain men to take the view of the Castle' at that very hour. No one was punished. We may picture the inspection party entering the castle in a thoroughly official manner and walking round, seemingly in all innocence of what was cooking; taking as long as possible, peering into every nook and cranny, making pompous comments on the state of this and that, asking the soldiers inane yet apparently very searching questions which necessitated lengthy answers. While this went on the soldiers stood about self-consciously trying to look as if things were perfectly normal and to avoid giving the impression of being impatient for the visitors to go away. And on the other side of no-man's-land the Cornish combat team lay concealed behind hedges awaiting the signal to move in, until eventually they came to the conclusion that they had been played for suckers, and stood down cursing the go-between who had made fools of them, vowing vengeance should he fall into their hands.

This particular piece of sport was probably spoiled by members of a group of about 100 men who made a solemn compact to defend the city to the limits of their strength. They had planned that in the event of the enemy effecting an entrance they would meet at the former house of the Dominicans, now belonging to Lord Russell, and make a concerted escape through a postern which led out of the garden; if they met with opposition they would stand together to defend themselves. They appointed one of their number as captain for the enterprise. While they waited for this final act to begin they worked unobtrusively for the more effective defence of the city, arranging among themselves that at all times a certain number of them should undertake, over and above their normal spells of watch and ward, periods of unofficial duty patrolling the streets and ramparts on the look out for possible acts of treachery. Their vigilance, indeed, was the chief, and perhaps, in the last analysis, the only cause of the preservation of Exeter from disaster, for there was no service or precaution that they omitted to take by day or by night. They belonged of course to the Protestant party, 'all bent together to honour God, obey the King, and to serve in their common-wealth'. They believed the defence to be a sufficient and just cause in itself, and were greatly heartened by the manifest determination of the mayor and magistrates, regardless of their dislike of the reformation. The latter, acknowledging their zeal, naturally favoured and encouraged these vigilantes. And it was they who were ever to be found taking the lead whenever action was called for, however dangerous. They were conspicuous in sorties which they never missed, and indeed frequently they made up an entire raiding party. Inevitably sympathisers with the rebels maligned them and impugned their motives, looking for ways of discrediting them, but this only drove them closer together, strengthening their conviction that their unofficial activities were amply justified.

It happened that one of their fighting patrols scored a noteworthy success. Dashing out of a sally port they violently assailed a party of rebels, taking prisoners and bringing back much spoil including one or two small guns. They suffered some casualties themselves, leaving several of their number behind in enemy hands. John Drake, who had been receiver and sheriff of the city the previous year, returned with an arrow through both cheeks, while John Symons, a cook, was mortally wounded. The most spectacular exploit was performed by John, a Fleming, and servant of Richard Helyard, the goldsmith. He was carrying a loaded arquebus when suddenly he found himself face to face with one of the rebels who had his bill raised ready to strike. Caught at a momentary disadvantage, John threw himself to the ground, shouting that he surrendered. The rebel lowered his weapon, not realising that the gun was loaded; John rolled over, took aim and shot him through the heart. He then stripped the corpse of weapons and strolled coolly back to the gate.

This skirmish was to have an unfortunate sequel. Its success greatly encouraged the company, and after a number of meetings they decided to venture another sortie to see what further damage they could inflict on the foe. In the course of their many activities some rivalry had grown up between two of the more prominent members of the band. These were John Courtenay, the fifth son of Sir William Courtenay of Powderham, a young man of proud and ancient lineage, already knowledgeable and experienced in warfare, and Bernard Duffield, a servant of Lord Russell and keeper of his Exeter house, a man of rather obscure origin who had advanced in his master's service by dint of zeal and ability. These two strove incessantly to outshine one another in devotion to duty and bravery in combat. The former, as a very junior member of a great aristocratic family, was in the position of having to win his spurs in order to keep his status, the other was clearly out to prove that personal merit was no whit inferior to birth. Unhappily, what began as zeal for the cause degenerated into a competition for personal advantage.

The project for another raid brought the antipathy of the two men to the surface. Courtenay, speaking as a soldier with knowledge of how these things were managed in a regular campaign, asserted that action of this nature by part of the garrison of a beleaguered fortress was not permissible without the express sanction of the commander-in-chief, except in some extreme necessity. Duffield, 'very loth to lose any part of his credit', and 'to desist from that [which] he with others had determined', insisted that the raid should go ahead as planned. It is clearly implied that hitherto these expeditions had been undertaken without reference to higher authority, and that Courtenay was raising a novel objection to a plan of which Duffield was clearly the chief architect. Unable to make any impression on his comrades, Courtenay resorted to the mayor to whom he disclosed the entire project, putting forward various arguments designed to prove that it was certain to endanger the security of the whole city.

Blackaller was greatly alarmed by the suggestion that a prominent and influential citizen, who so far had done nothing but set an excellent example to his fellows, was about to jeopardise the safety of the whole community in order to feed his own self-esteem. He convened a meeting of the common council and ordered Duffield to appear before it. Both men were examined. The question was thoroughly debated, but in the end Duffield had to be told that it was necessary to forbid the sortie, which was probably planned on a very big scale, because the anticipated risks were too great to be acceptable. Blackaller entreated him not to take the decision hard. He praised Duffield's services, assuring him that no one could possibly think any the worse of him for yielding to the opinions of the city fathers backed up by professional advice. Duffield, none the less, was furious with Courtenay (whose action probably infringed the unwritten rules of the band) and accused him of slandering a comrade for personal advantage. He stubbornly refused to abandon the plan, completely lost his temper and ranted so wildly at the council that they ordered him to be locked up in order to avoid possible violence. Unhappily for Mayor Blackaller, Frances Duffield was every bit as pugnacious as her father. As soon as she learned that he had been thrown into gaol to cool off, she rushed round to the mayor's house to demand forcibly that he should be released immediately. When the mayor demurred she became extremely angry, abused him in most unlady-like language, and finished by slapping his face. Her conduct was widely resented in the city, and since Duffield's

riends no doubt defended it warmly there was danger of a violent
quarrel developing, had not the mayor 'with great patience wrapped up
his wrong and injury [and] so moderated the matter as he pacified
the broil and salved the sore'.

Exeter was fortunate in its mayor. As the siege dragged wearily on,
nerves became increasingly frayed, and the smallest differences easily
became magnified into bitter disputes in which men all too easily
imagined their honour and loyalty to be questioned. It needed a man of
tact and strong personality to smooth over difficulties and keep people
working harmoniously together. How young Courtenay came out of
his shabby affair is not recorded. Blackaller must have had his own
opinions about his reliability, but being a wise man kept them to himself. And so as day succeeded tedious day, belts were pulled a notch
tighter, spirits sank a degree lower, and from the battlements anxious
eyes scanned the surrounding countryside hoping at length to sight the
dust raised by the army marching to their rescue.

Chapter 6
War of Words

With the forming of the siege of Exeter the swift movements and dramatic encounters which had marked the second half of June ceased abruptly, and for the greater part of July the campaign was waged largely on paper. Hamstrung by the unexpected resistance of Exeter, very probably deprived of a strong detachment of Cornish troops vainly seeking to reduce Plymouth castle, Arundell had perforce to abandon any plans to present the rebels' demands to the King at the head of an army, and instead sent them ahead by messenger. The Lord Protector returned a reasoned reply, still evidently hoping to talk the insurgents into abandoning their enterprise. Concurrently he conducted a protracted verbal battle with his commander in the West, endeavouring at once to allay the latter's very real apprehensions, and counter his repeated requests for men and munitions with excuses and advice, hoping perhaps that, other considerations apart, if troops were dribbled westwards as slowly as possible the storm might still blow itself out before full scale military measures became unavoidable.

I

In their final form the Articles of the Rebels were completed 'in divers camps by east and west of Exeter'. Odd references suggest that a short preliminary list peculiar to the Devonshire people had been gathered by Sir Hugh Pollard and transmitted by the hand of Sir Peter Carew, featuring prominently an objection to the subsidy on sheep which would have been particularly upsetting to a largely pastoral shire where there was no enclosure problem. The ultimate list was, however, restricted to religious and political issues, and seems preponderantly to have represented the Cornish case. Several versions of the Articles exist, differing slightly in their wording, but all to the same effect; the sixteenth, however, the demand for hostages, is found in one version only, and could have been a verbal addition.

The full list ran as follows:

1. We will have all the general councils and holy decrees of our fore-fathers observed, kept and performed, and whosoever shall gainsay them, we hold as heretics.

2. We will have the laws of our sovereign lord King Henry VIII concerning the six articles to be used again as in his time they were.

3. We will have the sacrament hung over the high altar, and thus be worshipped as it was wont to be, and they which do not thereunto consent, we will have them die like heretics against the holy Catholic faith.

4. We will have the Mass in Latin as it was before, and celebrated by the priest without any man or woman communicating with him.

5. We will have the sacrament of the altar but at Easter delivered to the people, and then but in one kind.

6. We will that our curates shall minister the sacrament of baptism at all times, as well on the week days as on the holy days.

7. We will have holy bread and holy water made every Sunday, palms and ashes at the times accustomed, images to be set up again in every church, and all other ancient ceremonies held heretofore by our Mother the Holy Church.

8. We will not receive the new service because it is but like a Christmas game. We will have our old service of matins, Mass, evensong and procession as it was before; and we Cornishmen, whereof certain of us understand no English, utterly refuse the new English.

9. We will have every preacher in his sermon, and every priest at the Mass pray, especially by name, for the souls in purgatory as our forefathers did.

10. We will have the Bible and all books of scripture in English called in again, for we be informed that otherwise the clergy shall not of long time confound the heretics.

11. We will have Doctor Moreman and Doctor Crispin, which hold our opinions, to be safely sent unto us, and to them we require the King's Majesty to give some certain livings to preach among us our Catholic faith.

12. We think it meet, because the Lord Cardinal Pole is of the King's blood, that he should not only have his pardon, but also be sent for from Rome, and promoted to be of the King's Council.

13. We will that no gentleman shall have any more servants than one to wait upon him, except he may dispend of a hundred marks in land, and for every hundred marks we think it reasonable that he should have a man.

14. We will that the half part of the abbey lands and chantry lands in every man's possession, however he came by them, be given again to the places where two of the chief abbeys were within every county

where such half part shall be taken out; and there to be established a place for devout persons, which shall pray for the King and the Commonwealth. And to the same we will have all the alms of the church box given for seven years.

15. For the particular griefs of our country, we will have them so ordered as Humphry Arundell and Henry Bray, the King's Mayor of Bodmin, shall inform the King's Majesty, if they may have a safe conduct in the King's great seal to pass and repass with an herald of arms.

16. For the performance of these articles we will have four lords, eight knights, twelve esquires, and twenty yeomen pledges unto us until the King's Majesty have granted all these by Parliament.

The most striking feature of this manifesto is its peremptory tone, every article commencing with the challenging 'We will have . . .'. Once these non-negotiable demands (as they may realistically be termed) had been conceded in full, the insurgents' representatives could settle details with the government on terms of equality. Over the religious issue they insisted on the complete reversal of every change which had taken place since 1529, including the resumption of full communion with Rome, as the reinstatement of Cardinal Pole clearly implied. Crispin and Moreman, both canons of Exeter, were highly regarded in the West and were now languishing in prison for having preached too vigorously against the Reformation. Even more surprising is the utter consistency of the rebels; they did not flinch from the revival of the draconian Act of Six Articles backed by all the horrors of the ancient penalty for heresy.

Although the authorities could not bargain with traitors, the Articles were treated with great seriousness, and at least three official replies were drawn up. The Lord Protector addressed himself directly to the rebels in a reasoned statement couched in the language of sorrow rather than anger, urging them to abandon the course of disaster before it was too late. The divines Cranmer and Nicholas Udall — the latter commissioned by the Council to make an 'independent' critique — were concerned to refute the militant Catholic line and justify the Protestant position at large.

Somerset chose to ignore the pugnacious tone of the Articles and confine himself to what were obviously the substantive grievances. It is of course feasible that he was dealing with an earlier, less provocative version which covered rather different ground than the final one; some of the points could have been communicated to him verbally.

Baptism, he insisted, would continue as ever to be available at all times. As to confirmation, it was the job of the parish priests to prepare children to receive it; there was no compulsion on them to attend school for the purpose, a condition which of course would have been

uite out of the question in country districts. Some wild mis-
pprehension had evidently arisen concerning Holy Communion: 'Doth
:ceiving of the Communion either make matrimony or give authority
nd license to whoredom?' he enquired. In the past both sexes had
lways communicated at the same time, and it had never been suggested
nmorality resulted. The Six Articles, along with sundry treason laws,
e continued, had been repealed because Parliament had petitioned for
'almost on their knees', for they thought no man could rest assured
f his lands and goods when at any moment a careless word could place
im in imminent danger of death. Did the rebels really wish to be
agged again in this fashion? Granted the law could be re-enacted if the
hole nation demanded it,

> but we fear that they that most desire it will soonest and sorest
> repent it. When we are content to rule like a father with all mercy
> and clemency, do you call for the bridle and whip? Ah! our loving
> subjects [technically it was the King who spoke], who be these
> that put this into your heads? Do ye know what ye demand and
> what the end would be of that request?

ismissing for the nonsense it was the insinuation that Parliament had
nuggled the recent changes through without the King's knowledge,
omerset went on to deflect criticism of the clergy. Agreeing that they
ailed all too often to set forth God's truth, he argued that on the
:bels' own showing they were behind the present upheaval. Moreover,
 priests did refuse to perform services they should be punished for it;
neir dereliction of duty should not be made the pretext for rebellion.
   On the subject of language Somerset was frankly scornful. How
ould the people have learnt their prayers in Latin when they did not
nderstand it, and was it really impossible to teach their children the
asic prayers in English? Why Cornishmen should take offence over
ne use of English completely mystified him, more especially since
ve are informed that there be very few or no towns in Cornwall but
e shall find more in them that understand English than that under-
tand Latin'.
   Finally, he attempted an involved explanation of the economic and
olitical situation, stressing the obvious points that rebellion could
icrease scarcity as a result of wanton destruction, raise the level of
nemployment, and necessitate measures which must involve even
igher taxation.
   Archbishop Cranmer dealt with the Articles systematically. His
:futation of Catholicism and exposition of Protestant doctrine seems
:ss significant than the overwrought, even hysterical language. Consider-
ig that the ridiculed Prayer Book was his personal achievement, it is
ot remarkable that his opening words were, 'When I first read your
:quest, O ignorant men of Devonshire and Cornwall', adding, however,

'You were deceived by some crafty papists which devised those articles for you, to make you ask you wist not what.' But it was when he came to consider the first article that he exploded: 'Is this the fashion of subjects to speak unto their prince, "We will have?" . . . Have not all true subjects ever used to their sovereign this form of speaking, "Most humbly beseecheth your faithful and obedient subjects"?' He was still harping on this 'rude and unhandsome manner of speech' when he came to deal with the third article. In the fourth they were 'ignorant people' again. In the seventh he affected horror at 'superstition and idolatry, how they prevail among you', turning at the thirteenth to sarcasm with 'you wise disposers of the commonwealth'. Nice words from a man of God, but then he dedicated his life to licking the boots of the mighty.

Nicholas Udall put the case calmly, avoiding abuse, and stressing the error into which the people had allowed themselves to be led. Like Cranmer, but more objectively, he dwelt on the folly of rebellion, echoing the ever present fear of it in the Tudor age:

> Oh! my countrymen, if ye knew how ill a way ye take for your own safeguard . . . for the redress of your griefs, for the surety of your goods, chattels, houses, wives, daughters, heirs and all your succession, yea, and for your very own persons too, ye would abide great wrongs, grievous oppression, yea and extreme tyranny, ere ye would thus unnaturally move a tumult against your prince and sovereign.

Both priests were puzzled by Article thirteen, and so have most historians been. The customary complaint against the gentry was that they failed to employ as many servants as they could afford, thus condemning people to avoidable idleness and want. In the circumstances it seems to propose some limitation on the armed strength at the command of the upper classes which they could, and did, employ to enforce their will on the peasantry.

Whether or not these rebuttals ever reached the insurgents, there was no rejoinder. In any case, as we have already suggested, the contributions of the two divines may have been intended primarily to discourage waverers in the rest of the country.

II

From the relative security of London the Protector meanwhile plied Russell with exhortations to move swiftly and decisively against the rebels whom he supposed to be insignificant in numbers and poorly armed. The Lord Privy Seal, uneasily poised in his exposed forward position at Honiton, countered with a stream of letters (unhappily lost) n which he did his best to convince Somerset of the real dangers of he situation.

Humphry Arundell might be immobilised by the gallant defence of Exeter, but equally Russell could do nothing except look on impotently while awaiting reinforcements. Such force as he had brought with him was pitifully small: his personal retinue together with a handful of West Country gentlemen and their servants who had rallied to his standard. It is unlikely that the total exceeded 300, if as many; most were horsemen. It seemed to him, moreover, that his situation was even more perilous. Wild reports put the numbers of the rebels far higher than they could possibly have been in reality. He firmly believed that there were enough of them simultaneously to maintain the siege and fall on him in overwhelming strength. In Hooker's succinct words 'he lived more in fear than he was feared'. From the correspondence with the Council, which on his side cannot have been notable for coherence, he emerges as the type of general who dwells in a perpetual nightmare in which he is beset by an enemy so powerful that he dare not meet him in pitched battle. To be fair, it must be recalled that he was exercising an independent command for the first time at the advanced age of 65. Only the determination of the aggressive Sir Peter Carew prevented him from retreating. Whether or not the knight had formed a correct estimate of the rebels' strength, he certainly had a low opinion of their fighting qualities, a prejudice which in these circumstances happened to be a decided advantage. Had the enemy showed more aggression it could have proved a dangerous delusion.

Russell's weakness was only too evident. He was short of money and munitions. While the insurgents increased in number with every day that passed, the handful of common people who had at first joined him was rapidly melting away. Even the gentlemen were beginning to slink off. The morale of those who remained was shaky, while their retainers, he reported on 8 July, were becoming restive because he was unable to pay them. This was a serious matter for soldiers had to purchase their own food. In the first instance he had been advanced £300 'as parcel of his diets', and shortly afterwards got an imprest 'for conduct, coats and transportation of soldiers levied in London'. Coat and conduct money covered the cost of clothing men in the livery of their contingent and conveying them to the base of operations. Here Russell was guilty of some exaggeration. If his command did not exceed 300 horse, £300 should have sufficed for nearly three weeks' pay. The Council was not unmindful of his needs; on 10 July it ordered the Mint at Bristol to deliver £100 to him for distribution to the gentlemen's followers at the standard rates of sixpence a day for foot soldiers and ninepence for light horsemen. The gentlemen themselves were expected to feel sufficiently rewarded with individual letters of thanks. When later on

Russell signified his intention of raising thousands of infantry, the Protector ordered the Comptroller of the Mint, the King's Receiver in the region, and the receiver for his own estates, a man named Croch, to honour all bills presented to them. Russell was further authorised to raise loans from merchants, which would be gratefully repaid. Fortunately for him there were three Exeter merchants at Honiton, detained on their way home by the rebellion: Thomas Prestwood, a former mayor, John Budleigh, and John Periam whose brother was a tower of strength to Blackaller throughout the siege. All of them men of great wealth and fully aware of the Lord Privy Seal's needs, they raised on their own credit large sums from their fellow businessmen in Bristol, Taunton, Lyme and other towns, with which he was able immediately to procure all the stores he required and proceed to the enlistment of a large number of troops.

One consequence of Russell's weakness was that he could not make up his mind on a suitable base for his operations. He feared in particular that having concentrated so far forward he had exposed his rear to any rising that might break out in Somerset or Dorset. The threat was lively enough. There had already been minor disturbances there a few weeks earlier, and now his summons to Sir John Arundell to take the field had been ignored.

Sir John was first cousin of the rebel general and head of the Lanherne branch of the family. In Dorset, where he resided near Shaftesbury, he enjoyed wide influence. There were persistent reports that he had caused Mass to be celebrated and that his conduct in general smacked of disloyalty. The Council recommended sending him to Sir William Herbert (who was busy recruiting in Gloucestershire and Wiltshire) to be conveyed to London for questioning, but the difficulty, as Russell pointed out, was how to do so without causing provocation. Somerset agreed that if sent for suddenly Arundell might become desperate, and decided on 12 July that 'we will work at the matter for the time, and so shall you well to do also', unless an opportunity of delivering him to Herbert should present itself. When, however, a few days later the Council directed that Arundell should be taken to Portsmouth, he evidently went without demur, and by 26 July was in London and being examined by them. He then claimed to have been confined to bed very sick when Russell's first summons reached him: this may well have been true since it was necessary to carry him to Portsmouth in a litter. He declared that he had only received one more letter, which he produced, and insisted that although he had not been summoned 'upon his allegiance' he had fully intended reporting to Russell as soon as he was fit. But even so, he claimed, it would have made little difference, for as a relative stranger in Dorset he discounted his ability to attract recruits there. He admitted that when he had heard people talking wildly about the rising in Devon he had permitted two Masses to be said in order to appease them, but apart from that, and a procession on Corpus Christi day, he had used nothing but the Prayer Book services. The Council bade Russell check his statement locally and apprise them of any incriminating facts that might come to light. Apparently none did, and Arundell was merely bound over with sureties not to leave London.

The air was thick with rumours. Few of them ever turned out to have any foundation in fact, but in the prevailing state of suspicion and uncertainty it was difficult to discount them. Persistent lurid tales of outbreaks of disorder in other shires were sedulously fostered by the rebels in order to spread despondency, and did nothing to lessen Russell's feeling of insecurity. Fearing encirclement, he contemplated abandoning Honiton, and pessimistically discussed the prospects of holding the insurgents at Sherborne where a castle barred the road to London. Perhaps at the back of his mind was forming the idea that if they had to progress from one siege to another they would not get very far. Certainly it was out of the question for his puny force to engage them in battle. There were not even enough men to picket the 40-mile gap between the estuary of the Parrett at Bridgwater and the Frome at Dorchester. The latter stream, moreover, was fordable throughout its length, and although the country from Langport to Bridgwater and thence to the sea was 'very strong', the fact that it was for the most part the morass of Sedgemoor rendered it unfit for cavalry. In any case an army could easily penetrate between Bruton and Sherborne, or to the south of it through Dorset where only the marshy district of Blackmoor presented any sort of obstacle. He concluded that from Sherborne he could cover Dorset, Somerset and Wiltshire for just as long as the enemy did not emerge in force from Devonshire. If they did advance he would have no choice but to retire along whatever line their movements might dictate.

Although undated, this appreciation was probably made about 9 July, the day after Russell had noted the rumours of fresh disturbances threatening his rear, and a week after the investment of Exeter had begun. Without doubt these few days were the most anxious of the campaign. First reports had been to the effect that there was only enough food in Exeter to last for two days. Despondently Russell informed the Council that its surrender would have to be expected at any moment, and intimated that he was contemplating a desperate attempt to break through the siege lines with his handful of horsemen. Not surprisingly they concluded that it would be pointless to send reinforcements to Devonshire, and that the logical course would be to make preparations to hold the rebels farther to the east. To add to the confusion rebellion broke out in Norfolk on 8 July, and the next few days brought news of serious disturbances in Buckinghamshire and Oxfordshire.

In all probability it was Sir Peter Carew who was burning to make the dash for Exeter, but during his frequent absences — his own home at Mohuns Ottery was only a short distance from Honiton — Russell's resolution faltered. Before the plan could be activated reports came in simultaneously that Exeter had surrendered and a riot or rebellion had broken out in the neighbourhood of Salisbury. Although there was no substance in either, the fact that Wiltshire had been convulsed only a few short weeks earlier could not be overlooked. Russell consulted the Dorset gentlemen. Alarmed, naturally, about the safety of their homes and families, they unanimously recommended a withdrawal to Dorset-shire until such time as the strength of the army could be built up. Now was the moment to get off a brief, non-committal communication setting out the advantages of Sherborne, to prepare the Council for news of the retreat itself once it had been completed. And so the next morning saw the troops saddled up and streaming out of Honiton on the road to Taunton without waiting to notify Carew of the change of plan, or rather, as Hooker insinuates, trying to give him the slip. The news of their departure, a few hours later, filled him with alarm. Vaulting on to his horse he galloped after the column, overtaking it on the summit of Blackdown. He argued long and earnestly with Russell: bleak as the prospect might look, a withdrawal at this stage could lead to nothing but disaster; showing a bold front was infinitely preferable to advertising their weakness by running away. Eventually the soldier succeeded in convincing the politician of his error and persuaded the reluctant Russell to return to Honiton where he remained for the next three weeks or so, except for one half-hearted foray in the direction of Exeter which took him a mere five miles to Ottery St Mary where his resolution failed, and after a miserable night, although 'as it fell out he was more in fear than peril', he pulled back to Honiton again.

He probably deemed it prudent to keep this episode from the Protector. The likely sequel is that Sir Gawain and Sir Peter Carew stood over him while he wrote asking the Council to approve their formal appointment as members of his council of war, making sure that there would be no repetition. Somerset was relieved: '. . . We refer it to yourself to choose whom ye think meet to be called unto you for advice and for understanding of the state of the country'.

But for this change in the command structure the Lord Privy Seal might still have retreated, for on 10 July the Council gave him a free hand to select any base from which to harass the insurgents and maintain peace in adjoining counties most effectively. In the short term it was essential to deny them access to supplies of food and dis-courage recruits from joining them. He was advised to stimulate hatred

them by spreading rumours of their alleged atrocities. Horror stories
ere indeed already circulating; this psychological warfare seems to
ve left its imprint chiefly on such 'establishment' writers as Hooker
d Richard Carew who were at pains to insist that the rebels freely
actised intimidation in order to win recruits, whereas the reality was
at scarcely anyone supported the government. All semblance of con-
liation had to be abandoned as it became clear that not merely did the
bels, scornful of the consequences, reject the proffered amnesty, but
e majority of the populace, including even many of the gentry were
aiting to see which side would prevail before committing themselves.

was necessary to authorise Russell to treat as traitors men who
fused to rally to his standard. The government recommended 'sharp
stice': the sword was the only argument these people were capable
understanding. The people of Somerset were wavering: very well,
lect a few and hang them *pour encourager les autres*! Similarly the
mes of men who excused themselves from service should be noted
ith a view to appropriate measures after the rising had been put down.
uthenticated atrocities committed by the rebels were few and far
tween; the government, in contrast, practised systematic terrorism
maintain authority. Active support of the revolt was of course
other matter. Security was a constant worry, and the spy who was
ught bearing a letter from the rebel council to be published from
lpits throughout Wessex deserved his fate.

The unhappy Lord Privy Seal continued his vigil at Honiton 'in an
ony and of a heavy cheer', but so long as the rebel army did not
sume its advance the risk was justified, for the malcontents of the
ljoining counties prudently refrained from hostile acts against a
vernment which still appeared to be in control.

I

recisely what Russell did or did not tell the Council can only be
njectured. For much of the time he failed to make clear his require-
ents, mainly because he was unable to formulate a positive strategy.
he original straightforward plan of campaign had had perforce to be
placed by a desperate defensive strategy limited to relieving Exeter
d containing the rebels should they show signs of resuming their
stward thrust. This meant trying to bottle them up in the peninsula,
d the point at which to insert the stopper was the 'straits' between
ridgwater and Weymouth where it narrowed to only 40 miles. What
as lacking was the stopper. Two or three hundred horsemen could
ot possibly cover a front of this length, and it was only the valiant
efence put up by the people of Exeter that saved Russell from the

necessity of facing up to this crisis. Convinced that Exeter was on the point of surrender, that even if it held out the enemy was numerous enough to sustain the siege and push eastwards simultaneously, and nagged by fears of risings in his rear, he continued to transmit a hopelessly confused picture to the government who, consequently, inclined to the belief that the worst was about to happen. In their estimation the immediate response should be the formation of a mobile force to harass the enemy and slow down his progress. They did not understand why their general kept on demanding infantry in order to be able to go over to the offensive: he had not informed them that the rebels' own offensive had been at a standstill since 2 July. This misunderstanding did much to delay the dispatch of troops to the West.

It was infuriating for Russell that this was the one occasion on which veteran professional troops were actually available for immediate service, so that there should have been no need for him to lose precious time in trying to recruit local levies — half-trained men! Had his mission remained one of pacification a personal escort would have sufficed. As it gradually became clear that sterner measures were needed, it was at first assumed that the commotion was so localised that he would experience no difficulty in raising a force locally, and incidentally minimise outlay on conduct money. Of course, even if this had not proved well nigh impossible, it would have been quicker and simpler from a military standpoint to commit the mercenaries in the first place.

But there were cogent political objections to employing mercenaries. It would have been a highly unpopular decision, a precedent no government could lightly contemplate. Even the hard men on the Council recognised that foreign soldiery were particularly obnoxious to the English. The House of Commons subsequently branded them as 'a handful of an armful to follow, driving on the design to subject England to the insolence of the foreigner'.[1] Hooker states that those who served in the West were 'abhorred of the one party [the rebels] and nothing favoured of the other'. The truth was that all mercenaries had a reputation for savagery. The Venetian diplomat Sebastian Giustiniani, had written in 1516 of the 'inhumanity of the Germans who do not content themselves with plundering, but burn and kill, filling every place with death and slaughter', and of the Swiss who boasted of 'irrigating and inundating the earth with human gore'. Equally relevant was the purpose for which this costly professional army had been assembled. The duke of Somerset was naturally loath to disperse it and postpone, perhaps indefinitely, the invasion of Scotland. Finally, and perhaps most material of all, he had an understandable fear of allowing the mercenaries to pass out of his immediate control to become part of an army under the command of a potential opponent which could later be turned against himself. As it was thus manifestly in his interest to assure the Lord Privy Seal that the situation as a whole was not menacing, Somerset's evident preference for leaving Russell to collect whatever raw levies he could find needs no further explanation. Should the political crisis eventually come to a showdown, even a large force recruited in the shires would be no match for 2,000 or so veterans under his own command.

The Protector, as we have seen, planned initially to reinforce Russell with cavalry whose speed and mobility would outweigh mere numbers in a war of movement. The latter, on the contrary, stated his unwavering preference for infantry, local advice having convinced him that they could operate with infinitely greater freedom than horsemen in a countryside cut up by deep, narrow lanes and thick hedges. The difficulty, he complained, was to find trustworthy men, so thoroughly disaffected was the whole district. By 8 July a few local gentlemen only had joined him, and they were despondent. Declaring that he would not be strong enough to take the offensive until he had assembled at least 2,000 foot, and despairing of recruiting anything like so many, he implored the Council to provide them as a matter of urgency. The reply was that there was little prospect of finding this number anywhere without some delay. (If they had to be obtained from any distance, it would take two or three weeks at least to muster and march them to Honiton.) However, Somerset was so far impressed by the general's note of desperation that on 10 July he consented to release a few of his precious mercenaries. He ordered 150 Italian arquebusiers to proceed to Devonshire forthwith, and Lord Grey of Wilton with 300 or 400 horse to advance to Salisbury ready to join Russell if required. In addition 300 foreign horse and 1,000 German foot were placed on standby, and Sir William Herbert was commissioned to raise levies in Gloucestershire and Wiltshire.

These dispositions were as much political as military. Almost certainly Somerset would have liked to relieve Russell of the command and give it to Grey who was not only an able and distinguished general, but also personally devoted to the duke. But equally certainly the majority of the Council would have vetoed it. Hence a compromise: Russell was to have a minimal number of mercenaries, while Grey was posted half along the route so that he would naturally assume command of any larger force that might follow.

Before this offer could reach him, Russell further confused the picture. As Exeter had only enough food for eight days (which were now up) he hourly expected news of its fall, and since his pleas for support had been ignored he had decided to try and raise 2,000 foot himself, planning to bypass the local gentry, whose loyalty was suspect, and recruit them directly. Somerset was bewildered. Having been given to understand that Exeter had not more than two days' provisions he had assumed that it had already surrendered and the rebels had resumed their offensive in overwhelming strength. Accepting Russell's assurance that it was impossible to find reliable infantry he had concluded that the formation of a mobile force offered the only real prospect of effective resistance. 'If we had at the beginning known so much', he wrote, 'we had not stuck to have relieved the matter otherwise.' Relieved now to learn that local resources would suffice, he commended Russell's plan to raise 2,000 foot, 4,000 if he needed them — 'we stick not at it' — and gave orders for the additional bills to be honoured. For the present, alarming new developments in the Midlands made it imperative to divert Lord Grey and the promised reinforcements, although there was every hope that he would be able to complete his mission within a week.

IV

As uproar mounted in many widely separated parts of the country the situation as it appeared at the seat of government became daily more confused, all the more so in the absence of concerted measures to deal with it. The Home Counties remained sullen, liable to burst into flame at any moment. Precautions were taken but with no clear end in view. Orders were issued, for example, to break down the bridge over the Thames at Staines; the inhabitants protested that their livelihood would be ruined, and apparently no further action was taken. It is difficult to see what the purpose was. It may have been connected with the summons sent out on 1 July to some 300 noblemen and gentlemen to assemble at Windsor with all the horsemen and footmen they could muster, and designed to forestall any sudden concentration of rebels to threaten the capital. Subsequently, on 16 July, the Council ordered that 4,000 horse and 2,000 foot, inclusive perhaps of mercenaries *en route* for the North, should be held near London to guard the King.

None of this looked likely to bring the rebellion in the West to a speedy end, and to make matters worse the Protector's persistent attempts to play down the crisis was patently a transparent façade. Sir William Paget was in Brussels endeavouring to negotiate an alliance with the Emperor Charles V. At first he was hopeful of obtaining advantageous terms, since war between France and the Empire appeared imminent, but as England more and more gave the appearance of relapsing into civil war her value as an ally slumped. Thanks to the vigilance of his ambassador, Francis van der Delft, Charles was kept fully posted of developments, and a warning to Paget on 4 July to minimise the extent of the disturbances was instantly nullified by intelligence of the demands of the Cornishmen. Soon afterwards the talks were abruptly terminated.

Much disturbed at what was going on in his absence, Paget had
ritten trenchantly to Somerset urging stern measures, recalling how
he peasant wars in Germany a generation earlier had escalated:

> call to your Grace to Council six of the gravest and most experi-
> mented men of the realm, consider what is best to be done, and
> follow their advice. Send for your Almayn horsemen; send for
> Lord Ferrys and Sir Wm Herbert to bring you as many horsemen of
> such as they dare trust out of Wales. Let the Earl of Shrewsbury
> bring the like out of Shropshire, Derbyshire, Nottinghamshire,
> Staffordshire, of his servants and keepers of forests and parks. Go
> yourself, accompanied with the said noblemen and their companies;
> and appoint the Chief Justices of England, three or four of them to
> resort, with commission of oyer and terminer, to that good town
> which shall be next to the place where your Grace shall remain.
> Attach to the number of twenty or thirty of the rankest knaves of
> the shire. Let six be hanged of the ripest of them, the rest remain in
> prison. And thus, sir, make a progress this hot weather, till you have
> perused all those shires that have offended. Your Grace may say you
> shall lose the hearts of the people; of the good people you shall
> not − of the ill it maketh no matter.

Jnhappily for Somerset he was unable to make up his mind whether or
ot to take the field himself, and, had perforce to cling to half measures
ntil it was clear that full scale government intervention was
navoidable.

In London the authorities were taking no chances. On 3 July the
nayor commenced a nightly inspection of the constables on watch,
seeing that they kept to the hours appointed for them by the last Court
f Aldermen who shared this duty until the end of September. Kent
emained uneasy following the disorders of the spring; disaffection was
ampant in Essex. The beginning of the month saw a fresh outburst of
isorder in Hampshire. On 13 July the Protector congratulated Sir John
hynne and his fellow magistrates for their effective handling of riots
t Odiham and other places, while simultaneously urging the cor-
orations of Winchester and Southampton, which were evidently slack,
o redouble their efforts. He commanded the mayor of Southampton
o arrest a certain Friar Wigg who was alleged to have advocated
estricting the power of the King. But after 10 days had elapsed the
nayor admitted to having been unable to trace him, and enquiries at
Vinchester, where he was also well known, proved likewise unavailing.

Around 12 July matters took a decided turn for the worse with new,
arger risings in Norfolk, and closer by in Buckinghamshire and Oxford-
hire, which demanded immediate military measures. Henry Haquefort's
and of heavy cavalry, which originally it had been intended to keep
round Guisnes and Boulogne, was suddenly brought over to London.
Jn 18 July martial law was proclaimed in the city. Two days later

preparations to resist a possible attack were put in hand. Picked livery
men from each company were detailed to maintain a watch at every
gate daily from five in the morning till eight at night when the gate
were closed. Every alderman and his company were ordered to hold
themselves in readiness with harness, guns, bows, etc., to defend the
walls. The Corporation's own guns were mounted on the ramparts
and brass cannons were borrowed from the Tower to be posted at every
gate; gunners were taken on to the payroll. On 21 July, Archbishop
Cranmer preached at Matins in St Paul's, exhorting the people to
prayer, fasting, and obedience to authority, as well as denouncing
rebellion with all the passion at his command. (Literary gifts apart
his fear and hatred of the lower orders was almost the only thing he
shared with Martin Luther.) After he had celebrated Holy Communion
his chaplain preached in like vein at St Paul's Cross, broadcasting his
words to a larger audience. Next day gibbets were set up at London
Bridge and Aldgate, where the Knight Marshall executed a rebellious
tailor arrested at Rainsford, Essex, and in Southwark where they
hanged a Boulogne man who had been found acting suspiciously in
Kent.

The affair in Buckinghamshire and Oxfordshire — Berkshire and
Northamptonshire were also affected — was directed chiefly against
gentlemen and graziers. The rioters disparked the park of Sir John
Williams at Thame, killing the deer, and went on to do the same at
Rycote. In several places they also slaughtered sheep. Over and above
this they were incited by some of their priests to protest against innovations in religion. Having completed their depredations along the
Buckinghamshire border they moved west towards Woodstock where
news of government counter-measures caught up with them. Reports
of this fresh outbreak had reached the Council just as Lord Grey's
force was being assembled for dispatch to the western front. Whether
it was the occasion of any disagreement or not, the decision was taken
almost immediately to redirect it to the Midlands, a total of 1,500
horse and foot: Delft reported that it included a great number of
noblemen — meaning of course gentlemen — and foreign troops such
as Germans and Albanians, accompanied by field artillery. An
experienced professional, Grey moved swiftly. Many of the insurgents
did not await his coming but slipped away to their homes. The remnant
retreated to Chipping Norton where Grey surrounded and routed them,
taking some 200 prisoners. In a hurry now to resume his march to
Honiton, after having broken the back of the rising, he left the final
pacification to the local authorities. On 19 July he called together the
sheriff and justices and gave his instructions. He handed over a dozen
prisoners selected for exemplary execution, three each to be hanged at
Oxford and Banbury, the remainder to be allocated to Dedington

Islip, Watlington, Bicester, Chipping Norton and Bloxham; the justices of the peace were to choose two more to be hanged at Thame. The majority were small farmers and craftsmen; four were priests who were hanged from the towers of their own churches. This was carrying out Paget's advice with a vengeance, and Grey's efficiency and ruthlessness won general approval. Sir Thomas Smith, Secretary of State, wrote to William Cecil, the Protector's secretary, that it was worth 10,000 proclamations in the existing deplorable state of affairs, a comment which he doubtless hoped would reach Somerset's ears to remind him that confidence in his kid glove methods had quite evaporated.

A few days later a further, and fleetingly serious affair developed in Yorkshire. On 25 July, Ombler, a yeoman, and Stevenson, his nephew, of East Heslerton in the East Riding, and Dale, the parish clerk of Seamer, met to concert plans for a rising, addressing themselves to the poor and those opposed to the Prayer Book. They planned to fire the coastal beacons so as to call out the local people as if to meet an invasion. If the gentry offered any opposition they were to be slain. The plan soon went astray. One of their agents became tipsy in an alehouse at Wintrington and let the cat out of the bag, giving the gentry time to take precautions. None the less, the beacons were lit at Seamer and Staxton. Ombler and his confederates descended on the house of Matthew White, a large purchaser of chantry lands, dragged out him, his brother-in-law, a visiting merchant from York, and a servant of Walter Mildmay, one of the local chantry commissioners, and took them to a spot a mile away where they stripped and murdered them. Their numbers swollen to about 3,000, many of whom were said to have been coerced into joining, they rampaged for some days along the border of the North Riding, chased by the gentlemen and their retainers. Ombler was arrested on his way to Hunmanby in search of additional recruits, the other leaders were picked up shortly afterwards, and all were executed at York on 21 September. From the start it was an ill conceived and virtually motiveless insurrection in which loot may well have been the main attraction. But although contained and put down by the local authorities relying on their own resources, coming when it did it must have been an alarming portent of a general flare up in the old stamping ground of the Pilgrimage of Grace, and discouraged any thoughts of withdrawing troops from the North at this time.

V

Although in temporarily withholding reinforcements Somerset had held out every hope that the Oxfordshire incident would be settled in a matter of days, as indeed it was, the harassed Lord Privy Seal's frustration may well be imagined. By way of consolation, however, the Council generously provided him with a new proclamation which they were confident would terrify and divide the Devonshire rebels. On 15 July he drily suggested that a similar one should be published in Cornwall in view of the fact that it was every bit as rebellious. Although, like Van der Delft, they must have known this for the past fortnight, the proclamation was duly forwarded without comment; it threatened the insurgents with forfeiture of lands and chattels, and slackers with the risk of being taken for traitors. But the Council's appreciation of the way things were remained sketchy, for they cheerfully advised that Sir William Godolphin was the best man to execute the proclamations in Cornwall, quite unaware that he had been a prisoner for weeks.

Meanwhile Russell's efforts to recruit men were poorly rewarded. Those who did offer themselves were the local Mouldys, Shadows, Warts, Feebles and Bullcalfs; the best men having very possibly already joined the rebel army. So by 15 July he was asking for the landsknechts to be sent. This placed the government in a dilemma. It had already committed these troops to Oxfordshire, and was now regretting a hasty decision. However they may have behaved in reality — and there is no direct report of their conduct — the mere fact of employing mercenaries against true born English rebels had provoked such violent resentment that Delft reported that the people were threatening to leave not one foreigner alive in England. So Russell had to be told that it was inexpedient to send the Germans, 'for that they be so odious to our people abroad in so much as we can hardly move them [the people] to receive them without quarrel here at hand'.

To soften this blow there was the announcement that Grey was now ready to move. In Whitehall it seemed that there was no longer anything to prevent Russell commencing operations. Yet still he continued inactive; worse, he appeared hopelessly irresolute, referring almost every problem to London for decision, and apparently incapable of distinguishing imaginary dangers from real ones. Having picked up yet another rumour of trouble in Dorset he worried lest some ordnance stored in the Isle of Purbeck should fall into the wrong hands. It was necessary to instruct him to organise the removal of the guns to a place of safety, either Corfe Castle or Poole: at least he ought to secure the powder and the light pieces — the rebels would not be able to find much use for the heavy ones which of course were made for arming batteries or ships. He also suffered from shortages of musket balls and arrows, and accused the government of failing to supply him with ammunition. They drily suggested, 'As to shot . . . shift is to be made there [to] buy lead whereof we doubt not there is plenty within the limits of your commission, and as for powder the same has been sent hence unto you.' When, a little later, he announced a scheme to blockade the Cornish coast, the Council responded, 'We like well your device for pinnaces to cut off their victuals by sea', but offered no comment, presumably because they did not wish to discourage initiative. At the same time they must have wondered precisely what Russell expected to achieve, and decided that he had some notion of interdicting possible aid from France.

It is hardly surprising that after three barren weeks the correspondence between Somerset and Russell was tending more and more to descend to mutual recrimination. There were faults on both sides. Russell was certainly not up to the job. This might not have mattered if he had belonged to the old nobility, for then the squires and yeomen of the district would have felt themselves in honour bound to rally to his standard as their 'good lord'. But since his name was not Courtenay the gentry regarded him as an upstart who was no better than they were, just richer and luckier. Somerset, under intense pressure, needed — and demanded — quick results with a minimum of fuss. Incapable of delegation, he had armed his field commander with precise and detailed instructions, and became exasperated with him for failing to carry them out to the letter. Russell in turn hardly made out the best case for himself. Although most of his letters are lost it is obvious that the information they gave was incomplete and contradictory. In addition, verbal messages were entrusted to the couriers, one of whom, a certain Captain Travers, seems from the few oblique references to him to have been concerned primarily to enhance his own reputation by claiming the credit for anything achieved by the army. In brief each felt, with some justice, that the other was letting him down.

Russell indeed was open to criticism for failing to harass the enemy. He could have argued that inactivity on his part would have the effect of beguiling the rebels into a false sense of security; apparently he did not do so for the reason that the idea never occurred to him. His one declared aim was to build up an army worthy of the name, and until this was done the stark truth was that he was powerless to raise the siege of Exeter. In addition to some 500–700 horse he had managed to get together some infantry for which he requested an additional trumpet and guidon. But there were not more than 1,000 altogether, of dubious quality, and he insisted that to raise as many as 2,000 men, let alone 4,000, was a sheer impossibility, since the local men would as soon join the rebels who were gaining strength daily and now boasted of mustering fully 10,000 troops: he actually asserted that he was outnumbered 10 to one. Reiterating the need for an effective striking force, whether to relieve Exeter or meet the rebels in the open, he now pleaded for the earl of Warwick to be ordered west with the entire army, meaning the one being prepared for the Scottish campaign, of which Warwick was commander designate. Nothing less would answer since he greatly feared that the rebels, who were planting bogus deserters to spy on his movements, were far better informed about his situation than he of theirs.

Within the next day or two the first reinforcements arrived, 160 Italian arquebusiers commanded by the Genoese nobleman, Paolo Batista Spinola, though it is possible that the companies of horse led by Jacques Jermigny and Pietro Sanga had already joined him. By 20 July it is probable that the strength of the army had increased to some 1,800 men, including 350 foreign horse and perhaps 300 English, the 160 Italians and approximately 1,000 native foot.

Almost immediately they saw action. Around 21–2 July there was a skirmish with some rebels 'in the straits', a column detached by Arundell to probe round the army's exposed flank, or maybe an independent group from Somersetshire. Thanks largely to Spinola's arquebusiers and the steadiness of the local billmen gallantly led by the gentlemen, he got the better of the insurgents who, armed only with bows and bills, stood little chance against the accuracy and penetration of the professionals' disciplined fire. Russell's own archers were not very effective; far too many of their shafts flew wide, and the rebels retrieved them and shot them back, something that could not be done with spent bullets.

Faced with a rapidly deteriorating situation in East Anglia the Council could not spare Warwick, although they promised on 22 July to send him once the commotion there was over. But when the next day Norwich was occupied by rebels, the government had to reconcile itself to the fact that it now had two major revolts on its hands at once. In addition, alarming intelligence had come from Plymouth which, it seemed, had been treacherously surrendered by its mayor, making it necessary to divert a naval squadron there to recover the castle, as well as sending William Hawkins with a party to arrest the mayor. Fortunately, within a day or so it proved the report had been much exaggerated, and the Council was able to reassure the Lord Privy Seal that the castle continued to hold out.

The Protector was sceptical about the shortage of recruits: 'It were strange to us that they should not be able to make 4,000 or more, and to prevent from joining with the rebels, yea to make them serve with you.' There was, however, no reason for Russell's continued inactivity. He had his Italians; he should commandeer horses for them and as many other of his men as possible, and by virtue of mobility increase his effective strength, more effectively harass the enemy and, incidentally, deny them use of the horses. Mobility was in fact the corrective to the enemy's numerical superiority. The infantry should be disposed in road-blocks to constrict the rebels' ability to skirmish and forage. Mounted arquebusiers could scour the countryside using hit and run tactics to harass small bands, withdrawing when larger numbers appeared, and thus wear them down — 'abate their pride after they have met with men of conduct'. So long as Russell took care to keep his lines of retreat open at all times disaster could be avoided. Meanwhile Lord Grey was on his way with 250 horse and 160 arquebusiers 'sent by Spinola', a phrase which implies that the company had been divided, and was reunited when Grey's column reached Honiton.

While this advice was on its way, Captain Travers reached London with the encouraging news of the first minor success for which the Council

> gave therefore to you the King's Majesty's and our right hearty thanks, requiring you to impart the same to such gentlemen and others as at this present have done . . . good, faithful and painful service. And trust of good success to follow. . . .

Travers also carried the now normal string of complaints. One was that the government was failing to keep up the supply of ammunition. They assured him, and Travers would 'further show unto your contentation', that supplies were now on their way. They hoped also to satisfy once and for all his demands for infantry, having commissioned Mr Aleury to recruit men in South Wales and Gloucestershire where an abundance of troops should be available, and ended: 'Now we trust you shall have enough of both to encounter and subdue the rebels.' Following this up, on 24 July they ordered Sir William Herbert to raise as many men as Russell asked for in Wiltshire, adding that 'Mr Herbert is of such courage that he saith he is able rather to bring too many than too few'.

Still Russell was not satisfied, complaining bitterly that apart from Spinola's small band all he had been sent was cavalry. Galled by criticism he considered unmerited, he expostulated angrily on 25 July that he was experienced in the art of war and knew perfectly well what he had to do. It was the Council that failed to understand the difficulties and hazards of the situation which confronted him, and he resented them cavilling at every decision he took, every request he made. In the face of violence proclamations were worse than useless: mere words would not turn the Somerset men from their treasonable ways and rally them to his standard, even though he had dealt with the ringleaders and hanged an agent of Arundell's caught trying to incite rebellion.

The correspondence had become increasingly strained as Somerset's patience became exhausted. He assured Russell that neither his judgment nor his military competence were in doubt, and that the fact that advice as to the conduct of operations had been tendered did not imply want of confidence. But, he insisted, his own experience of soldiering far exceeded that of Russell's, and he had formed his conclusions about the progress of the campaign from Russell's own reports: 'Marry! ye wrote as though they had now passed the straits.' If the situation was that bad even the bravest and wisest captain could come to no harm from sound advice, and the Lord Privy Seal would do well to reflect that the ultimate responsibility was the Protector's alone, that his head would roll should disaster be upon them. Barely concealing his contempt for the general's ineptitude, he continued with an elementary lesson in strategy and tactics, condescending even to give instructions for the casting of shot! Ignorant of the calibre of the guns, which were not standardised yet, the government could not send bullets; 'we should peradventure send you shot as fit as a shoe for a man's hand'. It was thanks to Russell's own reports that the need for cavalry appeared obvious. Exeter was evidently on the point of surrender, after which it would be impossible to hold the line of the 'straits'. The rebels would be able to break out of the peninsula where a mobile force could contain them far more effectively than slow-footed infantry; the Protector added a reasoned evaluation of the relative merits of the different arms. The thing that annoyed him as much as anything was the small thanks he had received for the Italian arquebusiers who, as he pointed out with asperity, had already proved their worth in action making up in fire power what they lacked in- numbers.

In a personal note he took the opportunity to bolster Russell's morale, and drop the hint that it was time for some positive results by remarking that the rest of the country was now at peace, 'saving some of the light sort remaining fickle, but to no great number, namely at and about Norwich' whither the marquis of Northampton had gone to mop up. He did not admit that Northampton had been sent off in a great hurry with what few troops remained available, under strict instructions not to take any risks at all.

Before there was time for Russell to make any more complaints the Protector was staggered to hear from Herbert his intention of furnishing no fewer than 10,000 men which the Lord Privy Seal had asked for. The build up was getting out of hand, he wrote on 28 July. There could not be more than 4,000 rebels in the field, 'for the most part unarmed' as eye-witness reports confirmed. Russell already had as many, 'better armed with arms and having arquebuses which they have none'. In a word he considered the army large enough for its task already, and should Herbert bring 2,000 or 3,000 men from Wales, 'well appointed' with 2,000 from Gloucestershire and Wiltshire, 'taken but of the best appointed and most willing', they would serve Russell better than any greater number

> for the multitude should not only pester and consume your victuals but of so many some doubtful and hollow hearted should turn to the rebels' part. You should be in more danger of your own company than of the rebels themselves.

The problem of feeding a growing army had already prompted Russell to complain of shortages in the vicinity of Honiton. How did he propose to manage if he concentrated even more men there? 'The one of you should be ready to eat another for want.' Somerset was afraid that this could be made a pretext for withdrawing to a better stocked district. As it was, scarcity was threatening to push up prices beyond the reach of the soldiers' wages — the rebels enjoyed a marked advantage through making free with church goods — and Russell had already been authorised to fix food prices, indeed to raise wages if that would hasten the decision.

This is the only definite statement made at the time as to the sizes of the opposing armies. As regards the insurgents, Somerset may, in contrast to the despondent Lord Privy Seal, have underestimated their true strength; so much depended on the exact proportion of their manpower that Devon and Cornwall had returned. They could certainly have fielded the better part of 3,000 effectives, without reckoning partially armed men, and doubtless the cause attracted much more support than the official musters ever could. One thing must be regarded as certain in view of events yet to come: their armament was far from negligible. As no muster of the royal army survives, the figure of 4,000 presents some difficulties. A total of 1,800 on 20 July has already been suggested, and it looks extremely doubtful whether Russell had managed to procure any more than the 1,000 local footmen he then had. Grey's 250 horse and 160 arquebusiers, which had not in fact arrived by 28 July, brought the total to not more than some 2,200. It is impossible, therefore, to escape the conclusion that the Council had reversed its earlier decision and sent the landsknechts, the emergency in the Midlands having removed doubts about the wisdom of employing them. They must have been assigned to Grey for he could not have acted with such speed had it been necessary for him to begin by calling out militiamen; indeed in view of the generally mutinous state of the southern half of the country such troops would have hampered his operations. Having no doubts about his loyalty Somerset could safely entrust the Germans to him. It must also be noted that they were not available for service in Norfolk at this time. Their inclusion would bring the total for Russell's army to 3,000 or 3,200, depending on the exact strength of the band, when concentration was eventually completed; artillerymen and pioneers would further increase it. Finally we may suspect that Somerset in effect was writing 'nearly' 4,000, as opposed to 'over' 3,000 with a view to silencing Russell's demands: he made it abundantly clear that he would send no more.

The build up of the army having reached the point at which it was at least feasible to go over to the offensive, the anxious days of waiting were drawing to a close. This itself created a new uncertainty in Somerset's mind: the inexperienced general might all too easily squander the forces so painfully assembled in some ineptly conducted operation. Once more he outlined a tactical plan. In view of the great numbers of the enemy it would be unsafe to attempt to engage more than 2,000 of them at once, unless the army were divided into two columns to attack simultaneously from different directions, not indeed, the soundest advice to give an untried commander even though his force might be 'sufficient considering the good order and armoury against fearful rebels and unarmed', especially when they were any thing but unarmed. If in spite of everything the insurgents succeeded in breaking out of Devonshire his strong mounted arm could still head them off as they would all be on foot. To the very end the Protector was determined to justify having sent all those cavalry!

Even as Somerset sat writing those lines battle was at last being joined, although in a very different manner than had been foreseen.

Chapter 7
The Norfolk Rising

I

It had long been the custom of the country folk of central Norfolk to come together every summer in the pleasant little market town of Wymondham to celebrate the feast of the Translation of St Thomas of Canterbury. Long ago a chapel had been raised to the memory of the martyr which over the years had become the local centre of his cult.

In 1549, as in years past, great numbers of people attended

a certain night and day play which was played there the Saturday night, being the 6th day of July, and held on the 7th and part of the 8th day, being Monday, which day the people [were] to depart.

But as the festivities proceeded many a merrymaker felt a gentle tap on the shoulder followed by a few muttered words in his ear from someone who melted rapidly back into the crowd. Thus it turned out that on Monday morning, instead of taking the road home, they hung about the town awaiting the commencement of a meeting which had been arranged by several of the inhabitants. There speaker after speaker expounded the burning issues of the day. Months had gone by since the investigation of enclosures had been ordered, yet nothing had come of it. With every day that passed the prospect of effective remedy was made more remote by the wilful obstruction of the gentry who, while responsible for enforcing the law, were at the same time the very men who profited from enclosures and the abuse of the commons. Locally indeed results had only been achieved when the peasants acted for themselves, as at Attleborough the previous month. The example was there; with much of England in uproar the time was opportune and might not come again.

Tempers rose. Someone suggested making a start at Morley, two miles out of town, with the land of Mr Hobartson, a lawyer turned squire, a breed much detested in Norfolk not merely for their opportunism in buying up land but also for the professional skill with which they exploited local customs for their own gain. A party set out forthwith, levelled his fences, and returned to Wymondham. But these were only the first to go down that morning; among others were some which had been put up by another lawyer, a certain Serjeant John Flowerdew who lived at Heathersett. It would not be far wrong to blame him for all that now followed.

There were sound reasons why Wymondham should become the centre of disturbance. Flowerdew, a prominent landlord of the new, acquisitive type, was intensely disliked throughout the district. Ten years earlier, when the abbey had been dissolved, he had removed the bells and stripped the lead from the choir of the church, nearly wrecking the structure in the process. The townsmen were inordinately proud of their noble church, with its two great towers, which they had shared with the monks, and had petitioned the King to spare those parts of it which were scheduled for demolition, offering to pay the full value of the lead, bells and other items. Their tender had already been accepted and the money paid over when Flowerdew made his raid. Thanks to his legal expertise he had been able to get away with it, but two leading townsmen, the brothers Robert and William Kett, who had taken the lead in the negotiations with the King, had never forgiven him.

Rightly or wrongly, Flowerdew jumped to the conclusion that the Ketts, with whom he also had private differences, had engineered the invasion of his property this 8 July. Furious, he hastened to town, sought out some of the levellers, and offered them 40 pence to go and throw open a piece of common land near the Fairstead which Robert Kett himself had fenced off. They went in a body to Kett and demanded that he should restore the rights over the land of which he had wrongly deprived them. Had Flowerdew not been present – he must surely have gone along to watch the fun! – Kett's reaction might possibly have been different. As it was, he readily acknowledged the justice of their demand and offered to lead them in a bid to curb the power of the great landowners, holding out the prospect of sweeping changes that would rudely confront the nobility and gentry with the nemesis of their arrogance. And without more ado he set the example by organising the destruction of his own hedges.

That evening he led a party back to Heathersett where they made short work of Flowerdew's remaining enclosures. The lawyer confronted his enemy, bitterly accusing him of having assembled this mob in order to pursue a personal vendetta. But he and his servants were roughly shouldered aside.

Before departing from Heathersett the people gathered by the side of the Thetford road under the tree known to this day as Kett's oak, and acclaimed Robert as their leader. In turn he solemnly pledged himself and all his possessions to their cause, bade them have courage and strike a determined blow for their liberties, promising: 'The office which the tate has bestowed upon me I will never lay down until you have got our rights.'

Robert Kett was eminently fitted to become the spokesman of the narticulate masses. Although something more than a mere man of the people, the particulars of his life up to that fatal day are every bit as obscure as any of theirs; even his age is unknown. Although he carried on business as a tanner he was in fact a man of some property. He owned land reckoned to be worth 40 marks (£26 3s. 4d.) a year, and had been assessed on goods worth £160 in the subsidy of 1545, sufficient to entitle him to be considered a minor gentleman. Another and perhaps more realistic estimate credited him with £50 a year from land, ·and personal wealth totalling £666 13s. 4d. He was in fact descended from a gentle family of great antiquity. A Roger le Chat was recorded in Norfolk as early as the reign of King John, and his line has been traced from 1316 down to the death of Henry le Cat in 1433. After a break we come across a John Kett at Wymondham in 1483, and William Kett in 1545, possibly Robert's father. A case of bastardy at some point may be suspected, for the Wymondham family were always identified as Kett *alias* Knight. What emerges beyond any doubt is Robert Kett's exceptional gift of leadership. His brother, a butcher, acted as his right-hand man throughout and was highly esteemed for his courage.

Having completed the work about Wymondham, Kett set out for Norwich with a small band, moving slowly as frequent halts were made to root up more hedges. At first it numbered no more than five or six men, but it swelled rapidly: with serving men and vagrants according to prejudiced contemporary reports, although modern research has proved that the backbone consisted of highly respectable yeomen and tenant farmers.

Already the spark of revolt had spread as far as the county town. Inspired in part by gossip picked up at Wymondham games, in part by spontaneous impulse, a mob had assembled and gone to lay open the Common Close, a pointless action, as it happens, for on this field were grazed the cows which supplied the city with milk. The ominous overtones of this unlawful assembly alarmed the more responsible citizens. Thomas Codd, the mayor, went out to reason with the rioters and tried with conciliatory words and offers of money to persuade them to desist. But they ignored him and he came back to the city empty handed.

On the evening of 9 July the aldermen convened in anxious session. They dispatched Edmund Pynchyn to London to apprise the Protector (whom he found at Windsor) of the commotion, allowing him 40s. for expenses, with a further seven for the hire of a horse and harness; he got another 10s. on his return. Messengers were sent to warn the local gentry; one was paid 5s. 4d. for carrying letters to Sir Roger Townsend, another 2s. for going to Sir William Paston at Oxnead. The meeting dragged far into the night, fortified by six pennyworth of beer. But the city fathers, nervous and unsure of themselves, failed to reach a clear decision. There were a few who forcibly advocated tough measures to suppress the rising immediately. The majority, however, were more conscious of the hazards. Admitting the dangers threatening them, and acknowledging the courage of the hard-liners, they none the less opposed any rash action, arguing that the prospects of success were gloomy and that if they were to fail they would be blamed for making matters worse. Someone else raised the awkward point that to assemble an armed force without the King's sanction would be illegal. In the end they decided to wait and see, and meanwhile put in hand preparations to defend the city by issuing arms to reliable citizens and manning the walls. This, it was hoped, would earn them a breathing space until instructions could arrive from London. They might as well have taken vigorous action, for the youthful King bitterly confided to his journal the belief that their decision (or lack of it) arose from 'the town being confederate with them [the rebels]'.

The next morning, 10 July, Kett and his band crossed the river Yare at Cringleford and advanced as far as Bowthorpe just outside Norwich where they uprooted more hedges, gained many new recruits, and pitched their camp. Here the sheriff of Norfolk, Sir Edward Wyndham found them. In the King's name he commanded them to disperse and go home peaceably. His manner gave offence: the crowd surged around and tried to drag him from his horse. Luckily for him he was well mounted. He managed to break free and galloped the two miles to Norwich, but soon left again hurriedly and thereafter made not the smallest attempt to control the situation. That night a multitude of people, encouraged by his discomfiture, flocked into the camp from the city and the countryside, bringing whatever arms they had managed to collect.

Kett was not happy with the camp site; it was wide open and provided no cover. People were pouring in from all directions and settling down anyhow with no thought of organisation. He wanted a place which could be defended against any possible interference, and where he could impose order through planned occupation. Men coming from the city carrying green boughs (the agreed recognition sign) confirmed the existence of several locations which both answered his requirements and lay conveniently close to Norwich. As first choice they recommended Eaton Wood which was but a short walk from where they lay. Kett inspected it but judged it unsuitable. After further consultation it was decided to occupy Mousehold Heath.

At that moment they were encamped south-west of Norwich. As Mousehold lay on the opposite side the most convenient route was through the city, and Kett sent messengers to the mayor requesting free passage, and giving an undertaking that no harm would be done to either person or property. But in view of the peasants' evident hostility to the authorities Codd refused, upbraiding them with 'many sharp and bitter checks for their disorders', and tried to convince them that they were heading straight for disaster unless they abandoned their enterprise forthwith.

As the crowd straggled towards Hellesdon Bridge on 11 July the gentry put in its second and final appearance in the person of Sir Roger Woodhouse of Kimberley. Thinking to mend the damage done by Sheriff Wyndham he ordered his servants to load one cart with food and two more with barrels of beer, and set off with them to treat with the insurgents. While no doubt correct in his estimate that they must have been experiencing difficulty in feeding themselves, his gesture badly misfired. Ignorant that the rising was directed primarily against the gentry, his approach must have been so intolerably patronising as to strengthen the smouldering antipathy of the peasants. They pulled him from his horse, tore off his clothes and dragged him to a nearby ditch, which belonged to one Morice of Nether Earlham, and chucked him in. In his account Alexander Neville asserts that they actually meant to murder him, and would have done so had it not been for the courageous intervention of one of his servants,

> Edgerley the stout
> Him rescued while courageously he fought.
> His servant's valiant act and loyalty
> Him recompensed with forty pounds in fee.

So they kept him as a prisoner instead — their first — and resumed their march across the bridge which was so narrow that they had to supplement it with a rude causeway improvised from tree trunks and faggots.

The next morning they continued on their way round the north side of Norwich, grubbing up every hedge they came across, and halting at Sprowston where they had an altercation with Mr Corbet, another lawyer. Some of them threatened to burn down his house, but in the end they contented themselves with wrecking his dovecote. Dovecotes were a privilege of the gentry which gave much annoyance to farmers on account of the depredations committed by the birds on their crops; among their grievances was the plea that 'no man under the degree of knight or esquire keep a dove house except it hath been of an old ancient custom'. Corbet's was a disused chapel which he had lately taken over and adapted. The rebels were far from being reactionaries in matters of religion, but they deeply resented any and every manifestation of the grasping habits of gentlemen.

At that time Mousehold Heath was a large open space up to six miles wide in places. Kett sited his camp on the hill which rises steeply from the river Wensum, opposite the cathedral precinct, and just north of Thorpe Wood and village. Formerly it had been called St Leonard's and had been a place of pilgrimage for sufferers from various maladies. More recently it had come to be known as Mount Surrey after the large, handsome house which the late earl of Surrey had built on it. News of the establishment of the camp was broadcast by beacons and church bells, and recruits poured in by the thousand until, it was claimed, more than 16,000 had assembled, more than the population of Norwich itself. A regular township sprang up as Thorpe Wood was stripped of timber to build shelters.

Hard on the heels of the stir at Wymondham came more outbreaks. Insurgents from King's Lynn, Downham Market and other places formed a camp on Rising Chase which was promptly dispersed by the local gentry. They reassembled at Watton from where they blocked the passage across the Little Ouse at Brandon Ferry and Thetford for about a fortnight until, towards the end of the month, Kett ordered them to Mousehold.

There were other disturbances as far away as Landbeach, on the edge of the Fens, and in Cambridge. On 10 July, 100 men assembled with a drum, and destroyed the fences surrounding a close at Barnwell belonging to Mr Smith, one of the bailiffs of the town. However, the mayor, the vice-chancellor of the university and some of the college heads succeeded in pacifying the rioters very quickly, for by 13 July Somerset was commending their prompt action. Some of the trouble-makers were hanged in due course.

In parts of Suffolk the news from Norwich brought the people out in force for a surprise attack on Great Yarmouth. But although initially both of the bailiffs, John Millicent and Nicholas Fenn, esquires, were taken prisoner, they escaped and organised the inhabitants to drive off the rebels who withdrew to Mousehold to swell Kett's ranks.

For a few days at least the confusion was so great that the whole of East Anglia seemed to be in uproar. Nevertheless, as the situation began to take shape it became clearer that the rising was effectively confined to Norfolk north and east of a line drawn between Lynn and Diss. This was the main arable farming region, the most thickly populated, and the one peculiarly subject to tensions arising from both population pressures and conflicts over land use. From the origins of the rebels it is clear that the great majority of the people of this district were involved, the disaffection being spread evenly throughout it, with only hints of concentration: one along the Attleborough-Wymondham-Norwich axis, the other within the area immediately to the east of King's Lynn. The seven hundreds not represented in the camp coincided

most exactly with the poor south-west quarter, the marsh and breck-
nd where the same pressures did not make themselves felt. The
:solate character of much of this area served very largely to isolate the
:at of rebellion which Kett made no attempt to expand, for having
:tablished himself at Mousehold he simply stayed there.

Incredibly, having thrown Norfolk into uproar, Kett, almost casually,
linquished the initiative, and although Norwich, in contrast to Exeter,
:as a ripe plum there for the picking, he made no move to occupy it,
uch less to march on London to force his demands on King and
ouncil. Instead, a situation developed that was wholly without
:ecedent: he proceeded with all due and proper form to take over the
)vernment of Norfolk.

This astounding decision was the outcome of several interlocking
:ctors. The first and most obvious was the vacuum left by the dis-
)pearence of the gentry of whom nothing further was seen after
'yndham and Woodhouse made their single-handed gestures in the
:rst few days. Thereafter they either fled the county incontinently or
:ent to ground. This fact is significant. Alarmist reports of the
nprisonment and mistreatment of a great number of them turned out
 the end to have been a legend. Only a few were in fact taken, nearly
l of them belonging to the immediate vicinity of Mousehold. The
:ajority of the 46 resident justices of the peace, not to mention many
f the lesser gentry, simply funked it and waited for the government to
:scue them, joining the relief columns and howling for blood after
:ther men's arms had gained the victory. William Woodhouse fled in a
:oat across the Wash into Lincolnshire, leaving his brother and sons as
:ostages, and came back as bold as you please in Lord Willoughby of
:arham's force. The failure of the gentry followed from their complete
:ss of authority. The people simply refused to treat with, or even
:sten to them. They had forfeited the authority which normally was
:ccepted unquestioningly as the natural order of things, because by
:lfish pursuit of their personal interests they had forfeited all claim
) respect.

One man alone offered any resistance. Sir Edmund Knyvet from
:lingham mustered a small company of his servants, attacked a band
f rebels near there and scattered them. During the mêlée several of
:is men were unhorsed and in danger of getting killed, but with a fine
:isplay of valour he rallied them and withdrew into Buckenham castle.
:lis opponents repaired to Kett for help. For a moment he contemplated
:n attack on the castle, but it was strongly fortified and he judged that
:nce Knyvet had too few men to be able to risk a sortie he might as
:ell be left in peace.

II

Most of the rebels' grievances were complaints about the gentry. Si
dealt with rents: the various feudal dues which the lords of manor
who were in law liable for them, sought to make freeholders pay; th
enhancement of rents for meadow, marshland and copyholds above th
levels customary in 1485; the exaction of unreasonable fines from
copyholders, and the buying up of freehold land to be let out a
competitive rents. Four more sought to restrict the commercial activitie
of the gentry. No lord of a manor was to serve another as his bailif
No gentleman should be permitted to graze more sheep and bullock
than were necessary for his own housekeeping if his income was les
than £40 a year: this drew a distinction between the genuin
squires and the upstarts whose selfishness was a chief cause o
complaint. Lords of manors ought to be barred from using th
commons which were to be reserved for the use of the tenantry so as t
protect them from deliberate overstocking. Further, lords were not t
sell the wardship of their tenants' children for profit or exercise an
control over their marriages. Enclosure as such received only one brie
mention: existing saffron fields were approved because of the expens
of planting them, but no new ones were to be permitted. Tw
complaints referred to game: no one below the degree of knight o
esquire was to be permitted to keep doves or rabbits on their ow
freehold or copyhold land unless they fenced them in, 'so that it shal
not be to the commons' nuisance'.

The peculiarity of this rebellion, as Professor Bindoff has pointe
out, was that the insurgents departed from the ordinary course o
appealing to the King against his evil counsellors, but rather invoke
the aid of the good councillors against corrupt and oppressive loca
officials. Here they particularly hit out at lawyers. The feodary — th
officer who enforced feudal obligations owed to the King — was no
to act as legal adviser to any layman: Flowerdew had been feodary th
previous year! No man who did not hold £10 a year in land directl
from the Crown was to be obliged by the feodary or escheator t
undertake any office. One radical reform was proposed, the feodar
should in future be a man of 'good conscience . . . yearly chosen to th
same office by the commons of every shire'. Also, to penalis
oppression, 'those your officers that have offended your Grace an
your Commons and so proved by the complaint of your poor Common
to give unto those poor men so assembled iiij^d every day so long a
they have remained'. They also prayed the King to revoke from th
lords of manors all leet jurisdiction, i.e. the regulation of village affairs

Among miscellaneous requests were the standardisation of th
bushel at eight gallons, free passage and fishing in rivers, and th

surance to mariners and fishermen of 'the whole profit of their
shings, as porpoises, grampuses, whales, or any great fish . . .' on
hich landlords tried to claim royalties. Finally a reminder that
rfdom lingered on in parts of the county, more than in most: 'We
ray that all bond men may be made free, for God made all free with
is precious blood.'

This programme has been well summed up as an attempt to cut
ack the growth of rural capitalism. In advocating the cause of the
nall independent producer it was essentially populist, and hence,
oupled with the stated desire to revert to the conditions of the happier
mes of the first year of Henry VII (which of course no one could
member), was unmistakably conservative — the Commonwealth
ovement in action. It contains no hint of the egalitarian rumblings
nat were to be heard here and there. The significance of calls to
ecimate the gentry and equalise the distribution of wealth is
ebatable. So far from reflecting considered opinion, they stand on
cord as intemperate outbursts in pubs or slogans shouted by rioting
obs. Individuals prosecuted for uttering them appear uniformly to
ave been servants, labourers and the unemployed. The articles accepted
ne social structure, seeking merely to restore the *status quo* by
eversing the recent deterioration in conditions. The farmers, the
niddling sort of people, gathered on Mousehold, were anything but an
isignificant group. In 1522 men worth £5–19 in goods comprised
lmost a fifth of the community and owned upwards of a third of its
ealth; the complete range from small husbandmen to substantial
eomen, assessments of £3–39, amounted to a full 40 per cent sharing
0 per cent of the wealth. Gentlemen, although individually affluent,
ccounted for less than half as much. The farming community was
larmed not only at pressure from the landlords above, but equally
om landless labourers below, and these were very numerous in
orfolk. Proposals for restricting the farming activities of gentry and
lergy can be construed as an attempt to deflect the question of re-
istribution of land away from their own interests: landlords in fact
ought to profit from the rising demand for land by splitting up holdings
hen they could. Everyone knew that the labourers constituted a
erious and growing problem, but contrived to ignore their existence
y labelling them vagabonds and beggars, and insisting that they were
aused solely by enclosures and engrossment. Interestingly, the articles
id not protest against the recent draconian anti-vagrant legislation.
ersisting ambivalence towards this class was to bedevil the avowedly
galitarian aims of the Levellers a century later, deeply dividing them
ver the question of whether servants and paupers could be regarded as
ill citizens. Antipathy towards the gentry was rife in 1549, but princi-
ally in the form of resistance to disturbing innovators — enclosures,

rackrenters and, in the West, Protestants. The existence of a genui
egalitarian movement cannot be convincingly demonstrated.

The Lord Protector had already announced these very reforms. F
had urged patience, but obstruction by the landlords had proved
well nigh insuperable obstacle. Nevertheless, he still held the reins
power; his actions lent confirmation to the people's belief that he w
on their side. In May he had reiterated his denunciation of enclosure
in June he had offered a general pardon to all who had anticipate
the outcome of the enquiry. To uncomplicated minds governme
policy looked unequivocal. But its execution depended on the ve
men who stood to lose financially through it, and whose entire reco
proved beyond doubt that they would sabotage it if they coul
Somerset himself contributed the final touch by directing magnat
and justices of the peace to repress the disorders he himself had u
wittingly encouraged, and thus achieved nothing except to provi
them with an additional opportunity of manifesting their malevolenc
In the end, therefore, there was nothing for Kett but to shoulder tl
gentry aside and set up an alternative administration in order to car
out government policy.

The creation of a camp council — two deputies from each of the ?
Norfolk hundreds and one of Suffolk — was only the beginning. To
was grafted an embryonic machinery of government which scrupulous
adhered to the proper legal forms. It was alleged that the rebels inte
cepted royal writs addressed to various gentlemen ordering measur
for the preservation of the peace, erased the names of the addresse
and substituted their own; that they detached the seals from roy
documents and affixed them to ones they concocted themselves an
exhibited in public places. They may have done so. One thing the
certainly did was to capture Thomas Godsalve, a lawyer and son
Sir John Godsalve, sometime Clerk of the Signet and Comptroller
the Mint, and force him to write bills, complaints, writings an
commissions. He penned all instruments issued at the camp in tl
King's name as well as the list of grievances. The King's authority w
invoked because the Norfolk men were out to enforce his ordinance
and they prayed him for instructions and plenary powers. Their 27
article reads:

> We pray your Grace to give licence and authority by your gracio
> commission under your great seal to such commissioners as yo
> poor commons have chosen, or to make as many of them as yo
> Majesty and Council shall appoint and think meet for to redress an
> reform all such good laws, statutes, proclamations, and all oth
> your proceedings, which have been hidden by your Justices of yo
> Peace, sheriffs, escheators, and other your officers from your po
> commons since the first year of your noble father. . . .

Kett ordered the citizens of Norwich to hold themselves in readiness to turn out under arms to help defend the King's peace, and the mayor was required to supply money from the treasury: evidently the door was forced at some stage because the cost of repairing it subsequently amounted to 34s. in labour and materials. For the support of the camp, contributions were laid on the countryside, warrants being issued in a form similar to that used by the Crown purveyors:

> We, the King's friends and deputies, do grant license to all men to provide and bring into the camp at Mousehold all manner of cattle and provision of victuals, in what place soever they may find the same, so that no violence or injury be done to any honest or poor man, commanding all persons as they tender the King's honour and royal majesty, and the relief of the Commonwealth to be obedient to us the governors and to those whose names ensure.
> [signed]
> *Robert Kett* [and two delegates from each hundred]

Bands of rebels foraged for supplies and money. 3,000 bullocks and 20,000 sheep, to say nothing of pigs, fowls, deer, swans, and thousands of bushels of corn, were driven in and consumed, it was said, in a few days. Men whose ordinary diet was too often sparse and monotonous revelled in the abundance of flesh, and there was reckless waste. It tasted all the sweeter for coming from the beasts which were the root of so much resentment.

As is only to be expected since they ended as losers, the conduct of the rebels was misrepresented in every way. It was alleged that the camp became a Mecca for every dissolute person in the county. Certainly they had very little cause to display any love for the landed class, or to trust them:

> they cried out of the Gentlemen, as well for that they would not pull down their enclosed grounds, as also understood they by letters found among their servants how they sought by all ways to suppress them, and whatever said they would down with them, so that within a ij or iij weeks they had so pursued the gentlemen from all parts that in no place durst one gentleman keep his house, but were fain to spoil themselves of their apparel, and lie and keep in woods and 'lownde' places where no resort was: and some fled out of the country; and glad they were in their houses, for saving of the rest of their goods and cattle, to provide for them daily bread, meat and drink, and all other viands, and to carry the same at their own charge home to the Rebels' camp; and that for the saving their wives and children and servants, notwithstanding, were divers gentlemen taken and brought to prison, some in Norwich prison, and some in Norwich Castle, and some in Surrey Place.

But although the report was apprehensively spread about — and like th
above lovingly collected and recorded in due course by Neville — th
they had put many harmless folk in irons, manacled two by two, an
and systematically ill-treated them, only two instances of person
molestation were actually recorded. A certain Mr Wharton was mac
to run the gauntlet down the hill from the camp to the city gate; h
was pricked with spears and knives, and subjected to blood-curdlir
threats, but apparently not otherwise harmed. A lawyer from Multo
'a very subtle fellow and a man set to sale for money', who was widel
known for his vindictive nature and reputation for dabbling i
necromancy, had concealed himself in a thicket of thorns and briar
A woman betrayed him to a passing band of rebels who dragged hir
out. As they were hauling him off to the camp 'mighty showers fe
mixed with hail which covered the earth and was very deep'. Proper
awed by this display of occult powers, his captors took good care t
avoid doing him any further injury. Other charges of brutality a
vandalism were uniformly generalised, and so far as can be ascertaine
little harm was done to either life or property throughout the rebellio
The peasants confined themselves to systematic destruction of th
hedges and ditches whose appearance in the landscape had robbed ther
of their ancient rights.

Anarchy was the last thing Kett was prepared to tolerate, or inded
could afford. The rebels were nothing if not decent God-fearing fol
with standards to maintain. The point they were out to make was tha
since the gentry had signally failed in their duty they themselves wer
perfectly capable of taking up the reins of government and making
very much better job of it. In order, therefore, that 'the people b
admonished to beware of their robbings and spoiling and other the
evil demeanours, and that account they had to make', Kett sat dail
under 'an old oak with great spread boughs [which] they laid ove
with rafts and balks across, and made a roof with boards', and there h
held court, sentencing thieves to prison. The tree came to be known a
the Oak of Reformation.

Gentlemen were also brought before Kett to be tried. The assemble
people, it was alleged, formed the jury and pronounced their verdic
by shouting in unison, 'A good man!' in the case of one, 'Hang him!' i
the case of the next, and so forth. Judgments such as these wer
handed down

> although they were utterly ignorant of the man in question, whethe
> white or black, old or young (as one whose name was never hear
> before) but led by a certain blind and headlong rage of the mind (a
> by a mighty tempest) oftentimes without a word, and as it were wit
> a mad nod of their furies, they inflicted most cruel punishment
> upon innocent and just men.

t is, however, virtually certain that none save proven malefactors uffered in this court. Accounts of it sound very much like the pologists of the gentry whining at the prospect of them being subjected o the brutal criminal law which they habitually meted out to the ower orders.

II

he Norfolk rebels were nothing if not God-fearing men. Among Kett's oremost advisers was Robert Watson, a 'new preacher', on whose ecommendation Thomas Coniers, the minister of St Martin's on the alace Plain, was appointed to read Morning and Evening Prayer daily rom the new Prayer Book. It comes as no surprise to find their basic opulism complemented by a pronounced anti-clericalism, with five f their articles directed against the abuses of the Church. The purchase f land by priests was to be prohibited, and what they already owned nould be let to laymen; tithes, ever a fertile source of wrangling, were o be limited to a strict tenth of the produce of the soil. Priests were ot to be allowed to serve gentlemen as private chaplains or household fficers, but were to minister in their parishes, and the incumbent or npropriator of every living worth £10 a year was to be compelled to erve there in person or provide a curate. Finally there was a clear ndorsement of the new confession, combined with another hint of emocratic action:

> We pray that priests and vicars that be not able to preach and set forth the word of God to his parishioners may be thereby put from his benefice, and the parishioners there to choose another, or else the patron or lord of the town.

Quite the most extraordinary feature of the whole episode was the pirit of toleration which pervaded it. Kett sought earnestly to promote hat we should call dialogue. He permitted anyone who wished to do o to come to the Oak to try his hand at talking the people into bandoning the rebellion. Among these were Thomas Codd, the mayor, nd Thomas Aldrych of Mangreen Hall, Swardeston, 'a man of good isdom and honesty and well beloved' — also a former mayor of orwich — who had reluctantly consented to join Kett's council in the ope of being able to exercise a moderating influence. Nevertheless, either he nor anyone else was able to shake Kett's hold over the eople.

Nor did any greater success attend the efforts of Dr Matthew Parker, ae Master of Corpus Christi College, Cambridge, and future archbishop f Canterbury, who had been born at Norwich in 1504. Highly esteemed

as a preacher, he daily from his pulpit exhorted the citizens to walk th
paths of righteousness.

One sultry day, accompanied by his brother Thomas (a futur
mayor) and several friends, he entered the camp where he found Ket
holding council under the Oak. Thomas Codd was there too, bein
pressed to surrender the keys of the city and resign his office, to whic
he stoutly replied: 'I would rather lay down my life than by villain
treacherously desert my city or through fear and cowardice mos
shamefully fail in the duty I owe my King.'

Parker noted the interest taken in the question of resignation; h
also 'saw the miserable common people drowned in drink and excess
and thinking 'that sober and wholesome communication would littl
profit drunkards overcharged with meat and drink, and stricken wit
the heat of the weather and sun', he quietly withdrew.

But the next morning he went back up the hill, arriving whil
Mr Coniers was reciting the Litany. Having waited until it wa
concluded he approached the Oak and began to preach.

He extolled the virtues of temperance and sobriety, and by appealin
to the congregation to refrain from self-indulgence in the consumptio
of food, which was God's gift, sought by inference to reprove them fo
the unreasonable demands they had made the previous day. He went o
to urge them to show charity, to renounce anger and private enmities
and to refrain from tormenting and murdering their enemies. As he wa
a 'charming' preacher the crowd listened attentively until, reaching .
climax, he adjured them to abandon their reckless course in the interes
of the common good, to honour the young King and have faith in hi
emissaries. At this one man interrupted abruptly:

'How long shall we bear with this hireling doctor? He is hired by th
gentry, and so he comes with words for which they have paid him
and his tongue bribed by them. But for all his prating we will bridl
their intolerable power, and will hold them bound by the cords o
our laws [in] spite of their hearts.'

In a flash the mood of the assembly became menacing. The situatio
was retrieved only by the intervention of Mr Coniers. He had with hin
three or four choristers from the cathedral whom he now caused t
begin singing the *Te Deum* in English. The overwhelming beauty o
the music, which must have been one of the great polyphonic settings
'with solemn music and distinct notes elegantly set for the delight o
the ear', completely enthralled the peasants, 'they being ravished (fo
they were unwonted to Music)'; in their village churches they hear
only the plain, spoken (or hitherto mumbled) liturgy.

While they listened raptly Parker slipped away and strode rapidl
down the hill towards Pockthorpe Gate. But a few harder heade
members of the congregation followed and overtook him. Surroundin

im, they asked questions about his licence to preach. He answered
at he had been licensed by the archbishop of Canterbury for the past
6 years, but, realising the danger of becoming involved in an argument,
e faded away as soon as he could, leaving his brother to carry on the
ialogue. Subsequently it transpired that he had been in no actual
anger as most of the people in the camp held him in high esteem.

In St Clement's the following morning he preached against rebellion.
group of rebels waylaid him in the porch after the service, informed
im that they were aware that he owned three or four good horses, and
emanded that he should give them up. He made no reply, but having
ached his lodgings he sent for a farrier whom he ordered to unshoe
e horses and pare the hoofs of two of them to quick, and rub nerve
il into the hoofs of the others so as to make it look as though they
ad been lamed by excessive work. Thus the rebels were deceived into
inking the animals not worth taking away.

By this time Parker had come to the conclusion that he was a
arked man. A few days later he strolled casually out of town down
e road to Cringleford bridge where he had arranged for his horses to
e brought, and so made good his escape to Cambridge and the
omfortable security of the Master's lodging at Corpus Christi.

V

these early days relations between camp and city were ambivalent.
aving initially denied passage to the rebels, Mayor Codd allowed him-
lf to be pressed into taking a seat on Kett's council along with
ldrych and Watson. His attitude is hard to determine. On any reckon-
g irresolute where Blackaller of Exeter was inflexible, his apologists
aintained that he was coerced into participating in the administration
f the camp, and countersigning both Kett's warrants and the schedule
f grievances. And so as to be in a position to restrain the rebels from
nticipated excesses he had frequently to agree with decisions he
isliked. In fairness to him it must be conceded that his position was
eak. The great perimeter of Norwich was virtually undefendable; the
alls were decrepit, and beyond the cathedral precinct there were none
t all, only the shallow river Wensum which presented hardly any
bstacle to a determined assault. Also he had little enough to guide his
ctions apart from the Protector's commission under the Great Seal for
e reformation of agrarian abuses which had been delivered to the
orporation on 13 July, the day following the occupation of Mousehold.
s a policy statement it did not exactly provide a basis for the
ondemnation of Kett's action, although of course it had been drawn
p before the latest development could have been known. The city

council sat up till after midnight discussing it, but their only decisi
was to reward the poursuivant who had brought it 40s., while the on
immediate beneficiary was Mrs Pynchyn who charged them 6s. f
bread, beer and candles.

Certainly there would have been a large element in the city wl
sympathised with the insurgents, probably the lower class, as in Exet
since many of them must have been recruited from the surpl
population of the countryside, squeezed off the land for want
employment. Unlike Exeter, Norwich possessed no nucleus of leadi
citizens who were of a mind to show a determined front. It is diffic
not to suppose that from the mayor downwards a good many mo
shared the rebels' point of view.

To Kett good relations were something to be valued. As he at
time contemplated a march on London, having made up his mind
stand fast and address himself to the task of reforming Norfolk,
needed the willing co-operation of the citizens. Thus he made no mo
to occupy the town against their wishes, but merely posted men at tl
gates to control movement in and out, though not, it would seem, ve
rigorously. There was probably a wide measure of truth in the asserti
that a good many arms were seized and carried away. Compared wi
the peasantry the inhabitants were well equipped. In the musters
1522, 410 out of a total of 721 able-bodied men had been ful
harnessed, compared with less than one in four in the rural area. The
is no evidence that the ratio had changed in the interim. Rumours th
the rebels intended to pillage the city were no doubt great
exaggerated, though not entirely lacking in foundation, for they cou
enter it more or less at will, and among so large a company there mu
have been many rough characters.

It was inevitable that in the midst of so much uncertainty a deepeni
uneasiness should have pervaded the atmosphere. An eye witne
remembered how:

> The women resorted twice a day to prayer, and the servants (exce
> what must needs stay at home) did the same. When Kett
> ambassadors were sent to any private house, they were fain to ba
> or brew, or do any work for the Camp, else they were carried
> traitors to the Oak. As for trading there was none in the City, peop
> being forced to hide up their choicest goods, and happy were the
> that had the faithfullest servants. They that did keep open the
> shops were robbed and spoiled, and their goods measured by tl
> arm's length, and dispersed among the rebels. Their children the
> sent away for fear of fire. I the writer (who was then 22 years
> age . . .) was present after prayer during this dolorous state, whe
> people met [and bewailed] the miserable state they were in, and lil
> to be in, holding up their hands to heaven, praying with tears th
> God would deal so mercifully with them that they might live to ta
> of it, thinking it impossible at the time, they were so devoid of hop

Some of the wealthy took refuge in flight. They would! Leonard
otherton made for London, possibly getting robbed on the way, for
e was afterwards compensated to the extent of £3 6s. 8d. He obtained
n audience with the Privy Council to whom he painted a black picture,
though on being pressed he admitted that the offer of a pardon would
mollify the majority of the insurgents and bring the affair to an early
onclusion. It is by no means improbable that he was sent to explain
way the signatures of Codd and Aldrych on the list of the rebels'
omplaints which must have reached their lordships almost
multaneously.

To the vacillation and demoralisation of the authorities in Norfolk was
dded the impotence of the government. For the Protector himself it
vas acutely embarrassing. Reluctantly, as well as belatedly, he had had
o sanction the formation of a sizeable army in the West Country. Even
s the camp was forming on Mousehold he was having to divert some of
he troops assigned to it to the Thames valley to cope with the new,
nd fleetingly more menacing, disturbances in that quarter. With
imultaneous tumults breaking out as far apart as Cambridgeshire and
Hampshire, and alarums and excursions in many more places, all
vailable forces were tied down, including upwards of 6,000 men,
etained to guard the King, whom Somerset, understandably, was loath
o release from his immediate control. There were, doubtless, voices on
he Council demanding immediate tough measures, and once again he
ound himself having to head them off. The formation of yet another
ounter-insurgency force would gravely imperil the prospects of the
cottish campaign. Once more he was reduced to hoping for something
o turn up; indeed at this juncture there was very little else he could do.
The total collapse of the traditional machinery of law and order in
Norfolk was something that could not have been foreseen, nor could it
ave come at a worse moment. And yet there appeared a glimmer of
ope.

It is probable that Somerset had on his desk at the same time the
emands of both the western and the Norfolk rebels, and perhaps some
rom other districts too. He cannot have failed to observe the striking
issimilarity in tone: the demands of the Cornishmen, each commencing
vith the challenging 'We will have . . .', contrasted strongly with the
ustomary humble form, 'We pray that . . .', employed by Kett. He was
ndeed impressed by the coincidence between Kett's objectives and his
wn. He could, therefore, afford the hope that the Norfolk men would
e amenable to reason and that it would not prove necessary to take
ilitary measures against them.

The reply he drafted was conciliatory, even cordial, in tone. Whil
deploring their resort to arms, he stressed the powers vested in th
commissioners to reform abuses, 'whereof, doubtless, some had b
this time been redressed had not those disorders given impediment t
these designs generally'. Although only an Act of Parliament coul
restore rents to the levels obtaining in 1485, the King 'would so fa
extend his authority, royal and absolute', as to direct his commissione
to reduce those due at Michaelmas next to the levels of forty year
back, with confirmation by Parliament to follow. Landlords would b
prohibited from engaging in business as farmers or clothiers, and n
one would be permitted to follow two occupations or hold more tha
one farm. Recalling his proclamation of 8 July against excessive foo
prices, he undertook to reduce the price of wool by one third; probabl
influenced by complaints from other counties. In conclusion h
promised that Parliament would reconvene in October,

> against which time they should appoint four or six of their count
> to present bills of their desires, and in the mean season apply them
> selves to their harvest and other peaceable business at home, an
> not to drive him to necessity (whereof he would be sorry) by sharpe
> means to maintain both his [the King's] own dignity and th
> common quiet.

But it was no more than a hope. Although Cranmer preached a
impartial sermon condemning enclosures, this undertaking to invok
the royal prerogative to enforce unprecedented restrictions on propert
owners, on the supposition that they could subsequently be steam
rollered through Parliament, must have provoked stiff opposition i
Council, and strengthened misgivings about his conduct of government.
The only realistic way out was for Kett to climb down. Although no
unsympathetic to the aims of the rising, Somerset's attitude toward
rebellion was exactly the same as that of any other contemporar
statesman. However, not only would the customary ruthless repressio
signify the collapse of the reform policy to which he had lent hi
authority, simply to admit the existence of a second full-scale revol
would seriously diminish his credibility as head of the government
York Herald arrived in Norwich on 21 July bearing this missive
After suitable entertainment laid on by Mrs Pynchyn (bread, wine
fruit and other dishes costing the city 3s. 4d.), he put on his gorgeou
ceremonial dress and proceeded to the Oak to meet the rebels. Havin
proclaimed the King's general pardon to all who would disperse quietly
he read out what really amounted to the acceptance of everything th
Norfolk men had asked for. It made a deep impression. Many fel
inclined to put their trust in the government, and 'on their knees fe
down, giving God and the King's majesty great thanks for his Grace'
clemency and pity, whilst others cried out: "God save the King
majesty!" '

Kett, however, suspected that he himself was destined to be
cluded from the amnesty; it also struck him that acceptance of the
rdon would constitute an admission of guilt. Signalling silence he
claimed:

'Kings are wont to pardon wicked persons not innocent and just
en; we for our part have deserved nothing [i.e. punishment] and are
ilty of no crime.'

He poured scorn on much of the herald's speech as irrelevant, and
lled on his followers to stand fast and insist on the government
cognising that they had in no way broken the law, but on the contrary
forced it to the letter.

York thereupon charged him with treason and commanded John
ttibone, his swordbearer, to arrest him. A tremor of rage rippled
rough the crowd and the situation began to look ugly. So the herald
treated to the town accompanied by a large number of men who cast
wn their weapons and threw themselves on the King's mercy. The
rporation rewarded him with 'viij pieces of good old sovereigns'
rth £4.

The sole outcome of the day's proceedings was a hardening of
titudes. Convinced of the righteousness of their cause, and the
sential legality of their actions, the peasants refused to accept that
eir conduct amounted to treason, and made up their minds to stand
eir ground until their demands had been met in full. The city
thorities for their part now had the guidance they had previously
cked. Kett stood outlawed. There could be no question of further
alings with him; the gates must be closed to the rebels.

There had already been some build up of armaments on both sides.
e insurgents had been ransacking the homes of the gentry. Artillery
d been obtained from Old Paston Hall and other places, powder from
rwich and towns as far away as King's Lynn. The city had acquired
o iron guns from Caister Hall belonging to Sir William Paston. Con-
ering that cannon are supposed to have been a royal monopoly, the
own's ultimate sanction against the feudal baronage, it is remarkable
w many could be found lying about the country for anyone to use.

All that night men toiled to put the city in a state of defence.
pposite Mousehold there were no walls, only the shallow river; to
fend this gap earthworks were thrown up on either side of Bishop's
te. Extra guards were posted at all vulnerable points. As there was
insufficiency of round shot, Robert Raynbald, the chamberlain,
ganised the casting of 80 rounds, using 214 lb. of lead; evidently the
ns were all small. Everything else had to be prepared in a similar
rry: 15 lb. of slow match (made by boiling cord in vinegar) and a
ge bundle of brown paper for wadding; ladles, sponges and quoins;
rows and bowstrings. The locks on the gates were mended; in half a
ntury of Tudor peace the citizens had not bothered to keep them in

repair. Orders were confused. Gentlemen whom the rebels had lodged in the town gaol were freed, but on second thoughts they were locked up again for their own safety in case the town should fall. One cannon was dragged to the common staithe where two brothers named Appleyard kept watch over it for the night, while Paston's two guns were removed from the staithe to the castle where Thomas Godsalve (Kett's erstwhile secretary) guarded them with a large company. Ten of the largest guns were mounted in the castle ditch, but there, in the centre of the town, there was no target for them to shoot at, and therefore they were transferred to the Hospital Meadow to strengthen the weak sector along the river bank. Nerves were tense, and much of the night was 'spent in fearful shots on both sides'.

As expected, the attack began in the morning, but in a bizarre fashion. Soon after first light the rebels brought their cannon down to the foot of the hill and opened fire at easy range. After a short bombardment they stopped, and the defenders were surprised to see a flag of truce approaching, carried by two men who were recognised as Ralph Sutton, a hatter, and James Williams, a tailor. These proposed a few days' truce to enable the camp to stock up with provisions, and actually wanted to do their shopping in the city. They added that they had had to go without breakfast. The immediate result of closing of the gates the previous day had been to cut them off from the city markets on which, apparently, they had been relying for most of their supplies. If this favour should be refused them they threatened to storm the city and lay it waste with fire and sword.

Codd was staggered. He came out to the rampart and began upbraiding Sutton and Williams for their crimes and their presumption in asking for admittance to the city to enjoy the rights of citizens. A bitter personal note crept in: they expected too much of a man they had lately humiliated and virtually held prisoner, and were quite mistaken in supposing that the citizens could be intimidated. Norwich was loyal to the King and defied Kett to do his worst: sooner or later he and all his confederates would be hanged as traitors.

From a military standpoint there was no need to attack Norwich Kett was not out to wage war on anyone. By now he must have formed a poor opinion of Codd and most of his colleagues, and calculated that it would be safe enough to disperse most of his men in foraging parties But since he was purporting to rule the whole county he could not afford to tolerate any defiance of his authority. He was, indeed, beginning to experience the same dilemma as Somerset – how to pursue an enlightened policy while not at the same time abdicating his responsibilities. Thus, according to the position he had adopted, it was Norwich that was in rebellion against the authority he claimed to wield on behalf of the King, and so it had to be reduced to obedience.

Equally material was the stark fact that his men were famished, as well as infuriated by Codd's attitude.

Towards the middle of the morning, therefore, dense waves of yelling rebels poured down the hill, almost certainly directing the main weight of their assault against the sector on either side of a gate between Bishop's Gate and the Hospital Tower where a battery of six guns (supplied with 2 cwt. of shot) had been sited, with archers and billmen in support. Braving a hail of arrows, the rebels pressed their attack right up to the river bank and into the water. To the consternation of the defenders men could be seen coming on with arrows sticking out of their arms and legs, or even wrenching shafts out of their bodies and handing them, dripping with gore, to their own archers to shoot back. Faced with an enemy who, as they could plainly see, were possessed by the Devil, the defending bowmen began to waver and desert their posts. But the gunners stuck to their task with ferocious determination until the assault was held and thrown back with heavy loss.

Near noon the alarm was raised that other rebels had broken into the city on the other side. A large number of men rushed away to hold off this new thrust, leaving the waterfront under manned. In any case the defenders were all too few in number, since many of the citizens had skulked 'in their houses and about their business', regardless of the common danger.

It was probably a carefully executed diversion by a few picked men, intended to throw the defence off balance. For at this moment Kett hurled a fresh wave down the hill and across the Wensum, taking the defenders there by surprise, even the gun crews, who panicked and ran, forgetting to fire their pieces. The 22-year-old eye-witness had fought there all morning, and during the lull,

> being sent for a barrel of beer for the dry army, was met by a great number which came through the river, and so scared the gunners away and others, that some ran to raise up the City for more help, for the rebels had broken up the rampires, opened the gates, and carried up 6 pieces of ordnance to the hill, and the rest in such numbers as the citizens could not deal with them, ran crying about the streets: 'Traitors! Traitors!' and a great number entered houses, robbed shops and did much violence.

York Herald and the mayor somehow forced their way through the streets to the market cross, 'cried, howled and shouted' the whole way, to the 'great admiration' of the populace. There, looking faintly ridiculous in the midst of the pandemonium, they tried bravely to command the intruders to throw down their arms and go away. Not surprisingly they were told, in effect, to 'get lost', and this is precisely what York did, galloping back to London which he reached next day, 23 July, finally convinced that the rebels were not going to be moved by speeches, and that they rejected the offer of a pardon as nothing more than a trap.

The insurgents looked for Leonard Sotherton but he managed to hide, along with many of his colleagues. They arrested the mayor and cast him into prison along with William Rogers and John Hamerson, aldermen, William Brampton, gentleman, and many other men of good standing, keeping them in irons in Surrey Place for the duration of the rebellion.

A man called John Fishman sought to curry favour with Kett by retailing the story of the casting of the roundshot overnight. Acting on his information, Robert Isod, a tanner, John Baker, a butcher, and a miller from Heigham named Edward, led a party of 80 men to Robert Raynbald's house. They forced him to conduct them to the Guildhall from which they removed an assortment of munitions: a whole barrel of gunpowder and the remains of another, iron and lead shot, and a number of morris pikes which were stored over the assembly chamber. They needed some cord to bundle the weapons up and baskets to carry the shot in. Too honest to steal them, they obliged Raynbald to stump up 6d. from his own pocket. Then they went back to his home and helped themselves to some of the cannon balls which had been cast overnight — the contemporary account says 120, a mistake, perhaps, for 20 — some serpentine powder and some paper, as well as a quantity of corn, all of which he claimed was his own property and worth £6 or more. Again with scrupulous regard for propriety, they made him purchase for 5d. a firkin to pack the shot in, and for 3d. a rope to truss up the remainder of the loot. The next day 100 men ransacked the house and unearthed various arms including two sets of almain rivets, 'as fair as any in Norwich'. This time they took Raynbald away, to the Oak of Reformation, intending to put him on trial. However, by producing a further 3s. 4d., he persuaded them to bring him home again.

Some at least of the citizens were uneasy about the fate of their mayor, their concern deepened as a result of overhearing rebels swaggering about the streets and in the alehouses making coarse jokes about a cod's head going for 6d. They deputed Thomas Aldrych to intercede with Kett: already his popularity with the rebels had enabled him to retrieve much of the plunder to which they had earlier helped themselves. He earnestly advised the leader to set Codd at liberty. Kett heard him out in silence and then sat for some time rapt in thought. Aldrych went on to take him to task for persecuting a good man whose only offence was loyalty to his sovereign — a shrewd point in view of Kett's assumption of something resembling the lord lieutenancy of the county. He also appealed to Kett's finer feelings, concluding by virtually ordering him to release the prisoner. It worked. Codd's detention was

nitigated to a kind of open arrest which allowed him to pay fairly
egular visits to the city. None the less, he was too restricted to be able
o perform his duties adequately, and so nominated a predecessor,
Augustine Steward, as his deputy who, assisted by the sheriff, contrived
o preserve some semblance of order.

With the forcible occupation of Norwich and, whatever his own view
of the matter, the defiance of the herald and rejection of the royal
pardon, Kett had to accept that he was now committed to actual
ebellion, and that his only hope lay in avoiding defeat. Accordingly
ie sent out secret agents in all directions to drum up support, and it
vas probably at this juncture that the number assembled on Mousehold
eached its estimated maximum of 16,000. The inference is that all of
hem were men more or less fit to bear arms, but although this was
ertainly not beyond the resources of the shire it might very well have
ncluded many non-combatants, women especially. There is no record
of casualties in the affair of 22 July, but, with the possible exception of
he initial assault, they were probably light on both sides; the citizens
after all had not really put up much of a defence.

The insurgents now settled down to wait and see whether the government, having had proof of their determination, would be prepared to
negotiate on equal terms.

Chapter 8
The Battle of Fenny Bridges

I

As the month of July drew to a close Humphry Arundell must have been becoming acutely aware of the need to regain the initiative. With his spies scouring the district he can hardly have avoided 'understanding of [Russell's] distressed state', yet at the same time signs of a growing concentration of royal forces at Honiton warned him of the danger of delaying his next move. Exeter could not hold out for much longer; its capture would restore his freedom of action.

On paper the advantage lay with the rebels. They still outnumbered Russell, possibly by as much as two to one in fully equipped men, with numerous lightly armed reservists. About one third were probably archers, the remainder billmen. The Cornish bow was a formidable weapon in the hands of a determined man. Cleaning up after the engagement on Blackheath Field in 1497, Englishmen had observed with wonder that it was fully six inches longer than theirs. The army was well equipped with field artillery and not lacking in skilled gunners; 16 guns were taken from them at Sampford Courtenay at the end of the campaign. What it lacked was offensive weapons. The classical English tactic was to stand on the defensive, for the archers to break up the enemy's oncoming formation with their shot, and the billmen to charge home when it was halted and in disorder. Modern continental tactics employed two shock arms: the massed phalanx of pikemen, originally evolved by the Swiss to fight on its own, but now universally supported by the fire of arquebusiers, and the fully armoured medieval cavalry given a new lease of life by supporting artillery, and more recently by equipping the troopers with pistols.

The royal army was much more varied in its composition. The West Country levies were armed in the same way as the rebels, with the possible addition of some arquebuses issued from the Tower armoury: about one English soldier in 10 carried a gun at the siege of Boulogne in 1544. Assuming, therefore, that this corps numbered 1,000 men, it may be envisaged as comprising something like 100 arquebusiers, 250 archers and 650 billmen. The Italians were all armed with arquebuses, heavy matchlock pieces which, as their length and weight increased, were beginning to be supported on forks when fired. Though slow to load, in the hands of trained, disciplined men they had already decided the great battles of Bicocca and Pavia a quarter of a century earlier.

The English horse consisted of demi-lances and light troops. The former wore three-quarter armour, the chief components of which were a close helmet, a pair of cuirasses, bullet proof in front, and arm and thigh pieces. Their main weapon was an 18-foot lance supplemented by a sword or battleaxe. The Venetian ambassador about this time reported that most of them were gentlemen, and he was probably correct. His statement that they wore only a mail shirt and a sallet, and were mounted on horses of indifferent quality, probably applied to their servants who would fight in a supporting role in the rear ranks, though less wealthy gentlemen mobilised in an emergency such as this may not have been able to afford the more elaborate harness. He added that they were unsuitable for shock tactics and could only charge in flank. The mercenary cavalry led by Jacques Jermigny consisted of 12 officers and NCOs, 29 men-at-arms in full armour with barded horses, 159 demi-lances clad in three-quarter armour, and 59 'horse gunners', similarly protected, a total of 259 of all ranks. It is not clear whether by the last group is meant arquebusiers or pistoleers. The greater part of the company might have been armed as *reiters,* a term which was just coming into use, who carried as their principal weapon the wheel lock pistol which had been invented about 1540 and had rapidly been adopted all over the continent. The usual practice was to carry two in holsters attached to the saddle, with a third thrust into the top of the right boot. Their tactics were to trot up to the enemy formation, troop by troop, fire, and retire to reload, until it was sufficiently disorganised for them to be able to charge home with the sword. Pietro Sanga's company was described as 'Albanois' — his contract stipulated men of 'Hault Burgundy at the least' — which meant light cavalry from the Adriatic region, originally Albania itself. In fact it consisted not of light armed men, but demi-lances, 216 officers and men, and it is very possible that many of them also used pistols.[1] It is far from clear when these companies, one or both, reached Honiton; they may well have been still *en route* there under Lord Grey's command.

There is no information about Russell's artillery train but we may safely assume that thanks to Henry VIII's loving provision it was ample for all his needs.

II

On 27 or 28 July, Arundell pushed out a detachment towards Honiton seeking either to test out Russell's strength or to seize the bridges over the river Otter at Feniton two miles to the west. They drove in the pickets, which must surely have been stationed there, and raised the alarm, but made no attempt to force their way across. The pessimistic Russell was in no hurry to offer battle, but convened his council of war on which the Carews were its leading members. The deliberations dragged on most of the day, with Sir Peter undoubtedly pressing for an immediate attack, 'and in the end after many speeches it was concluded that they should march towards them and give the onset to them. And accordingly without further delays or much talks it was done out of hand.' The next morning, a holy day, the army marched out to offer battle.

John Leland, the antiquary, had described the scene 10 years earlier:

> I rode to Feniton Bridge where Ottery water is divided into 4 arms by policy to serve grist and tucking mills. Upon 3 of these streams I rode by fair stone bridges. The first [western] arm of the 4 was the least and had no bridge that I marked. On the north side of the first bridge was a chapel now profaned.

The rebels, probably all Devonshire men, may not have been more than a reconnaissance in force. They held one end of the bridges, but as soon as Russell's column came in sight the majority of them were drawn up in the meadow below, no doubt in the traditional formation, billmen massed in the centre with archers on each wing.

The position was a strong one, and at first Russell tried 'all the policies' he could devise to take it without incurring undue losses. These having failed he had to fall back on 'bold adventuring', to force his way across the bridge by weight of numbers, the arquebuses and cannon sweeping the other end with their fire to clear the way for the bills. It was won at the cost of some few casualties including Sir Gawen Carew who was wounded in the arm by an arrow. Such wounds may well have accounted for most of the casualties if dismounted heavy horsemen formed the storming party since their body armour was proof against arrows. The main body of the rebels waited in the meadow, making no move to counter-attack, while the loyalists streamed across the bridge and deployed. Pausing only for a single volley, the royal troops charged, and in the fierce mêlée which ensued many fell on both sides until the rebels, heavily outnumbered, broke and fled, leaving Russell in possession of the field. It was instantly assumed that the enemy had been completely routed; the cry 'havoc!' was raised, and the mercenaries and serving men fell to stripping the bodies of the slain, while the gentlemen rested on their arms, congratulating one another on a gallantly won victory, and carelessly forgot to post sentries.

A shower of arrows from the nearest hedges brought them abruptly to their senses. Led by Robert Smyth of St Germans, a band of 200 Cornishmen had been marching to the support of the outpost at the bridge. Undeterred by the sight of the routed mob streaming back past them, they pushed stubbornly on, deployed silently and caught 'these spoilers napping [and made] many of them pay dearly for their wares'. Somehow Russell's captains contrived to sort out the confusion and reform a semblance of a line of battle. 'The fight for the time was very sharp and cruel, for the Cornishmen were lusty and fresh and fully bent to fight out the matter.' But they too were borne down by sheer weight of numbers and finally driven headlong from the field. 'Their captain, whose comb was cut, showeth a fair pair of heels and fled away', back towards Exeter.

It was claimed that 300 of the rebels lay dead on the field, a not improbable total, for the basic lack of discipline in the armies of those days usually meant that a defeated company lost all cohesion and was massacred; many of the wounded would be knocked on the head by the spoilers, and in any case a great many would soon die for lack of treatment. The struggle had been fierce, for the Cornishmen 'were very tall men, lusty and of great courage, and who in a good cause might have done better service'. Russell's losses were not stated but probably did not exceed 100, if so many.

The victors pursued for three miles. Russell, a changed man, now took it into his head that he could follow straight through to Exeter until, still in full cry, he was brought to a sudden halt by Joll, his household fool, screaming hysterically at him 'with a foul mouth, "My Lord, all the country is up behind you and coming upon you!" ' Joll had stayed behind with the baggage in Honiton. While the battle was in progress a furious ringing of bells had broken out in the church tower, sounding exactly like the alarm signal used by the rebels. He leapt instantly to the conclusion that it was the prelude to an uprising in the rear of the army, and without further thought, or pausing to find out whether it was merely a sympathiser attempting to create a diversion, he vaulted onto a horse and rode hell for leather after his master. As he passed by Gittisham and Buckerell he could hear their bells relaying the tocsin, and by the time he caught up with Russell chasing the fugitives towards Rockbeare he was breathless, excited and barely coherent. After the fury and determination displayed by the rebels his tale made an immediate impression. The Lord Privy Seal was neither the first nor the last general to throw away the fruits of victory when gripped by a sudden fear for the security of his flanks and rear. He readily took for granted the approach of a large hostile band from beyond Honiton, had the recall sounded, and, with the army marshalled once more in fighting array, marched cautiously back to his base.

III

In spite of this setback the consequences of the battle of Fenny Bridges were important. The rebels had been encountered in the field. They had not appeared in the expected overwhelming numbers — indeed it is probable that they actually fought every battle of the campaign at a numerical disadvantage — and most important of all they had been roundly thrashed in fair fight.

And yet the disparity of numbers may not have been all that great. At this date the only mercenaries available to Russell were the Italian arquebusiers, and possibly Jermigny and Sanga's cavalry, giving probably fewer than 1,000 reliable troops in view of the extremely questionable loyalty and morale of so many of the locally recruited men. The gap between the professional soldier and the part-timer was still comparatively narrow, and in any case the Cornishmen earned high praise for their courage and skill.

According to legend the rebels carried the ultimate weapon, the longbow; in practice the arquebus won the battles. Which was the better weapon? English soldiers were to debate this vehemently for the next half century. Sir John Smyth emphasised the bow's simplicity, its superior range and accuracy, and extremely rapid rate of discharge; he insisted that only a few highly trained men could handle the musket efficiently, and even then they came nowhere near matching the top bowmen. And of course there was always the proud record of Crècy and Agincourt to silence the doubters. None the less, the fact is that the gun replaced the bow while still a cumbersome and somewhat primitive contraption. As it was very much more expensive to purchase it would not have done so had it not been demonstrably superior. The giveaway in the great debate is that all the participants conceded that the prowess of the archers was a matter of past history — 'their art is much decayed' — and indeed there is no record at all of the true effectiveness of archery; even stories of victories against overwhelming odds must be relegated to the realms of mythology. The bow had been decisive in the Hundred Years' War when the French had obligingly made suicidal frontal attacks; the archers shot down the horses of the leading ranks, creating breakwaters which threw the following waves into confusion.

There is no shred of evidence that archery had declined by the sixteenth century, but many other factors had changed. Plate armour was proof against arrows. At Flodden in 1513 the Scotch pikemen clad in corselets 'abode the most dangerous shot of arrows which sore annoyed, but yet except it hit them in some bare place, did them no hurt'. Another account says that 'few of them were slain with arrows; the bills did hew and beat them down'. Obviously, like riflemen in a modern army, only a very few archers were star marksmen. As Sir Roger Williams and Sir Humphrey Barwick pointed out, in the heat of battle many of them failed to draw their bows fully or take aim. Here the arquebus, slow as its rate of fire undeniably was, had a clear advantage; the range and penetration of the bullet did not depend on the man, air currents had much less influence on the accuracy of the projectile, while in general terms the more mechanical the weapon the less the premium in the skill of the handler.

The hard truth was that the rebels had obsolescent weapons. Somerset was an experienced soldier, and impressed on Russell the great advantage his guns gave him. He could recommend employing arquebusiers to harass the rebels from a distance because he knew they outranged the bowmen for practical purposes. How many sixteenth-century governments, teetering on the verge of bankruptcy, attempting to foot the escalating bills of modern warfare, would have gratefully adopted the inexpensive longbow had it in reality been master of the battlefield?

In the exhilaration of victory the Lord Privy Seal sent an optimistic letter to the mayor of Exeter, by the hand of a boy who had on several occasions slipped through the investment lines, to announce the day's success and his determination to march to the relief of the city without further delay. This cheering news came at an opportune moment, for morale was running low, the inhabitants being 'in a doubtful and dismayed state'. Yet so long had they waited for deliverance and so regularly had their hopes been dashed, they now could scarcely believe that their ordeal was nearing its end. The ensuing week, therefore, was critical. With many people starving, and even the most resolute doubtful whether they could hold out much longer, whether indeed there was any point in further prolonging the agony, it needed all Blackaller's iron resolution to keep the men at their posts on the walls and to silence the blandishments of the Catholic party. In the earlier weeks of the siege these had had perforce to dissemble, plotting in secret but not daring to make any overt move. But as food became scarcer and scarcer the determination of the poor inhabitants fast ebbed away, and they began to come out into the open, feeling that since they already formed the majority of the population their chance of taking over the city was rapidly improving. Exploiting the condition of privation, they began openly to blame it on the obstinacy of the handful of selfish, rich men who ran the city and who were prolonging the defence with callous indifference to the sufferings of ordinary folk. It was necessary only to overthrow them and open the gates to gain access to unlimited food. Granted there was the risk that the wild Cornishmen might plunder the city, but they had only the word of the rich men on the corporation for it — for what it was worth! The truth was that it was they who feared a sack because it was their bulging warehouses and wine cellers that would be looted; their silver plate and gold chains that would be carried off. The houses of the poor offered nothing worth the taking save an occasional cooking pot, and what use was this when there was nothing to put into it anyway?

The plan, such as it was, matured on the morning of Sunday, 4 August. By this date the inhabitants were reaching the end of their tether, the siege having now lasted for five weeks. Within the last eight days two messages had come from Russell promising early relief, yet still he had not come. At about eight o'clock, when many of the principal citizens were in church, a great crowd of people thronged into the streets ready armed and harnessed as though for a sortie, but in fact intending to seize the town. As they went they taunted the Protestants:

Come out these heretics and two penny book men! Where be they? By God's wounds and blood! we will not be penned in to serve their turn. We will go out and have in our neighbours; they be honest, good and godly men.

Had anyone of contrary opinion been foolish enough to show himself in the street they would have quarrelled with him, beaten him up and possibly lynched him. Perhaps instinctively on the alert for any symptoms of treachery, Mayor Blackaller and his senior colleagues were the first to hear of what was afoot and to go outdoors in response to the calls. The troublemakers had not expected so prompt a reaction, but since nothing like all their expected supporters had yet appeared they were much taken aback and at a loss to face up to the formidable and commanding figure of the mayor. He brusquely bade them behave in a more orderly manner, singled out various 'bell wethers of this flock' like John Vincent and John Sharke, and sent them back to their homes with strict injunctions to remain indoors. Much abashed at his displeasure they obeyed dejectedly. There was a brief scuffle in Southgate Street and around the gate itself, the keepers of which were inclined to admit the enemy. But it was soon over with nothing worse than a broken pate or two. Once again and for the last time John Blackaller had saved the situation. It would have been ironical had he. finally succumbed at the very hour when the battle for the city was commencing a couple of miles outside.

On a calmer reappraisal of the prospects Lord Russell had come to the conclusion that caution would pay the best dividends. So far he had encountered a small contingent of rebels who had given him a hard fight; it would be better to wait a few days more for the arrival of Grey with more mercenaries, and thus he came close to letting slip the chance to relieve Exeter.

Chapter 9
Fiasco at Norwich

York Herald's depressing report of the events of 21—2 July convinced the Protector that measures to contain the situation in Norfolk had become imperative. It was established beyond all doubt that the commons were in open rebellion, and intolerable that the second city of the kingdom should be in the hands of the rebels with the possibility of it becoming the focus of a much wider revolt. Perhaps, he may have thought, emotional exhaustion following the exhilaration of victory would bring the rebels to a chilling realisation of the peril into which they had blundered. Surely by this time they must be bitterly regretting having rejected the amnesty, and in desperation would welcome a renewed offer with heartfelt relief, especially were it to be backed up by a token show of force. At this moment a demonstration was all that was practicable, with nearly all the troops that could safely be spared either in Russell's force or on their way to him. But at least he seemed to be about to move, after much prodding; it was permissible to hope that the western rebellion might soon be crushed, releasing forces for service in East Anglia should they still be needed there.

The question of command posed a difficulty. Warwick, a soldier of great ability and already commander designate of the northern army, was Somerset's most dangerous rival; to entrust him with a commission authorising him to levy soldiers in the heart of England would be inviting trouble. The choice fell therefore on William, marquis of Northampton, aged 36, a man of mediocre talents. It could have been this feature that recommended him for the post, more especially since it was not intended that he should do more than keep an eye on things. This apart, his rank, coupled with the fact that his sister had been Henry VIII's last wife — and subsequently Thomas Seymour's — should be enough to make a deep impression. As important a consideration was the fact that he had supported Somerset's assumption of the Protectorship and backed him up in the destruction of their brother.

The nucleus of his force, to which Lord Sheffield was assigned as second-in-command, was a band of Italian mercenaries. There had

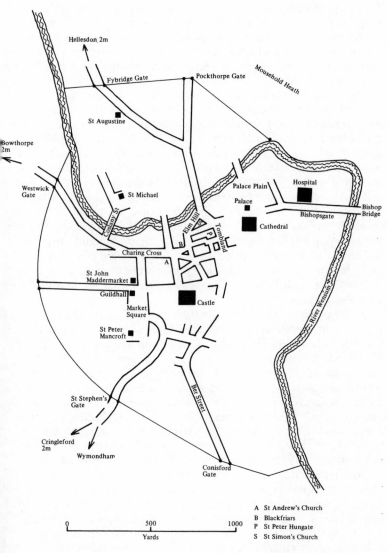

Hellesdon 2m

Fybridge Gate

Pockthorpe Gate

Mousehold Heath

St Augustine

Bowthorpe
2m

Westwick
Gate

St Michael

Coslany St

Palace Plain

Hospital

Palace

Bishop
Bridge

Bishopsgate

Cathedral

Elm Hill

Tombland

P

Charing Cross

B

A

River Wensum

St John
Maddermarket

Guildhall

Market
Square

Castle

St Peter
Mancroft

Ber Street

St Stephen's
Gate

Cringleford
2m

Wymondham

Conisford
Gate

0   500   1000
Yards

A   St Andrew's Church
B   Blackfriars
P   St Peter Hungate
S   St Simon's Church

Map 2 Norwich

lately arrived in London and impoverished soldier of fortune named
Malatesta, armed with letters of introduction from Paget and Hoby.
The only surviving son of Pandolfo Malatesta, who had been driven
from his principality of Rimini by papal aggression, he was looking for
a job, and hoped at least to be permitted to kiss the King's hand. He
was lucky. A stream of new recruits were passing through in ones and
twos on their way to the northern front, enough for a band to be
improvised for him. It was disbanded soon after the crisis was over,
and Malatesta was rewarded for his services — the last that was to be
recorded of one of the great princely families of the Italian renaissance.
Also available was Captain Thomas Drury's band of English foot
consisting, according to his contract, of 100 arquebuses and 100 pikes,
although he was eventually paid for 107 and 73 respectively. It was
one of the few companies of English professionals armed in the modern
manner. *En route,* Northampton collected some dozen or more knights
and many other gentlemen with their retainers, making a total force of
1,200 or 1,400 men, mostly horsemen. Drury was probably detached
to pacify Suffolk for on 11 August the Council awarded him £12 10s.
for capturing Peyn, a leading rebel there. Almost certainly the column
included the Spanish Captain Carlos de Guevara's company of 130
heavy cavalry, probably pistoleers, which were diverted on their way
to join Colonel Sir Pedro de Gamboa's command in the north.[1] There
were also 11 guns.

A three days' march in oppressive heat brought this column to
within sight of Norwich on the afternoon of 31 July. Northampton
was a foolish fellow. The Protector had given him precise instructions:
he was not to offer battle, but to station himself outside the city and
employ his cavalry to blockade the camp so as to make it untenable.
Athirst for glory he proceeded to do the exact opposite, 'seeking a
bubble reputation even in the cannon's mouth', so much had the
glamour of independent command gone to his head. Halting the column
a mile short of its destination, he instructed Norroy King of Arms, who
accompanied him, to ride forward in full panoply and formally
summon the city to surrender; if it refused he was to declare war!

Fortunately Kett had chosen not to install a garrison. Augustine
Steward, who was in charge, sent to Mayor Codd, now confined to the
camp, for instructions. Expressing regret that circumstances prevented
him welcoming the marquis in person, Codd authorised his deputy to
act at discretion. Accordingly, Steward placed himself at the head of
a deputation of citizens and went out to meet Northampton, carrying
the city Sword which he offered up in token of submission. The general,
enjoying himself hugely, kissed the Sword and ceremonially handed it
back, assuring the citizens of his intention to defend them against any
further attack, and restore peace. And so, with the Sword borne in state

head of the deputy mayor, the cortège solemnly made its entrance through St Stephen's Gate. The first stop was at the Guildhall where the marquis and his officers took refreshments laid on as usual by Mrs Pynchyn at a cost to the municipal treasury of 4s. 8d., including, a token of the guest's exceptional dignity, a pound of sugar purchased from Norman, the grocer, for 14d. After this, Northampton summoned the citizens to the market place and began to organise the defence.

But while he had been partaking of civic hospitality the first untoward happening had taken place. A party of Italians had gone out to reconnoitre and had been engaged by Kett's men in a skirmish. One of them, possibly their commanding officer, had incautiously ventured too far and lost touch with his comrades. The rebels pounced on him, and stripped off his clothes and armour, which were costly and richly ornamented. His men endeavoured to secure his release, offering a ransom of £100, but it was bluntly rejected and the wretched man was dragged to Mount Surrey where he was hanged from an oak tree by a man from Bungay in Suffolk. The executioner was himself hanged at the end of the rebellion. This, it must be observed, was the only attested case of anyone being done to death in cold blood by the insurgents, and it is evidence of the special hatred felt for the government's foreign hirelings.

Northampton seems not to have been unduly disturbed by the sudden death of one of his officers. He and his entourage supped with Mr Steward, and afterwards settled down for the night in the gallery of his house, sleeping as best they could in their harness, in spite of the sultry heat, in anticipation of an attack during the night.

The soldiers lit bonfires in the market place to minimise the effect of the darkness, while the sentinels were ordered to watch 'more painfully and diligently than commonly they were wont'. Sir Edward Ward, acting as knight marshal, divided the walls into five sectors, each under the command of a knight, and issued a watchword. The rebel guns opened fire several times, but their shots either fell short or whistled harmlessly overhead: one commentator even suggests that the gunners may have been bribed. Perhaps they intended to do nothing worse than rob the soldiers of their night's sleep, and they certainly succeeded, for on each occasion the sentries raised the alarm, until in the end Ward could stand it no longer and roused Northampton who had the entire army stand to for the remainder of the night. Several officers counselled the rampiring of a number of points on the perimeter farthest away from the enemy so that they could be held with fewer troops; there were of course not nearly enough to man the defences adequately. Gangs were set to work and remained hard at it until eight o'clock, but long before this the rebels had begun their attack.

Kett launched his assault before dawn, attacking many points simultaneously. The assailants attempted to hew down or burn Pockthorpe, Fybridge and St Stephen's Gates, among others. Scaling parties climbed the walls, while other groups forced their way through gaps where the walls had fallen down. Many came across the river. All of them displayed the highest spirit even when badly wounded;

> drowned in their own and other men's blood, even to the last gasp, [they] furiously withstood our men. Yea many also stricken through the breasts with swords, and the sinews of their legs cut asunder (I tremble to rehearse it) yet creeping on their knees, were moved with such fury, as they wounded our soldiers, lying amongst the slain, almost without life.

Twenty-five years later the (embroidered) recollections of men who had fought that morning made Alexander Neville's spine tingle with horror.

The struggle swayed back and forth for three hours. Northampton's men fought stoutly, the East Anglians, Sir Thomas Paston and Sir William Waldegrave, especially distinguishing themselves, until finally a counter-attack scattered the rebels and sent them fleeing pell-mell, leaving 300 dead and dying on the ground. Thanks to superior protection comparatively few soldiers lost their lives, but many were more or less severely wounded. The experience had been chastening. If there had been any disposition earlier on to despise the insurgents as mere rustic clowns, there was none now. The mercenaries, the backbone of the force, were more than a little shaken. They had come off none too well in the encounter of the previous evening, and, depressed as they were at the ignominious loss of a senior officer, any confidence they may originally have had in the commander-in-chief was fast being dissipated by the reckless manner in which he had led them into what was beginning to look ominously like a death trap.

While the marquis sat enjoying his breakfast at the Maid's Head Inn in Tombland, opposite St Simon's church, a group of citizens burst in with the news that many of the rebels were ready to surrender in consequence of the thrashing he had just administered, and that 50 of them were at that moment waiting outside Pockthorpe Gate (the one nearest to Mousehold) to be pardoned. He ordered Norroy to proceed there immediately with a trumpeter, to be shortly joined by Steward who 'was glad and for joy went with them'.

When they reached the gate and it had been thrown open they were amazed to find not one person waiting outside. They tried a flourish on the trumpet. This brought a certain John Flotman of Beccles down the hill accompanied by 20 or so other men. Norroy bade him return to the camp and announce that everyone who wished to accept the King's pardon must disperse and go home immediately. Flotman, 'an outrageous and busy fellow', replied coolly that Northampton was a fool and a coward, a born loser whom they despised, and hated as a traitor. In contrast (and voicing Kett's views) he asserted the loyalty of the men of the camp whose consciences were clear, secure in the knowledge that it was they who were upholding the King's interests as well as their own. Their purpose was 'to deliver the Commonwealth, vexed in many ways unjustly, from the detestable pride, lust and cruelty of their enemies'. Having committed no offence they merited no punishment. If the proffered amnesty was genuine why didn't Northampton clear off and set about hunting the real offenders? 'The Commonwealth is now almost utterly overthrown and is daily declining through the insolence of the gentlemen: our intention is to restore it to its former dignity.' And this they inflexibly resolved to accomplish, or die honourably on the field of battle.

Scarcely had he flung down this defiance when, with a wild yell, swarms of rebels came surging across the Wensum, over the flimsy breastworks along the Hospital Meadow, and crashed into the soldiers as they hurriedly emerged from the narrow streets to deploy on the Palace Plain. Gathering up what men he could, Lord Sheffield charged the attackers. He was too bold. Near the Cupid Inn he was thrown from his horse into a ditch and surrounded by a crowd of rebels. As he lay there helpless he called out his name and offered to pay any ransom, but his pleas were ignored and he was clubbed to death: this was no ordinary war in which professional soldiers fought for profit! Caught off balance, overwhelmed by weight of numbers, the tiny army just disintegrated and took to its heels in flight, leaving behind at least 100 dead and all their artillery; the rebels' losses were perhaps similar.[2]

The city was gripped by fear. Many men, the rich in particular, fled in terror, throwing away their gowns to make better speed; abandoning their wives and children, and even their possessions, though some of them prudently delayed their flight long enough to hide away their gold and silver and such like valuables. In the confusion many buildings were set alight and the fire spread rapidly, threatening to engulf the whole town until, providentially, the storm which had been building up broke, and the downpour quenched the flames. Long did the people remember how

lamentable and miserable was the state of the City at this time when nothing was seen or heard but lamentation and weeping of those that were vexed and troubled, and contrary the rejoicing of the enemy, the weeping of women, the crying of men, and the noise of them that ran about the streets. Then the clashing of weapons, the flames of the burning, the ruins and fall of houses, and many other fearful things which that I may not make less in speaking I willingly let pass, which so filled with horror not only the eyes and minds of the beholders, but struck with incredible sorrow the hearts and ears of all that heard it.

Confused and numbed, Augustine Steward went home to Elm Hill to find that his servants had fled in the wake of the army. Deprived of all advice and support in this his hour of trial, 'seeing the City empty of all assistance, and every man's door shut', he began to believe that he was actually watching his country collapsing into anarchy. Going up to the highest gallery in the house he looked out over the city and saw the houses on either side of Holme Street and most of the hospital out-buildings blazing; the Bishop's Gate was burning fiercely with molten lead running off the roof, so too were the buildings in Pockthorpe, St Mary Magdalen, St Augustine's, Coslany and Ber Street.

Beyond St Augustine's a great band of rebels was coming across the fields with drums beating. They began to set fire to the gate, and the flames soon threatened his house which stood next to it. He hurried downstairs to open the gate. The rebels poured in. They laid hands on him violently, tore off his gown and threatened to put him to a shame-ful death unless he revealed where Northampton was hiding. His reply that the nobleman had already bolted only infuriated them. They swarmed through the house, ransacking every nook and cranny, and only left after he had given them all the money he had on him. Later on another band came and looted his shop, leaving only when a man called Doo, a servant of Mr Smith of Huntingfield, warned that Kett would probably hang them for it, whereupon many of them sullenly threw their bundles back into the shop, and went off grumbling. To save the remainder of his stock, Steward sought to appease them by pressing on them lengths of fustian for shirts and doublets. When at length the looters had all gone Doo stayed behind with three or four other men to keep an eye on the place, and managed to turn away several other gangs. Many other houses were pillaged. In some of them servants who had not run away bought off the marauders by baking them bread and pastries.

The wild behaviour ceased as suddenly as it had begun when Kett entered the city and quietly reimposed his authority. He directed Steward to organise watch and ward again, and this was speedily effected. The insurgents were once more in undisputed control of Norwich, and this time they stationed a garrison which on wet nights camped in the cathedral.

In the meantime a gruesome little scene had been acted out in the camp. A violent quarrel had broken out over who was entitled to the credit for having battered Lord Sheffield to death. After they had nearly resorted to blows they acknowledged the claim of a man called Fulke, and much good it did him, because either for this or for some other misdemeanour Kett subsequently condemned him to be hanged on the Oak of Reformation.

As conditions returned to something resembling normality Steward

ndeavoured to improve the atmosphere by sending a Dr Barrett to
Mousehold to preach to the insurgents. But he failed to soften their
hearts, as did the pleas of women shattered by the barbarities they had
witnessed. Those citizens who had not fled and who feared that the
rebels might wish to settle scores with them, concealed their valuables
in cavities in walls and in cellars, and went into hiding in false roofs in
their houses; at least those who had reliable servants did so.

When Northampton, crestfallen, got back to London he had a sorry
tale to tell. At first no one was quite certain what had really happened.
The earliest reports, duly noted in the King's journal, were that Sheffield
had been taken prisoner; later the entry was struck out, and 'slain'
substituted. It was believed that several other gentlemen had fallen, but
they had probably gone missing in the rout, for later on they turned up
alive and well. Recriminations flew thick and fast. Sir John Cheke, who
was not an eye-witness, probably retailed Northampton's own lame
excuse when he asserted that the army had suffered less from the
onslaught of the rebels than from hit and run attacks on its rear made
by citizens from the sanctuary of their houses. At the same time there
does seem to be little doubt that there was some sort of fifth column
inside Norwich. But in the last resort nothing could disguise the fact
that he had brought on the disaster through his own incompetence in
leading a tiny force into a town which it could not hope to hold against
vastly superior numbers because the walls were dilapidated and much of
the long perimeter had no defences at all. By exceeding his instructions
he had delivered Norwich more firmly than before into Kett's hands,
and made a major military operation inevitable. Unhappily for the
Council there were no more troops immediately available, and all they
could do for the present was to appeal to the earl of Shrewsbury to
raise whatever forces he could in the Midlands and march to East Anglia
without delay. But shire levies could do no more than contain the
situation; at this point they must have written urgently to Russell
demanding the return of some of the mercenaries under his command.

Chapter 10
Clyst St Mary and the Relief of Exeter

I

Almost immediately following the engagement at Fenny Bridges, Russell received the long awaited reinforcements, 'the Lord Grey of Wilton with a crew of horsemen and one Spinola an Italian with three hundred shot'. Immured in Exeter, Hooker was probably somewhat vague as to details, for it seems that at least half Spinola's company had already arrived. In earlier correspondence Somerset had variously put its strength at 150 and 160. However, on 27 July he told Russell to expect Grey with 250 horse and 80 of Spinola's men, while earlier in the letter he pointed out that Russell already had 160 Italian arquebusiers. The conclusion must be that the band had been divided: Spinola in fact drew pay for 216 officers and men, and this we take as being his strength in the forthcoming campaign. Grey's horse may well have been English, for Somerset had written on 10 July that he was ordering Grey west with 300 or 400, and in addition placing 400 foreign horse on alert to follow if needed: the combined strength of Jermigny and Sanga was in fact just this number.

It is more than probable, moreover, that the landsknechts had come as well. At the beginning of September two ensigns of Almains (Germans) were paid in the same account as Jermigny and Sanga. An ensign consisted of upwards of 400 infantry; the two in question belonged to the command of Colonel Wilhelm von Walderden (or von Wallerthum) which comprised two, perhaps three, others, none of which served in the West. As we shall see, it is probable that they never actually reached Exeter to be observed by Hooker. Landsknechts had originally carried pikes like their rivals the Swiss, or great two-handed swords; by this date an increasing proportion were armed with matchlocks, and their tactics were based on the combination of the two arms, on the model of the Spanish *tercios*. They affected a flamboyant costume, and were protected by a steel cap, stout corselets round the body, with pauldrons, vambraces and trusses on the shoulders, arms and thighs respectively.

The arrival of William Lord Grey de Wilton stiffened the command of the army. An experienced veteran, he had led the horse in the decisive charge at the battle of Pinkie where he had been severely wounded. This combined with the fact that his title was very much older than the recently ennobled Lord Privy Seal's – they were equal in rank – gave solid grounds for him to assume the command-in-chief. Somerset, however, had assured Russell that the younger man was 'to have no place of name but a counsellor's, to give advice or to execute according as should be concluded', requesting him, nevertheless, to 'in favour prefer him'. In this limited capacity, his presence still constituted a useful safeguard of the Protector's interest, and indeed Grey was subsequently to be involved in his patron's fall.

The new units, the foreigners above all, were chagrined to learn how narrowly they had missed taking a share in a brilliant victory, and in consequence 'were in a great chaff, and much bewailed their evil luck that they had not come sooner to have been partakers of that service'. Engaged to fight the Scots, they had come to Great Britain eager for loot, and all they had done so far was to harry a handful of poverty stricken peasants in the Midlands.

With this substantial accession of striking power, and encouraged by Grey's aggression and competence, Russell at long last made up his mind to march without further delay. He wrote for the last time to the mayor of Exeter promising to arrive very shortly, and begging him to exercise patience for just a few days more. None the less, a further six days were to pass before he moved. The delay is not accounted for, but the newly arrived troops were entitled to at least a day's rest, the landsknechts may still have been on the road, and plans had to be finalised. It is by no means improbable that Russell had neglected reconnaissance, with the result that the enemy dispositions had to be probed before any move could be undertaken. It soon became apparent that the high road (now A 30) was blocked by a strong force well dug in, probably on the high ground near Rockbeare, leading to the decision to slip round its flank, if it could not be dislodged readily, with a view to making a dash for Exeter.

The order of battle can only be tentatively reconstructed from stray scraps of evidence. Hooker, who was locked up in Exeter, says the army numbered 'more than a thousand', which can mean anything; Somerset, who should have known its actual size, had stated it as 4,000. From the available evidence it may have looked something like Table 3. This gives a grand total of 3,012 of which 1,462 were foreigners. If the landsknechts numbered as many as 1,000, and Grey's own horse was 350 as originally stated, the aggregate would be 3,262, while Russell's escort and the local forces may have been more numerous than we have assumed. As there was also a train of artillery and some pioneers, a total of about 3,500 can readily be envisaged, which can be equally regarded as upwards of 3,000 or nearly 4,000, the figures specified by the Protector. Although the presence of the landsknechts rests on largely circumstantial evidence, it is certain that neither the timorous Russell nor the experienced Grey, like Warwick in Norfolk, is likely to have risked a critical battle without a force sufficiently strong and reliable to give some assurance of success. The consequences of failure were too dreadful to contemplate.

Table 3

Russell's retinue and local horse	300
Grey's English horse	250
Jermigny's horse	259
Sanga's horse	141
	950
2 ensigns of landsknechts (say)	850
Spinola's arquebusiers	212
Somerset and Dorset levies (say)	1,000
	2,062

II

The storm which had quenched the fires at Norwich on 1 August may well have swept across the West Country; certainly Exeter had had its share of rain that summer. By Saturday, 3 August, the weather had improved, and at last the army marched out of Honiton. Hooker's account of the campaign is sketchy and needs considerable supplementation. It says simply that the army turned off the direct road and marched to Woodbury Down where it pitched camp. There it repelled a fierce attack from a body of rebels stationed in Clyst St Mary. The rebels having reinforced Clyst, the decisive engagement was fought during the two following days. The interpretation of these movements gives the key to the operation.

Outside Honiton the army turned south through Ottery St Mary and across the desolate Aylesbeare Common along a by-road leading to the village of Clyst St Mary and its bridge over the Clyst, from where the final approach to Exeter could be made with the left flank protected by the estuary of the Exe. A detachment may have been left to make a demonstration against the rebel position astride the main road and occupy their attention. One wonders whether it was entrusted to the egregious Captain Travers who managed to convince the innocent little King that he had won the battle almost single-handed when in fact he was not there at all.

Near Woodbury Salterton they pitched camp on the down close to
a windmill owned by Gregory Carey. The army was organised in the
customary three divisions or 'battles'. A natural order would have (a)
the German infantry, (b) the locally recruited foot commanded perhaps
by Sir Peter Carew, (c) the horse and mounted infantry led by Grey and
Spinola. These last would naturally have formed the vanguard, a force
of some 1,200 men (less, perhaps, some casualties incurred at Fenny
Bridges) which corresponds closely to Hooker's 'more than a thousand'.
It must have been they who reached the mill first and went into camp
while waiting for the infantry, artillery and baggage train to catch up. It
was a long day's march for foot soldiers through narrow, twisting lanes,
the pace slowed to a crawl by the painful progress of the guns and
wagons. The van must have halted sometime during the course of the
afternoon, its position on the rolling downland being secure from
surprise attack and admirable for the deployment of the horse should
the occasion arise. It did.

Soon after they had halted, Spinola and his officers went into
conference together, at the end of which Spinola approached the
Lordy Privy Seal with a proposition. It was that the vanguard should
resume its advance without waiting for the remainder of the army.
Unlike the English, the Italians were seasoned campaigners inured to
gruelling marches under the burning sun, and since it was virtually
certain that the rebels were still guarding the main road there was every
prospect of seizing the bridge at Clyst St Mary and pushing straight
through to Exeter before the army's presence in the vicinity was
suspected. With only another five miles to go it was a gamble worth
taking. What Spinola is certain to have done was to bargain for double
pay for his men in consideration of the additional hazardous service,
while not forgetting the attraction of being the first to overrun and
plunder the enemy's encampments.

The rebel command had not been slow to appreciate that Russell
had stolen a march on them; by the middle of the day, at latest, scouts
must have warned of his movements. Once he succeeded in getting a
head start the only obstacle between him and Exeter would be the
tidal Clyst stream, and in consequence the bridge at Clyst St Mary
became the key to the operation. By this time Russell was closer to
it than the rebels, and, if he pressed on, he was bound to seize it hours
before they could march across country to stop him. A few hundred at
most were lying in the village. To gain time they were ordered to attack
the head of the royal army and halt it at all costs, hoping to achieve by
the suddenness of their attack what their small numbers could not
otherwise have done.

The two forces thus crashed head on into one another, each on the
alert, yet at the same time taken by surprise finding the other actually

advancing against it. In the first minutes the advantage lay with th rebels who, seeking battle, must have been already deployed in clump of billmen interspersed with archers. The royal generals found them selves in the vulnerable position of having to deploy from column int line under a hail of arrows as the billmen charged, yelling at the tops o their voices. In this crisis the limitations of the arquebusiers wer exposed: no time to prime their pieces and whirl their match around t bring it to life. But the pistoleers had only to wind up the locks of thei guns, and then peel off section by section from the column, trot up t the enemy, and fire their two or three shots apiece, wheeling away again to reload — the manoeuvre known as the *caracole*. Yet they coul not halt the onrush of the Devon men or stop them closing in for savage hand-to-hand struggle which swayed to and fro on top of th down. The rebels 'were of very stout stomachs and very valiantly di stand to their tackles', wrote Hooker. But once Spinola's men ha succeeded in taking up position on the wing they poured in an enfiladin fire to which the archers could make no effective reply (if indeed the had not already been swept into the mêlée) since they lacked groun advantage and there were no pikes to hold off the charge of Grey' lances. After a stout resistance the rebels gave way and were hurle down the hill, leaving behind scores, if not hundreds, of dead an prisoners. Russell's losses were not reported, but cannot have bee inconsiderable. With night approaching and the rear of the army stil coming up, no pursuit was undertaken.

Instead the army was paraded for a service of thanksgiving, and sermon preached by Miles Coverdale who was acting virtually a chaplain general. To offer thanks to the Almighty for victory gaine over the powers of darkness was one thing, to be obliged to endure a lengthy discourse on the subject another, particularly since it took precedence over supper. What the Catholics among the mercenaries can have thought about it, whether indeed they were expected to join in is not recorded. Whatever their confession, a homily in an unintelligible tongue can hardly be imagined to have roused their enthusiasm; most of them probably shrugged it off as the fortunes of war, an eccentricity of the incomprehensible English. No one can have felt much regret when Dr Coverdale was interrupted by a fresh alarm which made them reach hastily for their arms and remount.

It was not, as it turned out, the signal for another attack, but the sound of the main rebel force entering Clyst, having, it may be, conceded Travers an empty success when he overran their abandoned lines. Their comrades had not given their lives in vain. Precious hours had been gained and they had made certain that Russell would have to fight his way through to Exeter. Hooker's version is scarcely convincing: that the people fled the village fearing that they were about to be

ttacked, and sent out urgent appeals for assistance, 'whereupon forthwith in great troops resorted unto them a number of their companions
out of every quarter to the number as it was said of six thousand men'.
Bearing in mind what was to follow it is impossible to accept that the
newcomers arrived in any such haphazard fashion. While it is indeed
likely that during the static phase of the campaign a good many men
dispersed temporarily to their homes in order to ease commissariat
problems, it can hardly be doubted that Clyst was reinforced by an
organised contingent, augmented from the Exeter lines as well. The
number, moreover, may well be an exaggeration. The King's garbled
memorandum based on Travers's report mentions a figure of 2,000.
After the losses sustained in two recent engagements it is indeed
doubtful whether there were as many as 2,000 men in full harness,
although there must have been many more carrying some sort of
weapon if with little or no protective gear: 3,000 or 4,000 at most.
There were also some cannon, either those which had come originally
from the ships at Topsham, or perhaps newly brought up from Exeter.

The insurgents set to work energetically to fortify the village,
throwing up stout breastworks at all the approaches and turning the
houses into strongpoints. Thus prepared they waited for morning and
the coming attack.

II

Sunday morning. After his earlier hesitation, the Lord Privy Seal was
no longer in a mood to waste time, and soon after dawn the trumpets
called the troops to arms. Coverdale no doubt read prayers – a special
invocation before battle was a feature of the recently published *Primer* –
and grasped the opportunity to give another sermon exhorting the
Church militant to fight valiantly for the Lord's truth. Next, according
to a treatise on the art of war compiled for the education of the King,
the commander-in-chief ought to deliver an oration in appropriately
martial language, to be followed, more practically, by the treasurer-at-
war giving the troops further encouragement by holding out the
prospect of a bonus for a decisive victory; this, after all, is what the
mercenaries were there for, though it is by no means certain that they
got one.[1]

The preliminaries must have occupied some time. Towards nine
o'clock the army fell in and commenced the three-mile march down to
Clyst St Mary. Approaching the village it halted and deployed into the
customary three battles for the assault on the newly thrown up ramparts.

The rebels' position, which Humphry Arundell must have selected
with professional care, can be located with some certainty. Some 500

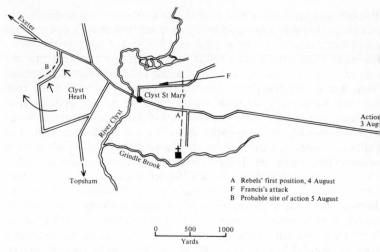

A   Rebels' first position, 4 August
F   Francis's attack
B   Probable site of action 5 August

0   500   1000
         Yards

Map 3 The Battle of Clyst St Mar

yards east of the village a deep lane runs between high banks from th
road down to the Grindle Brook. There is a hedge on the east side, an
very possibly there used also to be one on the west,[2] presenting
formidable natural obstacle to an advancing formation. The King
somewhat garbled account suggests that they took full advantage of i
stationing themselves 'at a certain hedge in a highway'. The line wa
continued with fieldworks across the Ottery road at least as far as th
lane leading to Clyst Honiton. The left flank may have rested on th
Clyst stream, or else been refused: the low lying ground near the wate
is likely to have been waterlogged at the time.

The assault was led by Sir William Francis, a Somerset knight whos
father had originally hailed from the nearby parish of Broadclyst, a fac
which suggests that the Somerset and Dorset militia were the spearhead
In view, however, of their unreliability, they were more likely to hav
been held in reserve. A more convincing array would place the mounte
contingent on the right wing where the defenders had only hastil
erected earthworks for protection, leaving the German infantry to cop
with the more formidable natural obstacle of the sunken lane. But onc
they became entangled in the hedges the pike column lost it
momentum, and the attack was reduced to nothing more effective tha
an exchange of fire across the gap. On the right it would have bee
natural for the English horse, unlike the foreigners, to dismount in th
traditional manner, and thus to form the first wave, supported wit
great effect by the volleys of the Italians. Led by Francis they storme
the rampart after a sharp fight — the gentry in particular being ampl

protected against arrows – and opened a gap for the supporting cavalry to exploit. Driven from their position the commoners fell back hurriedly to the village where they formed up for a fresh stand.

Inside the breastworks the royalists regrouped and advanced to the final attack. But whether by chance or design, Sir Thomas Pomeroy, whom Hooker imagined to be 'one of the chief captains' of the rebels, had got left behind in company with a trumpeter and a drummer, and taken cover in a furze croft. As soon as the advancing troops had passed by he bade the trumpeter sound the charge and the drummer beat a loud tattoo. The effect was electrifying. Men checked their stride uncertainly; those following collided with them. In a moment the entire army was reduced to disorder; in another, fear gripped every man from the general down to the humblest private. Was it the raw West Country levies who broke first? It matters little: the hardened mercenaries were just as terrified of an imminent attack on their rear. One and all took to their heels and fled as fast as their legs would carry them, discarding guns, pikes, helmets, anything to lighten themselves. Through the gun line they poured, past the wagon train, for two or three miles back up the hill until at length, winded, they gasped to a halt almost back where they had started out a few short hours earlier. Only then did it begin to dawn on them that they were not being pursued, and sheepishly they began to reform their ranks.

The insurgents had in fact pursued them as far as the wagons, by which point they too were probably out of breath, and Arundell prudently recalled them, for on the open slopes of the down they could fall easy prey to any sudden counterstroke by the opposing horse. He had no cavalry to continue the pursuit and complete the rout. If there was one moment when the battle was won and lost it was this. The want of but a few hundred horsemen quite certainly robbed the rebels of their victory, for in those days troops could rarely be rallied once they had been driven from the field in disorder.

As it turned out Russell's captains got their men sorted out again, morale seemingly none the worse for what had happened. The mercenaries at any rate were keenly aware of being in a hostile country where they could expect no mercy if they failed to fight successfully. It was now evident that the enemy were none too keen to maintain contact, but more interested in looting the captured train. The realisation that they had fled for no reason at all stiffened their resolution to win next time.

The rebels had indeed made the best of matters by helping themselves to the baggage, taking possession of an invaluable supply of arms, armour and ammunition, as well as the Lord Privy Seal's war chest. They also captured his guns which they dragged away to strengthen the defences of Clyst, thinking to convert it into an impregnable fortress. It

is not improbable that while thus engaged they were surprised by th
renewed advance of the royal army and chased back towards the villag
so fast that they were unable to re-occupy their original line. Th
captured guns may have been lost again, for they seem to have playe
no effective part in the subsequent struggle. In any case their rate o
fire was so slow that there was rarely time for more than one salv
before pikes were crossed. Nor would captured arquebuses have bee
much use in untrained hands; there were so many things to forget, lik
the priming powder, or the wad to stop the bullet rolling out of th
barrel, or removing the ramrod before firing so that reloading becam
impossible. Throwing stones was better, and some of the rebels did s
with effect. They lined the high banks which overhang the lane fron
Clyst Honiton as it dips down towards the village — the spot is un
mistakable. Striking directly for the middle of the village, Sir Willian
Francis charged down the lane at the head of his company. Rock
were rained down on them from overhead; one hit the leader, stov
in his sallet and fractured his skull so that he fell mortally wounded

Other units meanwhile had reached the outskirts of Clyst which wa
held by the rebels in force, with every house turned into a strongpoin
The troops advanced warily this time, setting light to the thatch of th
cottages. One after another went up in flames and the defenders wer
driven into the open where they were met by a hail of fire from th
waiting musketeers, while the wounded lay bleeding where they ha
fallen and were burnt alive. Soon the village became untenable, and th
defenders prepared to fall back across the river. A strong rearguar
formed up for a stand in the middle of the hamlet to cover the with
drawal. Russell's foot charged with levelled pikes and a bloody mêlé
developed until the western men were borne down by sheer weight o
numbers. Many fell sword in hand, adding their number to those wh
had already perished in the flames of the blazing cottages. Others threv
themselves into the stream — the tide was up — to be carried under by
the weight of their harness as they tried to swim across. A thousan
perished that day, according to Hooker — 900, the King wrote — an
he may not have been far out. Many were taken prisoner. Russell's ow
losses cannot have been light.

The majority of the rebels had, none the less, made good thei
escape across the bridge and were now drawn up on the opposite ban
determined to hold it. Grey was eager to get his horse over to the ope
ground of the heath where they could charge unimpeded. To force
way across the bridge would be costly, as would an attempt to ford th
stream, especially since the muddy state of the water indicated a soft
treacherous bottom. But in the ranks there was a gentleman of th
neighbourhood, John Yarde of Treasurersbeer. He remembered a for
higher up near the mill at Bishop's Clyst that was practicable for horses

and he led the cavalry to it. The foot soldiers had no option but to get possession of the bridge which, in addition to being blocked by tree trunks, was covered by a cannon. Volunteers were called for, Grey offering 400 crowns to the man who could silence the gun. Without hesitation one sprang forward and made a dash for the other side, 'more respecting the gain than forecasting the peril . . . but the gunner rewarded him for he discharged his piece and slew him'. But under cover of this gallant attempt, another man had slipped into the water and scrambled across underneath the bridge. Clambering the bank unobserved by the crew who were busy reloading, he struck down the gunner from behind, and called on his comrades. A party dashed across and secured the bridgehead. The way was quickly cleared of obstructions, and the remainder of the infantry poured over the bridge to link up with the cavalry on the heath. What was left of the rebel army pulled back towards Exeter.

A tragic misunderstanding enabled them to make good their retreat. As Grey pressed after them he reached the top of an eminence where he could scan the country for miles about. Looking back towards Woodbury, it seemed to him that he could descry a huge company assembling on top of Windmill Hill and marching towards Clyst. He urgently warned Russell that an attack on the army's rear was imminent; even the morning's false alarm had not taught them to stop worrying. By this time the troops were embarrassed by a large number of prisoners taken in two days of battle, who might prove dangerous in the event of a fresh attack. There was no time to make a reconnaissance. The rebels they had just driven from the field were still in good order and might counter-attack at any time. The decision was quickly taken: every man who had charge of a prisoner was ordered to kill him, and hundreds, it is said, were put to the sword on the spot. The bloody work completed, they prepared to repel an attack which never came. If there had been any gathering on the down it was nothing more than some curious country folk, perhaps come out to strip the dead. With contact with the enemy lost and night approaching, the army bedded down on Clyst Heath.

Even after the beating they had already taken the rebels were by no means finished. Arundell called up every available man from the trenches in front of Exeter, and prepared a new position on the lower side of the heath where it was broken up by small fields, and particularly along the hedge beside a road which they entrenched, toiling quickly and quietly throughout the night. At dawn they opened a galling fire on the bivouacked army. Its leaders decided to waste no time manoeuvring but to attack at once, 'and every man has his place assigned and order appointed unto him'. Russell's division on the left, facing towards enclosed ground, was unable to get directly at the enemy. He set his pioneers to hack openings in the hedges, and by this means worked round behind the rebel flank. Caught in a pincer their right wing could not escape. They chose to fight it out, and fighting they went down in a desperate hand-to-hand struggle until 'few or none were left alive'. Lord Grey afterwards avowed that in all the wars in which he had served he had never seen such bravery as that shown by the men of Devon and Cornwall that August day, nor ever fought in so murderous a fray.

IV

The fighting had taken up much of the day. When at last it was finally over there was no triumphant dash for Exeter: three days of battle had taught the army and its leaders that the rebels were not to be treated with disdain, and since the bulk of them had succeeded in withdrawing in fair order, it was by no means a foregone conclusion that the last had been seen of them. Having reformed, the entire army, therefore, made a leisurely march of one mile to Topsham where it quartered for the night. With it was borne the body of Sir William Francis, the only man of quality to have been slain, later to be carried to Exeter and buried with full military honours.

That same night Arundell pulled his much depleted force out of its position in front of Exeter and slipped silently away, still in good order with most of its artillery. The results of the three-day battle could not be disguised. A thousand men, or very nearly that number, had been killed, certainly in the first two days, to which Hooker's figure apparently refers. On the other hand the 900 recorded by the King in his journal may have been the number reported by Russell following a count of bodies on the battlefield. As many more were probably missing and unaccounted for. And this disaster had occurred on the very brink of success, dashing in fragments all hopes of taking Exeter. Now the rebels were irreversibly on the defensive. A majority of the Devonshire men probably dispersed and made for their homes on the chance that their association with the revolt might be forgotten. A few still adhered to John Bury who elected to accompany Arundell on the dismal march back towards Cornwall. The end was in sight and they knew it. The gentlemen whom they had confined in churches nearby now regained their liberty and made straight for Exeter, and it was they calling out to the sentinels on the walls who brought the joyful tidings that the rebels had decamped and the investment of the city had come to its end.

The citizens heard the news with joy and relief. All day they had listened to distant sound of gunfire, and when, late in the afternoon, it had ceased, and then night had fallen without further developments,

ιey had begun to fear that the relief column had been repulsed, and
ιat they would have to choose between starvation and surrender.
.fter five weeks of privation the one thing they could think of was
ɔod. Discipline was thrown to the winds. Without even waiting for the
ıawn hundreds rushed to the gates and poured out to ransack the
ɔandoned rebel camp, 'more for victual than for spoil', wrote Hooker,
ιnd yet they were glad of both'. If he himself joined in he was not one
f those who 'being more greedy for meat than measurable in feeding
ιd so overcharge themselves in surfeiting that they died thereof'.

Next morning, 6 August, the Lord Privy Seal's trumpets sounded
ɔveille at first light and, apprehensive of yet another hard day's
ιghting, he carefully marshalled his troops in battle order before
ɔtting out cautiously to march the last few miles to Exeter. As the
ɪrmy came in sight of the sentries at the South Gate at about eight
'clock the citizens went wild with joy now that there could be no
ɔubt their long ordeal had really ended. The fact that Russell had
ıst gained a notable and hard won victory did not occur to them at
ɪl; the mere fact that they had been delivered when at their last gasp
ιas all that mattered. He for his part seemed to Hooker to wear his
ιuccess coolly, as well he might since there was still much work ahead,
ɔossibly more fighting, certainly the long wearisome business of
ɔacifying a violently disturbed countryside. He knew too what they
ɪad been prevented from learning, that France was on the verge of
ɔeclaring war, and that he might shortly have to exert himself to
ɔefend from external attack the country he was now reconquering.

There was no triumphal entry. Mayor Blackaller had prudently
ιarned the general that the city was stripped bare of provisions and
ɪhat the council had made an order excluding all strangers for the time
ɔeing, requiring them to camp beneath the walls until such time as the
ɔlace could be revictualled. Accordingly Russell pitched his camp in
ɪt John's Fields next to Southernhaye, contenting himself with raising
ɪhe royal standard − the Red Dragon − on the city wall near the
ɔostern of his own house. As soon as he had set up his headquarters the
ιayor and aldermen waited on him, dressed in their best in honour of
ɪhe occasion. He embraced them all with great cordiality, graciously
ɪnd sincerely commending their loyalty, gallantry and endurance, and
ɔromising on his honour that their conduct would be well rewarded
ɪy the King.

The following day Russell dispatched his report by the hand of
ːaptain Travers who thus was granted the opportunity to impress
ιoung Edward with his own contribution to the success of the
ɪampaign to be dutifully entered in the royal journal. The Council
ɔceived the report with gratitude and sent Russell instructions to
ɔonvey their warm thanks to Grey de Wilton and the other gentlemen

for their services, and above all to the mayor and people of Exeter (not forgetting a Mr Bluett and other gentlemen who had aided the defence) for their loyalty and heroic resistance which had broken the back of the rebels' plan of campaign.

V

As the strategic key to the South West, Exeter was the obvious centre from which to reconstruct the shattered administration of the region, and the Lord Privy Seal planned at first to settle down there to supervise the protracted business of mopping up the last outposts of resistance and re-establishment of orderly conditions. The embers of rebellion still smouldered and might flare up at any moment in the least expected quarters. Indeed on the very day he reached Exeter a little knot of conspirators gathered at the Crown Inn, Winchester, to plot a fresh rising in Hampshire and West Sussex. The leaders were John Garnham, a Winchester carpenter, and a Sussex man called Flint. In theory at least it was an ambitious project. Garnham had been going around boasting that 1,000 men were waiting for the call to arms. At the 'Crown' they plotted to plunder the cathedral clergy in order to get funds, to seize three cannon which Flint knew to be stored in Selsey church, to acquire transport from sympathetic farmers, and to have a banner representing the Five Wounds of Christ made. Then they would march to Salisbury and behead the mayor. This was to be the signal for all Russell's reluctant conscripts to desert, opening the road to the western men, and united they would fall on 'the villain Herbert' to exact retribution for sundry local grievances. But Flint failed to make the rendezvous; possibly he was already in custody, for Garnham had been boasting widely of their alleged prospects in order to attract recruits, according to two serving men from north Hampshire who confessed on 12 August. In any case news of the rout of the rebels killed off any fighting spirit and the project fizzled out. Garnham was heard of no more, but Flint was still languishing in the Tower two years later.

In Exeter the most pressing need was to replenish the depleted larders of the housewives, which looked like becoming a major problem. Although communications with the outside world had been reopened, there were 3,000 or more ravenous soldiers encamped outside the gates, and almost immediately they were augmented by at least 1,000 more, Sir William Herbert's levies from Gloucestershire and South Wales. Paradoxically, this led to an easing of the situation. Although too late for the fighting, the Welshmen were 'yet soon enough to play' — too soon for the taste of the local inhabitants, for they took to plundering indiscriminately, gutting houses and driving away livestock until they earned themselves a reputation for cruelty and rapacity no whit inferior to that of the foreign mercenaries. Nevertheless, their blind greed rendered the citizens an unexpected, and certainly unintended, service. They so overburdened themselves with loot, far more than they could ever carry home, that they finished up by selling the surplus in the streets and market place. And having come by it so easily they were happy to part with it dirt cheap, with the result that the inhabitants were supplied with an abundance of grain and meat at give-away prices within two or three days.

No time was lost in proceeding with the pacification of the district. Gallows were erected in the city as well as various other places around the county, and many persons were summarily hanged, those especially who were reputed to be ringleaders. Against these the Lord Privy Seal was 'very severe and sharp', but towards the common sort whom they had led astray he was merciful 'and did daily pardon infinite numbers' who came in, made their submission and promised faithfully to behave themselves in future.

In this at least he was in complete accord with Somerset who commended the execution of the leaders — asking for numbers and particulars — and urged that they should be carried out in many different places in order to spread the terror as widely as possible. Far from being indiscriminate, the slaughter was consciously planned to make the greatest impact. The government was most concerned to apprehend and make a signal example of the key figures, above all the handful of gentlemen whose treason was so alarming and dangerous to the state; these men were regarded as individuals in contrast with the common people who, in the eyes of their rulers, appeared no more than an anonymous mass. There was keen interest in the details of Arundell's activities and especially in his behaviour should he be captured. Sir Thomas Pomeroy's reputation was familiar enough to enable him to be identified as the weak link in the rebel command. Russell judged it expedient to offer him a pardon in exchange for his collaboration in effecting the arrest of Arundell and the others. Somerset agreed to this, stipulating that the offer should be kept secret and that Pomeroy was to recant his popish errors and labour henceforth to promote the true religion. This alone would be a useful point gained, for by now the ideological motive of the rising was fully recognised, along with the consequent need to flush out papists, collect and burn the 'mass books of the old superstitious service', and see that the magistrates enforced the use of the Prayer Book. Russell also issued an order for the confiscation of church bells which had been used to summon the rebels into the field, but in the end it was not enforced.

Among priests who had figured prominently in the commotion and duly paid the penalty was Robert Welsh whom Russell himself had presented to the living of St Thomas. Hooker, who must have known him, was at a complete loss to comprehend how a man blessed with his advantages, 'descended of a good honest parentage', could have erred so far as to become 'an Archcaptain and a principal doer' in the rebellion. Welsh 'had many good things in him'. Not tall, but powerfully built, he was a noted wrestler, a marksman with longbow, crossbow and gun, a bold and accomplished huntsman. Devoted to every kind of sport, he behaved like a gentleman at all times. The plan to consume the city with fire had revolted him and he had insisted on its abandonment. The main charge against him was his vigorous opposition to the reformed religion, as evidenced by his successful preaching against it and refusal to give up popish rites and ornaments. The second charge arose from his responsibility for the hanging of Kyngeswell who, of course, had been acting as a messenger for Russell himself. It was also alleged that he had been involved in the murder of Hellyons at Sampford Courtenay. He was a difficult case:

> Some men in respect of his virtues and good gifts did pity and lament his cause, and would have gladly been suitors for his pardon, yet the greatness of his lewdness and follies being considered, they left him unto his deserts,

and he was condemned to death by court martial.

The fanatical Protestant, Bernard Duffield, was commissioned to carry out the sentence. Under his directions the gallows was erected on top of the tower of Welsh's own church, and the vicar, clothed in his Mass vestments, with a holy water bucket, sprinkler, sanctus bell, rosary, 'and other like popish trash' attached, was hoisted by a rope round his waist, and hanged in chains, long to dangle there as a warning to others. He met his end with contemptuous silence, and Hooker lamented, 'He had been a good member in his commonwealth had not the weeds overgrown the good corn and his foul vices overcome his virtues.'

Many prisoners were handed over to soldiers as a reward for good service, to be ransomed and to make what bargains they could to redeem their lands and goods. Few questions were asked and often the innocent suffered with the guilty, even people of consequence. John Furse of Crediton, sometime undersheriff, and steward of the Stannaries and the duchy of Lancaster, 'was greatly despoiled in the commotion . . . for he was then given body and goods like a rebel, and yet during all the time of that rebellion he was continually in his sick bed and not able to travel'. A great many people seem to have suffered sudden illnesses in that summer of 1549, but perhaps Furse's was genuine since he died on 14 February 1550. His demise might, of course, have been hastened by the worry of having to find £140 to pay his ransom. Later, in the county court sitting in Exeter castle, his widow was able to prove his loyalty and so she was discharged of the balance of the debt.

The full story was somewhat deeper. He had incurred the enmity of Sir Hugh Pollard for refusing to pay rent for certain lands which Pollard claimed belonged to his manor of King's Nympton. (It is remarkable how frequently this fellow's name turns up in events connected with the rebellion.) Furse was accused of some treasonable activity by a 'noftye pryste', the gravamen of the charge resting on the fact that he had once been in the service of the late marquis of Exeter and much in his confidence. Now this priest, none other than William Alley, had been presented to the living of Okeford by Pollard in 1544, and it was by the procurement of Pollard and his man Hansford that the information was laid. Nearly 20 years later, Alley, by then bishop of Exeter, happened to spend a night at Marches, the Furse home, where he admitted to John's daughter that the accusation had been false. Pollard was probably not the only unscrupulous man to exploit this time of troubles to settle private scores.

The punishment of the rebels and the rewarding of loyalists were the two sides of the same coin. In exercise of his plenary powers, Russell proclaimed the confiscation of the property of the leaders and awarded it to his principal officers, all the grants being subsequently confirmed. In doing so his primary concern was to strengthen the position of local men of proven worth. To Sir Gawen Carew he gave all Humphry Arundell's lands (subject to his widow's right to dower): the manors of Cassacwen, Helcett, and Helland in Cornwall, estimated to be worth £55 8s. 10d. a year, and Calwodely, Cadbury and Mere in Devon, worth £53 9s. 10d. Sir Peter Carew got all Winslade's property in Devonshire, including his house at Buckland Brewer, valued at £73 14s. 10d. The settlement on Mrs Winslade saved the Cornish estates, although even these were granted to Reginald Mohun to hold in trust for her, in consideration that he had been 'spoiled in the commotions by Arundell and Winslade; and for his faithful and chargeable service at that time'. John Bury's land went to William Gibb, an adherent of the Carews. Richard Reynell of East Ogwell was granted the demesne of Weston Peverell and the house called Pennicross near Plymouth; in command of a troop of horse, he had performed 'special good services, when in suppressing and confounding those traitors, he was sorely wounded and hurt'. For his services John Malory received the goods of the attainted vicar of Sutton, some of the mercenaries got annuities, and Thomas and John Harris of Crediton qualified for £433 compensation 'by reason they were spoiled in the last commotion by the rebels'.

Dr Coverdale was appointed to the bishopric of Exeter when Veysey was deprived in 1551. Nevertheless, he only enjoyed the dignity for two years, until Queen Mary restored his ancient predecessor, although, following a period of exile, he returned to assist at consecration of Matthew Parker as archbishop of Canterbury in 15 his views were considered too extreme to justify restoring him to episcopal bench, and it was the 'noftye' William Alley who got Ex in 1560.

In recognition of its steadfast resistance, accompanied by 'intoler costs, expenses and burdens', the city of Exeter was rewarded wit grant of the manor of Exe Island valued at £29 18s. 10d. a y Although relatively modest in monetary terms, it meant a good dea the corporation for its acquisition ended a centuries old dispute v the Courtenay earls of Devon who had held the authority of the poration in contempt. Since the fall of the marquis of Exeter t had made repeated attempts to purchase it from the King, fearing t it would ultimately be restored to the family. They had commissio their burgesses in Parliament to offer an inflated price for it, volunteered a handsome *douceur* to anyone who would further tl cause, all without success. Russell was additionally authorised confer a knighthood on the redoubtable John Blackaller.

As the rebel leaders were still at large it is possible to criticise Rus for celebrating victory prematurely, wasting 10 valuable days. Grey the Carews perhaps chafed at the renewed delay, but in the circu stances it was not unreasonable. By proceeding at once to sequestration of the traitors' property and executions of those who been caught, Russell was giving effective notice that after its ear hesitancy the government now meant to deal severely with its enem In handing out rewards he was taking a practical step towards secur once and for all the support of men whose loyalty had at one ti wavered. On both scores it helped to restrict further resistance to hard core of irreconcilables.

Chapter 11
Sampford Courtenay and the Pacification of Cornwall

I

With Exeter in his possession Russell had the remnants of the rebels bottled up in west Devon and Cornwall and could afford to deal with them at leisure. Almost certainly the army underwent a major re-organisation. Much of this has indeed to be inferred since there is a hiatus covering the critical period between 28 July, when the Council bluntly refused to send Russell any more troops, and 8 August when they briefly informed him of the outbreak of war with France. It is a fair assumption that on learning of Northampton's débâcle at Norwich the Protector, on 2 August, had ordered the immediate return of the two ensigns of landsknechts. This letter would have reached Russell while on the road to Clyst St Mary, and since the corps was already committed to battle, or about to be, he could justifiably defer releasing it. Having defeated the rebels, however, he had no excuse for continuing to ignore the order. Thus the Germans turned about on the battlefield and proceeded by forced marches to Norwich; the necessity of bringing them all the way from Devonshire explains why Kett was left undisturbed in Norwich for as long as he was. In view of the distance and the urgency it could plausibly be argued that if any mercenaries had to be transferred from the western theatre the horse, with their superior mobility, would have been the logical choice. The answer must be that there were already plenty of mounted troops in East Anglia, and that what was required — and as a professional soldier Warwick would have demanded — to complete a balanced army was a corps of regular infantry armed with up-to-date weapons. It is true that the observant Hooker never once mentions these troops, but the inference is that he never had the chance to see them, so abrupt was their departure.

To balance this serious reduction in strength, Sir William Herbert brought 1,000 Welshmen, and probably as many more from Gloucester-shire and Wiltshire; we may recall that at one point he had been asked to provide as many as 10,000. Furthermore, now that Russell was winning there was a sudden rush of recruits from the other counties of

the South West. All had to be organised and given some sort of training
before operations could be resumed.

Matters continued to be bedevilled by the want of *rapport* between
the Lord Privy Seal and the Lord Protector. A fresh irritant was the
anticipated war formally declared by the French ambassador on
8 August. To Russell's duties was now added the job of ensuring that
all ports and landing places in Dorset, Devon and Cornwall were put in
a state of defence, and preparing the country to oppose any attempt by
the French to land there; an impossible task when much of it was not
even under his control, and a depressing prospect when even a very
small expedition might be welcomed enthusiastically by disaffected
elements and cause the rebellion to flare up with renewed violence. He
was ordered to arrest all Frenchmen who were not denizens and destroy
their goods and ships, but this was not immediately practicable since
most of them resided in districts which had still to be pacified. Aliens
were a real danger: they had played a not inconspicuous part in the
campaign thus far, the majority of them being Bretons who had close
affinities with the Cornishmen, a potential fifth column in fact.

Since Russell probably contrived to give the impression that the
rebellion had been effectively crushed, and the Protector was only too
anxious to believe him, the new situation produced a conflict of aims.
The Council was in a hurry to disband the western army as rapidly as
possible, if only because it was costing a great deal and cash was scarce,
a major consideration in the case of the cavalry whose rate of pay was
twice that of the foot. They backed this up with the argument that
horsemen would have little value in the densely enclosed country west
of Exeter. In the first instance Jermigny and Sanga were urgently needed
at Boulogne. The levies of Somerset and Dorset, who had showed little
stomach for fighting their fellow countrymen, were obvious candidates
for early demobilisation, and this would release the gentry to resume the
task of local government. Moreover, 'some wise heads' would now be
required to organise the defence of the coastal districts: there was grave
concern for the security of Poole, the capture of which would give the
French a dangerous beachhead, and the Dorset men were to be specially
charged to guard it. By way of consolation Russell was offered the comforting thought that a reduction in the size of his now large force would
ease the problem of victualling it.

After this letter dated 10 August, the Council wrote again the
following day repeating their arguments with increased urgency, in
particular continuing to harp on the problem of supply.. There was
clearly, little to be gained from hanging on to the unreliable Dorset and
Somerset bands; a good many of the gentlemen must have been anxious
to get home again. The order for dispersal should be firstly, the mercenaries, secondly, the more expensive horsemen, and thirdly, the

levies from the more distant shires whose wage bill would be relatively high since they would continue to draw pay until they got home.

The chief difficulty over pay and other expenses was that the Council did not know Russell's exact strength. But although constantly worrying about the need to economise, they did not impose any definite financial limitations, merely stipulating that the reduction in strength should keep pace with the progress of pacification. They authorised the mayor of Exeter to advance him moneys repayable in London within eight days, or wherever else he might appoint after the accounts had been duly certified. The problem of paying off the soldiers was solved ingeniously. Each band should be sent home as soon as possible, having been paid such proportion of their wages as could be covered by the cash in hand, leaving behind one or two men to collect the balance when funds became available. One wonders how successfully this arrangement worked — for the payees. Russell himself was worried about his own pocket into which he had dug deeply in addition to running up heavy debts, and reminded his colleagues that they had not so far made any order to reimburse him. They assured him that he would not finish up out of pocket. A week later they sent him £6,000, earnestly praying him to observe strict economy as money was tighter than ever. In the long run he had no cause to complain. When it was all over and he had changed his allegiance at the right moment, he was rewarded with vast grants of land totalling £300 a year and created earl of Bedford. This was a pure bonus. Having, unlike nearly all other recipients of monastic property, been granted the estates of Tavistock abbey on nominal terms for the precise purpose of setting him up as the power in the West in place of the fallen Courtenays, he could quite reasonably have been expected to bear a large share of the cost of shoring up the government of the region.

After the first few heady days of victory it began to dawn on the Lord Privy Seal that the rebellion was by no means over. All the chief rebels were still at large, their men far from routed despite the severe hammering they had taken. So far from dispersing they had concentrated again at Sampford Courtenay and were preparing to resist to the death, strengthened perhaps by reinforcements from Cornwall. By 12 August, Russell had to admit that pacification was still incomplete, although he was evasive as to the extent of the problem. As a result the Council, now grappling with the problem of Kett, not to mention the state of war with France, continued to press for economy, arguing that the rebels 'at the first were in some dismay, and then one of your men, being in array, was worth three' of them.

The Protector had long lost patience with Russell and took little trouble to conceal it. Afraid that the dilatory general might not finish the job even before winter set in, he brusquely ordered him to make

the most of the resources he had. He did not even trouble to dis
Russell's fears that the rebels might seize some port and let the Fre
in: such a danger could best be forestalled by a swift campaign.
indignantly rejected a request for the army to be provisioned by
the available shipping was required for more urgent operations (
where, and Russell, as a seaman — a dry reference to his brief te
of the Admiralty — ought to have known that the onset of aut
gales would make it difficult. Instead he recommended dispersing
army widely to forage for its wants: 'All shift possible must be
to furnish yourself thereof that ye may' do so at the expense of
country people who, having previously supported the insurgents, o
in any case to sustain the Crown forces by fear of 'burning and spoil
It is evident from this that Somerset believed that the rebel forces
disintegrated, although he did not ignore the possibility that t
might yet rally, and warned Russell to keep his own under cont
ready to concentrate again.

Whatever his deficiencies as a fighting general, the Lord Privy
was an incorrigible opportunist. His next scheme was a request fo
expedition of 1,000 men to be landed somewhere along the Cor
coast in the rear of the rebels. This was altogether too much. It
patently obvious that he was exploiting the fact that a relief force
about to be dispatched urgently to the Channel Islands which had c
under heavy attack from the French who had already occupied S
Somerset effectively vetoed the idea. After the relief of Alderney
would order the Channel squadron to Plymouth to land whatever
could be scraped together, probably not more than 200 or 3
Naturally he was unable to forecast when this could take place, bu
would certainly take even longer for another squadron to beat d
Channel. So, if the operation was really essential, the best thing Rus
could do would be to find vessels for himself and use his own tro
He could if he liked also strike a bargain with a pirate named Thomp
who was then lying at anchor in the Severn, holding out the offer
free pardon in return for his assistance.

II

According to John Hooker's version Lord Russell had convinced h
self that his victory on Clyst Heath had terminated the campaign,
was much shaken by the intelligence that the rebels, both Devon n
and Cornishmen, had rallied at Sampford Courtenay 'fully bent
maintain their quarrel and to abide the battle'; he incontinently drop
all other business and reassembled his army to march against them
may have been that at his age he felt that the rigours of a four-

campaign of non-stop fighting amply warranted a pause for regrouping and fresh planning; it can hardly be doubted that he felt more at home in the council chamber than in the saddle. But within a week of reaching Exeter his council − general staff, one might almost say − had been reconstituted mainly with professional soldiers: Grey and Herbert, the brothers Sir Hugh and Sir John Paulet, Sir Andrew Dudley and Sir Thomas Speke, all of them advocates of swift and decisive action. And from London the Protector was demanding results.

With Herbert's troops and the accession of the local gentry and numerous common folk eager to purge their recent disloyalty, the army was now much larger than it had been, possibly a full 8,000, as stated by Hooker. It marched out of Exeter on 15 August but, since 'the way was very cumbrous', managed not more than the seven miles to Crediton that day. In justice to Russell he could well have been waiting for the end of a spell of bad weather and for the roads to dry out before starting. The march was resumed next day, Russell delaying his own start in order to write to the mayor of Exeter directing him to make a special levy on citizens who had refused to contribute to the cost of defence. The vanguard, which included the Italians and much of the horse, probably managed a normal day's march of some dozen miles, camping for the night in the vicinity of North Tawton less than three miles from its objective. The rest of the army, however, did less well, and seems to have finished up strung out over several miles of narrow road. Russell's report of the operation has survived, but is so indefinite as to times and locations that many of the details have to be conjectured.

The following morning, Sunday, 17 August, the scouts encountered a patrol under the command of Maunders, the shoemaker, which was perhaps patrolling the crossing of the river Taw. In a brisk skirmish it was brushed aside and its leader captured.

Although the van was now very close to the main rebel position, several hours were bound to elapse before the other divisions, including the baggage train, could arrive. Grey and Herbert, who were in command, had, none the less, 'a good part of the army' with them, and they were ordered to advance and reconnoitre in preparation for a full-scale attack.

Humphry Arundell's problem was that he was heavily outnumbered, by some four to one if, as is likely, he had no more than about 2,000 men left. His plan resembled that adopted by Montrose when faced with similar odds at the battle of Auldearn in 1645; he divided his army and set up an ambush. About a mile east of the village the ground rises to a well marked eminence marked at 593 feet on the Ordnance Survey map; it is the only feature which corresponds to what Russell called the rebels' 'camp' where they lay 'strongly encamped as well by the seat of the ground as by the entrenching of the same'. Here Arundell posted

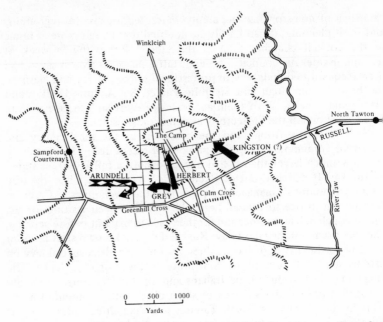

Map 4 The Battle of Sampford Courtenay – first pha⟨

what probably amounted to more than half his force, upwards ⟨
1,000 men, including almost certainly any who were short of equi⟩
ment. The inference is that they consisted of the Devonshire co⟩
tingent, led by John Bury, Coffin and Underhill. Well dug in an
dominating the approach to Sampford, they were intended to dra
on themselves the full weight of the royal army's attack. The remainde
a picked force of well armed Cornishmen under his own comman
Arundell concealed in the village itself, ready to be hurled against tl
flank and rear of the enemy once they were committed to an assau
on the hill.

Grey's approach must have been either by the direct road fro⟩
North Tawton or the present B 3216 which bypasses it about a mile
the south; both converge at Greenhill Cross, roughly 1,000 yards sh⟨
of the site of the 'camp'. As was intended, he discovered it and prepar⟨
to attack without delay. In the densely enclosed countryside he w⟩
unable to observe that it was only the bait in the trap – held only ⟩
the 'tag and rag' – which the Cornishmen were waiting to spring. T
natural pivot of his advance would have been a short distance beyo⟩
Greenhill Cross at Culm Cross where the Tawton road is intersected ⟩
a lane which leads straight up the hill and on to Winkleigh. Evidently
placed Herbert's Welshmen on the right wing and Spinola's arquebusi⟨

on the left, undoubtedly supported by other units since they numbered only a few score. Once again they immediately proved their worth, driving back towards the village rebel skirmishers who hovered on the flank of the assaulting column. The countryside is a patchwork of tiny fields surrounded by high banks and hedges, ideal for defence. Three or four of these obstacles had to be negotiated before the attackers could come to grips with the defenders, and pioneers were called up to clear passages, a slow, laborious business. While they worked their way slowly and methodically from field to field Arundell prepared his counterstroke. As soon as they were enmeshed in this maze he emerged unexpectedly from Sampford and struck 'with his whole power' at their rear, causing a momentary panic. But the Cornishmen became just as badly entangled, and Grey had just sufficient time to parry the thrust. Leaving Herbert to keep up the pressure on the 'camp', he collected his 'last' horse and foot – the rearmost line would appear to be what is meant – and turned them about to form a new front which held firm. Arundell's drive petered out. The Cornishmen no longer advanced with their former *élan*; they went to ground and contented themselves with a desultory exchange of artillery fire continued for an hour or so.

While this crisis was resolved fresh troops were reaching the field under the command of Sir Anthony Kingston. Herbert immediately threw them into the attack and at length stormed the rebels' position. Overwhelmed by numbers the defenders abandoned their posts and fled. Underhill was killed and with him, so Russell claimed, 500 or 600 men.

His plan having misfired, Arundell, with half his army routed, withdrew his own command from its exposed position for a last stand behind the defences of Sampford Courtenay. Russell arrived on the field just as Herbert was recalling his men from the pursuit, and although it was now late in the afternoon he ordered an immediate advance against the village. The attack was delivered in three battles. On the right Herbert and Kingston advanced from the 'camp'; in the centre Grey moved forward from the position he had been holding, while Russell's own command must have deployed south of the road by which it had arrived. Hopelessly outnumbered and with little fight left in them, the Cornishmen gave way and fled towards Okehampton without attempting any serious resistance. Russell's wing may have been late in deploying and moving off – almost certainly it contained inferior troops – and thus failed to cut them off. Nevertheless, he unleashed his cavalry in hot pursuit. Desperately Arundell strove to rally the fugitives to make a stand in Okehampton, but the pursuers were too close on their heels and they were swept on in the rout. When nightfall put an end to the chase hundreds had been killed or captured, and 16 brass and iron guns abandoned on the battlefield.

Throughout the night the royal army stood to arms for fear of a counter-attack. Too often in the past weeks men they supposed well and truly beaten had come back for more. But this time there was to be none, for the surviving rebels were scattered far and wide, bent only on saving their necks. Their losses had been nothing short of catastrophic Russell claimed 700 killed in the pursuit, in addition to 500 or 600 killed around the camp, besides many prisoners taken. There is no reason seriously to doubt him, even allowing for some element of exaggeration. A total of 1,200 rebel casualties seems not improbable and certainly spelt the destruction of their army. He admitted that many of his own men were wounded, but not more than 10 or 12 killed – perhaps he meant gentlemen. It sounds reasonable. There was no bald-headed onslaught; the enemy's morale had not been high and they had shown little taste for close combat. At the same time Hooker suggests that the rebels had resisted stubbornly and that the victory had been no walkover.

Arundell made with all haste to Launceston where Richard Grenville and various other Cornish gentlemen were held captive. He tried to incite the townsmen to murder the prisoners, but they would have none of it. Instead they released Grenville and joined with him in arresting Arundell and several other leading rebels, probably William Winslade, and Holmes in particular. In his deposition Arundell claimed that he had in fact gone straight to Grenville, 'declared all the matter' to him, and surrendered voluntarily. But by this time it could make no difference what he did. All a rebel captain without an army could look forward to was a noose, for no matter the shifts by which he might seek to put his conduct in the least unfavourable light, his treason was self-evident. Grenville sent urgently to Russell for aid, the message reaching him while the army was still mopping up around Okehampton. The Carews were instantly ordered to Launceston with a flying column, and Russell followed with the remainder of the army as soon as his hands were free.

This was the end of organised resistance in Cornwall. John Bury and Coffin managed to round up some remnants of the Devonshire rebels and led them eastwards via Tiverton towards Somerset. A strong column under Sir William Herbert was sent after them. Advancing up the Exe valley, he scattered a group which attempted to make a stand at Cranmore castle near Tiverton, hanging and quartering the prisoners on the spot. Under the impression that the main body had retreated to Minehead (where they are said to have taken ship to Bridgwater) he followed them there, detaching Sir Hugh Paulet and Sir Peter Carew to pursue the rest. Near King's Weston in Somerset, on 27 August, they caught up with the tired and hungry band, and destroyed it. A hundred and four prisoners were taken, including Coffin. It was a timely haul. Somerset had teetered on the brink of rebellion; now its people were given a grim lesson on the consequences. In Bath, Frome, Shepton Mallett, Wells and nearly every market town in the shire, one or two of the prisoners were hanged; the remainder were pardoned in batches.

Having crushed the Cornishmen, Russell retired to Exeter, taking with him the chief prisoners, Arundell, Pomeroy, the Winslades (John was captured at Bodmin), Holmes, Wise, Harris and Fortescue. They were lodged in the gaol there and shortly joined by Coffin and Bury. Soon they were all transferred to London.

III

To complete the pacification of Cornwall, Russell commissioned Sir Anthony Kingston as provost marshal, who set about his work with grim efficiency and evident relish. The Protector, it will be recalled, had given instructions to hang prominent rebels in order to terrorise the population into submission. It was not simply a matter of stamping on the last smouldering embers of disaffection, or even of meting out the punishments demanded by the law. It was not, that is, restricted to crushing the present rising, but was also designed to forestall the next by making certain that for a generation or more the people would be too cowed to dare attempt it. Once the army was disbanded the conditions in which it would be possible to start another would be restored. The only form of policing would be the local gentry who had behaved like frightened rabbits the moment their authority had been challenged. Despite all the panoply of arbitrary power, Tudor government rested on the consent of the governed in a very real sense, and that consent had to be secured willy-nilly. Much of the 'white terror' of that autumn took the form of the gentry's revenge for the mortal affront to their dignity, and it was in the interest of the government – at this moment identified with theirs even more closely than usual – to condone and profit by it.

No formal record was kept of the number who paid the price of treason over and above the thousands already killed in action. A few individual instances have come to light which give some inkling of the tragedy of those terrible weeks. Few parts of the county escaped Kingston's fury, and anyone holding a position of responsibility in the community risked being treated as an insurgent leader. Priests, as we know, were numbered among the 'principal stirrers' of rebellion. Hooker names eight who were executed; three or four of them can be identified with some certainty, and there could well have been more as a result of the concerted drive to purge the region of their reactionary influence.

New incumbents were instituted in many parishes in Devon and
Cornwall in the months following the rising. Not all, indeed, necessarily
followed men who had been executed, but any stipendiary who was
could have vanished from the scene unnoticed: at Pillaton the curate
was hanged on Russell's personal order. Parsons were hanged from one
end of Cornwall to the other. Robert Voyce of St Cleer was attainted
so also, as might be expected, was the vicar of St Keverne. In the far
west, William Alsa of Gulval was executed, as was Simon Morton, vicar
of Poundstock in the north east; his successor was installed later that
year. For some reason or other his fate inspired a Protestant ballad
popular in the streets of London:

> The vicar of Poundstock with his congregation
> Commanded them to stick to their idolatry;
> They had much provision and great preparation,
> Yet God hath given our King the victory.

Civic officials also suffered. The port-reeve of St Ives, one John
Payne, was hanged, as was the mayor of Torrington, unless he had
already perished in battle. (Other leaders such as Segar must either have
died fighting or been executed; Maunder, captured in the early stages
of the battle of Sampford Courtenay, was presumably executed
summarily soon afterwards.) The mayor of Bodmin was another — not
Henry Bray who disappeared, perhaps slain in one of the battles, but
Nicholas Boyer (or Bowyer) who had stepped into his shoes either as
deputy or successor. Although it was reported that he 'had been busy
among the rebels . . . some that loved him said that he had been forced
thereunto, and that if he had not consented to them they would have
destroyed him and his house'. He sounds like a moderate who tried to
steer the best course open to him in circumstances of great difficulty,
and succeeded in getting the worst of both worlds. Up to 17 August it
was risky to appear unco-operative with the rebellious townsmen of
Bodmin, afterwards even the most tenuous association with them was
fatal.

It seems that Boyer believed himself in the clear, for when Kingston
intimated his intention of visiting Bodmin in order to dine with the
mayor, Boyer 'seemed to be joyous thereof and made for him very
good preparation', welcoming him cordially to the town. According to
the story in Grafton's *Chronicle*, Kingston, before sitting down to the
meal, took the mayor to one side, explained that the true object of his
visit was to execute a traitor, and requested him to have a gallows
erected ready for use by the time dinner was over. Boyer set about the
preparations diligently. When he had done eating, Kingston called the
mayor over to him and asked if the gallows was ready, receiving an
assurance that it was. Then he took Boyer by the hand and asked to
be conducted to the place where the gallows stood. After gazing at it

a silence for a moment he turned to his host and enquired: 'Think you
they be strong enough?'

'Yea, Sir,' replied the mayor, 'that they are!'

'Well then,' said Sir Anthony, 'get you even up to them, for they are
provided for you.'

Aghast, Boyer whispered: 'I trust you mean no such thing to me.'

'Sir, there is no remedy,' Kingston replied flatly. 'You have been a
busy rebel, and, therefore, this is appointed for your reward.'

And at his signal, his retainers hustled the struggling mayor up the
ladder and hanged him.

This black comedy was remembered long after others had been
forgotten because even in that brutal age men were revolted by
Kingston's sick humour. Hangings as such could be regarded with
indifference; in 1598, after all, a normal year, no fewer than 74
criminals were condemned to death by the courts of Devonshire alone.
But the perverted enjoyment he evidently derived from his reign of
error was another matter. Even Richard Carew, while as a fellow
gentleman defending his cynical callousness as a necessary corrective to
rebellion, remarked that he left 'a name more memorable than commendable amongst the townsmen of Bodmin'.

An incident in a neighbouring parish provided Grafton with a
further anecdote, and shows that besides being addicted to sick jokes
Kingston could produce them on the spur of the moment. He had the
local miller on his visiting list, 'a very busy varlet in that rebellion'.
Forewarned of danger this fellow planned to cheat the hangman. He
called his servant, a tall, well set up lad, and told him:

'I must go forth. If there come any to ask for me, say that thou art
the owner of the mill, and that thou hast kept the same this four years,
and in no wise name not me.'

This, the man, a loyal servant, if a bit naïve, promised to do.

Now Kingston knew only that he was looking for a miller, he did not
know the man's name. So on arriving at the door he just called out for
the master, and the servant presented himself.

'How long hast thou kept this mill?' asked the provost marshal.

'Three years.'

'Well then,' said Kingston, 'Come on! Thou must go with me.'

Seizing the unfortunate man his servants dragged him to the nearest
tree.

Kingston explained: 'You have been a rebellious knave and therefore
you shall hang.'

In a torrent of words the man protested that he was not the miller
at all.

'Very well!' Kingston quipped. 'You are a false knave to be in two
tales.' And turning to his men he ordered: 'Therefore hang him up.'

As the hapless wretch dangled from the tree a bystander ventured the opinion: 'Surely this was but the miller's man.'

Quick as a flash Kingston chuckled: 'Well then! Could he ever have done his master a better service than to hang for him?'

William Mayow of Clevyan may have experienced another side of the provost marshal's humour when he was hanged from the sign post of a tavern in St Columb. If Grey considered it appropriate to hang priests on churches why should Kingston not have chosen pubs for the laity? Of course in this instance it might have been the nearest available bracket.

The broad swath of executions extending from end to end of the West Country burned deep into the memory of the people. 'Commotion time' became the point of schism in their lives, the event against which all others were reckoned until the passage of the years and, finally, the decease of all who had lived through that dreadful season assuaged the pain and gradually dimmed the memory of it. To compare its effect on the Cornish people with that of Verdun on the French in the present century is not fanciful; the death roll *per capita* was not dissimilar, and it broke their spirit.

And still this was only part of the story. Prisoners of war were liable for ransom, their goods and chattels at the disposal of their captors. As rebels, of course, their property was forfeit anyway, but in the confusion of the hour legal definitions held little meaning, with the consequence that nearly everyone found himself in peril. Proclamations in July had threatened everyone who countenanced the rebels in any respect whatsoever (whether by active support, communicating, or merely sympathising with them) with the forfeiture of their lands, these to be awarded to whoever should first lay claim to them. Inevitably this amounted to little short of incitement to the vengeful to settle private scores, and to the sly to bear false witness against their more guileless neighbours, all the more so when neutrality was held to be no better than treason itself.

One rebel prisoner named Thomas Boffin was assigned by Russell to a certain John Kemp. A complicated arrangement was entered into by which John Godolphin paid Kemp £20 for Boffin's liberty, presumably recovering it, plus interest, from the victim by instalments. Someone else seized the goods of the rector of Langton, Devon, who had been killed in action. Sir Anthony Kingston, as might be expected, had his own way with prisoners, discovering further ways of exercising his ingenuity. Gabriel Morton, vicar of Uny Lelant, was assigned to him by Russell. For once he did not hang his captive; it was more profitable to make over the tithes of the parish, for a consideration, to John Trewennick of Boscastle who received them for the remainder of Morton's life. Here pleasure could neatly be combined with profit.

Other soldiers armed with Russell's authority seized the property of
the rector of Bytton and held a sale of it at the church house in the
village. The rector had gone into hiding to wait for the tumult to die
down; perhaps he was fortunate to escape with his life. Other men took
full advantage of the proclamation of the general forfeiture of the
goods of the rebels. The looting was not confined to one side. There
could have been a good deal done by the insurgents, like William Webber,
one of the Devonshire captains, who had broken into the house of
Richard Pomeroy and taken goods and title deeds.

Not surprisingly the victors began to fall out over the division of
the spoils. One of the few Cornish gentlemen who actually got away
and served in Russell's army was William Lower of St Winnow. Assigned
to the party sent to apprehend the chief rebels after the battle of
Sampford Courtenay, he laid hands on one called John Bealbury,
seizing plate worth £8, together with other items. Then along came
another soldier armed with Russell's warrant authorising him to take
possession of Bealbury's property. How they eventually sorted it out
we are not told. Indeed, the few incidents that can now be recalled
have in general only been recorded for some extrinsic reason, in some
cases thanks to the chance of finding their way into a subsequent
lawsuit. The truth must be that so many took place that people's
sensibilities became dulled; besides, almost all the victims were persons
of no importance. The misfortunes of a family of good position held
far more significance, especially if it had played a prominent part in
the rising. A party of Lord Grey's troopers took advantage of the
general licence to plunder to descend on the Winslade home at Tregarrick
and pillage it, a terrifying ordeal for Mrs Winslade, left on her own with
her menfolk in custody. They broke open the chest in which her
husband kept his title deeds and other papers, and removed the
contents, including the one which made the family's Cornish estates
her jointure. Later on she did recover this document and the property
was thus salvaged from the wreck of the family's fortunes. Nevertheless,
there was a sad postscript. She subsequently married John Trevanion,
who made certain that her son never came into his birthright. This was
the more sophisticated way of despoiling the rebels, for William,
although pardoned for his part in the rising, failed to recover his inheritance in the courts, his record no doubt counting against him. After
him the Winslade family, once so eminent in Cornwall, disappeared
from the page of history.

In the first flush of victory Russell may well have felt inclined to
forget that his job was to re-establish law and order in the West; equally
he may have found it difficult to restrain his tough henchmen Grey,
Herbert, Kingston and the rest. At any rate the Council soon decided
that he was permitting the looting and confiscations to get out of hand,

and wrote to tell him so. This was not entirely fair, because t**
reprimand came a bare fortnight after they had advised him, in respon**
to his enquiry, to defer the publication of a general amnesty until **
could be certain that all the most dangerous rebels had bee**
apprehended. Now, however, he was told that the proclamatic**
threatening forfeitures had really been a piece of bluff designed **
demoralise the insurgents during those critical days when he had bee**
hanging on by the skin of his teeth at Honiton, and further accused hi**
of having taken it upon himself to alter its terms:

> which form and manner of seizure being by you altered, as yourse**
> confesseth, we see not that the proclamation is any warrant to yo**
> gifts. . . . and if you consider the end of the proclamation, it ma**
> manifestly appear that consideration was even then had that no ma**
> should lose anything otherwise nor in any other sort than the King**
> highness by means and right of the forfeiture ought and may by h**
> laws dispose of the same. And by his laws we do not think that ar**
> man should lose lands or goods before he be attainted of the crin**
> which meriteth that punishment.

In short the government now feared that the depredations of their ow**
troops might goad the people into another 'devilish enterprise'. Fc**
good measure they insinuated that Russell had been lining his ow**
pockets at the expense of the Treasury, and requested him to explai**
why the accounts he had submitted did not cover the whole of th**
advances which had been made to him.

Most of what took place in those dark days must remain a matter c**
conjecture. One thing is certain: Catholicism was stamped out, never **
reappear in Cornwall. The last English rebellion would take place ther**
in 1685, but by then it was to be a Protestant people supporting **
Protestant pretender to the throne of a reactionary Catholic kin**
Indeed they lost everything they fought for, since by the end of th**
century the Cornish language itself was to be little more than a memor**

Chapter 12
Dussindale

Kett's easy victory over the marquis of Northampton was a tactical one only; it led to nothing, indeed it gravely weakened his cause by reducing to absurdity his claim to be acting as the King's representative in Norfolk. Northampton, irrespective of the extreme foolishness of his conduct, held the King's commission; Kett did not. The attack on his column, no matter how gross the provocation, was just as crass a blunder; the fact that it had probably commenced spontaneously, against Kett's wishes, made no difference to the fact that it constituted an overt act of defiance which invited swift retribution.

At this juncture Kett realised that the sole remaining hope of achieving his goal, not to mention preserving his own life, was to spread the rebellion so widely that the government would be forced to negotiate a settlement. But although there were murmurings throughout the eastern counties, the degree of real support was negligible. Attempts to raise Essex made little headway; Lord Chancellor Rich had already decisively suppressed an incipient one in July. Secretary Petre also had his country seat there. John Chandler, parson of Alswinthorpe near King's Lynn, came to Colchester on 6 August. There, in the house of William Browne, a draper and tailor, he met Robert Peerson, a priest of the town, John Robinson, parson of Tardeston, Suffolk, and Richard Kent of Sturton, also in Suffolk. But the next morning the bailiffs of the borough were given a full account of it. They heard how Chandler had said, 'I would the town of Lynn and all the gentlemen there were on fire.'

He claimed that gentlemen's servants had been sallying out of Lynn to beat up the countryside, killing poor men toiling in the harvest fields, and pregnant women in their homes. The garrison had welcomed with a 'peal of guns' a certain Captain Bunting whom the insurgents had very much wanted to catch, but he had left his hat lying beside a well and fooled them into thinking that he had fallen in and drowned. But Chandler tried to convince his audience that at Bury St Edmunds he had met no fewer than 7,000 men who had come in from Langham,

Brandon Ferry, Ely and other towns, adding, 'where there is one man would there were ten', and this was too much for them, for they would quite certainly have already heard of a gathering of this size — more than he believed to be in the camp on Mousehold — in a town a mere 30 miles away. In fact most of Suffolk remained more or less tranquil thanks in part to the vigilance aand resolution of the authorities, and in part (one also feels) to the ineptitude of the rebels' agents.

Nor was force any more effective. The indications are that some desultory and probably very localised thrusts were made in the direction of King's Lynn. On 5 August, Kett and Aldrych ordered Nicholas Byron to take 100 men, commandeer horses and provisions for them and seize Great Yarmouth. Byron evidently expected the port to declare for him as soon as it was summoned to do so, otherwise so minute a force could hardly have been seriously expected to subdue the second largest town in Norfolk, which had a population of some 3,000.

The townsmen refused admission to Byron and his little band, and ignored Kett's 'commissions'. Instead they dispatched a delegation to the Protector who, in reply, exhorted them to resist, and promised to lead a relief force into Norfolk without delay.

Balked of an easy success, Byron turned away to overrun the Lothingland district of Suffolk, hoping to gather recruits. The people of Lowestoft evidently gave him a cordial reception for he acquired six guns there. These were taken to Gorleston and mounted in a close at the north end of the parish from where a bombardment of Yarmouth was commenced. A party from the town riposted by slipping across the haven to the west bank where they set fire to a haystack. A fresh northerly breeze blew the smoke into the faces of the rebels, and under its cover the raiding party took Byron's men by surprise and drove them in headlong flight from the field, leaving behind several dead, 30 prisoners, and all six guns which were carried back in triumph to Yarmouth to make a powerful addition to the defences.

To all intents the danger was now past. Other bands of rebels did indeed approach the walls in the course of the next few days, but all they accomplished was the destruction of much of the materials which had been laid in for the building of a new haven on the other side of the Denes. Eventually they were driven off by gunfire and were not seen again.

By 17 August, Sir Thomas Cleare and Sir Thomas Woodhouse had reached Yarmouth and taken command. They reorganised the defence, appointing a captain and petty captain in each of the eight wards, and ordering a strict watch for signs of incipient treachery. A ship called *The Dragon* and three doggers were anchored between the town and the new haven, the *Rose Lion* and the remainder of the doggers were

osted by the north end of the town, and the rest of the shipping
opposite the town between these two flotillas. To obtain early warning
of any fresh attack they dispatched a small pinnace, manned by 26
men and provisioned for four days, to Weybridge at Acle, and the
Broderers to Buckenham accompanied by a small boat. To scour the
landward approaches a band of 30 horsemen armed with pikes, 12 men
with half hacks (carbines or pistols) and 18 archers were assembled. On
19 August orders from the Council made the town additionally responsible for sealing off the route into Suffolk.

II

Once it had received Northampton's sorry report the government,
unable to postpone the reckoning with Kett any longer, immediately
set about assembling an army strong enough to inflict a decisive defeat
on him. This proved no simple matter. About 6 August a worried Henry
Hakfort called on van der Delft to ask what line he should take should
he be requested to lead his company of 420 heavy cavalry against the
rebels. The ambassador advised the young Guelderland nobleman to
reply that he had come to England with the Emperor's permission to
take part in the Scottish campaign, but not to get embroiled in religious
wars, and hence if the government needed him for the Norfolk army
they would have to seek the Emperor's agreement. Von Walderden's
landsknechts were equally reluctant to go: eventually the ensigns of
Wilhelm von Ardenburg and Clayne van Buren had to be bribed with
the promise of a whole month's pay for one day's fighting. Moreover,
they refused to move until the two ensigns serving in the West Country
had rejoined them.[1]

At first, according to van der Delft, Somerset was for rushing off to
Norfolk himself with Hakfort and the Germans immediately available.
Given time for second thoughts while they haggled, he began to weigh
the risks; whether, on the one hand, to take the field himself at the
cost of separating himself from the levers of power, or on the other to
place a powerful armament in the hands of an experienced soldier
which could mean only his chief rival, the earl of Warwick. By 7 August
the latter had in fact been appointed Lieutenant General and, taking
no chances, had hastened to Wales to recruit men. On 10 August he
issued orders to the East Anglian gentry to muster with their men at
Saffron Walden in a week's time. Then in the early hours of 11 August
he wrote from Warwick castle to William Cecil announcing his appointment to command in Bedfordshire, Cambridgeshire, Huntingdonshire,
Northamptonshire, Norfolk and Suffolk, but urging, none the less, a
different arrangement, namely that the marquis of Northampton should

continue as commander-in-chief — so that he should not appear to h
been disgraced — while he (Warwick) should act as second-in-comma;
He asked Cecil to arrange for this to be done. It was a smart pl
Northampton, although one of Somerset's original backers, had
doubtedly experienced the sharp edge of his tongue, and could
counted on to switch allegiance if handled tactfully. But irrespective
whoever finally commanded it, the army had come into being officia
by 7 August when John Hornihold was already acting as treasurer w
an imprest of £5,000.

Recruitment of the army and concentration at Cambridge v
completed in about two weeks, and since the full resources of the st;
were mobilised in an atmosphere of extreme urgency it could not rea
be maintained that Russell had done badly by comparison, left as
had been so long to his own resources.

Warwick's personal retinue comprised 106 demi-lances, 451 lig
horse, and 837 foot, and total inclusive of officers being 1,410. Wa
and the West Midlands provided 1,368 light horse commanded
Lord Bray, and 2,655 foot, of which Lord Powis was appointed capt;
general. These began drawing pay on 12 August. An artillery group w
added, although there is no statement of its establishment or t
number of guns. Three yards of taffeta were purchased for 32s. 8d.
make a banner of St George. Van der Delft reported that 8,000
9,000 men had been recruited by 13 August, although he wou
necessarily have been going by rough estimates; the King noted in
journal that Warwick had gone to Norfolk with 1,500 horse and 6,0
foot. Both estimates exceed the 5,431 men actually on the payroll by
wide margin, but they may have lumped in other units, includi
possibly various gentlemen and their followers who served without p;
On 16 August all Essex gentlemen in London were ordered home
await the King's commands, those of Suffolk to place themselves
the general's disposal, and those of Norfolk to report to him for du
by Saturday or Sunday 17 or 18 August. At Ingatestone, Essex,
William Petre laid out some £11 in arms, ammunition and clothin
including 12 bows, 14 pikes and three handguns — a further indicati
of the comparative rarity of firearms among the local defence forc;

Simultaneously Lord Willoughby of Parham had been commission
to muster Lincolnshire and Cambridgeshire. In the former county
raised 1,100 foot, while Cambridgeshire and the Lynn marshla;
district of Norfolk contributed 400 more. In fact there were 1,4!
officers and men on the payroll — 14 companies — with another ;
men forming the marshal's guard. There were also 123 light horse,
grand total of 1,599 officers and men. He purchased 482 lb. of powd
and a small number of bows and arrows, pikes and spears, presumab
to replace defective ones.

The city of London, meanwhile, prepared nervously to emulate the fortitude of Exeter — and avoid the fate of Norwich. On 3 August the own ditch between Aldersgate and Newgate, long abandoned to gardeners, began to be reconverted into a moat by seven score labourers. A week later spirits were cheered by the definitive news of Lord Russell's victory at Clyst St Mary which Archbishop Cranmer celebrated with a solemn *Te Deum* in St Paul's, while the chronicler noted with satisfaction that 4,000 of the rebels had been slain. The city had already been under martial law for a month. Now, on 16 August, two men who had shown symptoms of rebelliousness were hanged, one, Church by name, outside Bishopsgate, the other, called Payne, at Waltham. Four more were arraigned at the Guildhall and sent for execution at various places on 22 August: John Allen, pedlar of Southwark, at Tyburn, William Gotes, a shepherd from Hampton in Wiltshire, at Tottenham, and Roger Baker, falconer of Southfield, on Tower Hill; James Webbe, vicar of Barford in Oxfordshire, was dispatched to Aylesbury in order that his execution might serve as a deterrent to malcontents in Buckinghamshire. On 23 August the Court of Aldermen decided to ban the annual wrestling matches, fearing that they might become the occasion for a commotion.

Warwick concentrated the greater part of his army at Cambridge by 19 August. The suggestion made by some historians that his object was to keep Kett penned in Norfolk does not square with the fact that the latter never showed the least sign of leaving the vicinity of Norwich. The obvious explanation is almost certainly the correct one, namely that for most of his newly recruited contingents it was the direct route to Norwich and a convenient point at which to effect a junction with his other forces including his personal retinue, Northampton's command, less perhaps Guevara's company which (assuming that it had been in Norfolk earlier) seems to have been sent to the North, and with the probable addition of Hakfort's regiment. Willoughby, however, who was concentrating at King's Lynn, he ordered to rendezvous with him outside Norwich. Willoughby moved off on 20 August, making a detour through Walsingham rather than taking the direct route through Hingham since the district immediately west of Norwich was 'utterly as they lay spoiled both of malt, beef and muttons'.

The landsknechts commanded by van Buren and von Ardenburg had not yet arrived. They were halted further back awaiting the arrival of the other two ensigns marching up from the West Country, and presumably refusing to budge until they had been reunited. Warwick decided that since he already had sufficient troops to contain the rebels he could move on Norwich without delay, delegating an officer named Hudson to conduct the Germans there in a few days' time. He had no intention of attempting to attack until he had a large enough corps of

professional infantry to be certain of success, but he also hoped t
the sight of his already numerous army would persuade the insurge
to accept a peaceful solution.

III

On his own arrival at Cambridge, Warwick was greeted with marl
deference — understandably in view of the punitive character of
mission. The municipal funds were charged with 19s. to buy a gift
him, 4d. for getting out the gallows and purchasing a new rope, a
6d. for erecting it and putting it away after the executions. M
money was spent on the watch and the apprehension of rebels, a
Edward Loft who was sent scouting as far as Thetford was reward
with 10s.

Among the first people to wait on Warwick were the refugees fr
Norwich, those doughty citizens and aldermen who had abandor
their families to the mercies of the insurgents, and who now expatial
at length on the hardships and losses they had suffered in consequer
of their inability to stand up to the peasants. In extending the Kin
pardon he conceded the force of their argument, and with gentle iro
admitted that their panic had been no more than the natural reacti
but yet:

> notwithstanding in one they were somewhat imprudent that th
> withstood not these evils in the very beginning, for a few vali
> and wise men might well have dispatched those companies in
> moment if at the commencement they had opposed themsel
> for the health of their country.

After this mild rebuke he merely bade them arm themselves and foll
him.

Having put Cambridge in order the Lieutenant General left to jo
his army which by 22 August had reached Wymondham, 53 miles c
where it was joined by such local gentry as had remained at liberty, a
also by Willoughby who had covered a similar distance from Kin
Lynn. Next day the united force advanced as far as Intwood, just th
miles short of Norwich, where Warwick was entertained at the Hall
Sir Thomas Gresham, while his soldiers slept on their arms in the op
Nicholas Sotherton, an eye-witness, estimated the strength of t
army as 12,000, while Alexander Neville who investigated the episo
in the 1570s put it as high as 14,000. From extant records continge
can be identified as shown in Table 4. This makes a grand total of 9,42
Some provision should be made for other English troops, particula
East Anglian gentry, but not forgetting that during the summer vario

Table 4

	Horse	Foot
Warwick's retinue	560	860
Lord Bray	1,368	
Lord Powis		2,655
Von Walderden's landsknechts (est.)		1,100
Hakfort	420	
Willoughby	123	1,456
Northampton's force		
Drury		180
Malatesta (est.)		200
Other English (est.)	500	
	2,971	6,451

men-at-arms and demi-lances were in and around London prior to dispatch to the North or to Boulogne; a generous guess might be 500 horse and 500 foot bringing the aggregate to roughly 10,500 which the addition of artillerists, pioneers and sundry camp followers might well increase to between 11,000 and 12,000. Against this is the doubt whether Hakfort served in Norfolk at all. The difficulty is that the pay accounts are incomplete with the result that while they can be used to prove which bands served in any particular theatre, their silence as to the doings of others proves nothing. Apart from troops, the record of whose service has been lost, the number of mercenaries available – the core of Warwick's army – did not exceed 500 horse and 1,300 foot, less any casualties incurred in the previous engagements; quite possibly there was only the infantry, indeed the dependence of Warwick's plans on the arrival of the landsknechts rather implies that until they joined him he had scarcely any mercenaries at all.

As to the landsknechts on whom the success of the campaign depended, Sotherton estimated them at 1,040, Neville at 1,100, while the *Acts of the Privy Council* paid Mr Hudson for conducting four ensigns of them to Norfolk. The strength of the ensign was stipulated as 400; in fact von Ardenburg and van Buren had 864 men between them, and there should, therefore, have been 1,600 or more, in theory. This provides additional circumstantial evidence that two ensigns had been serving with Russell. When allowance is made for casualties, sick and stragglers, we can readily imagine that Walderden had established a depot for his unfit men, with a detachment to guard them against the hostile population, and marched on to Norfolk with a picked contingent of the fittest men, say 1,100.

The Germans had still not arrived by the morning of 24 August, so that although Warwick probably had a good 10,000 men, there were

only a handful of mercenaries plus Drury's company of English pro
fessionals. He could not, therefore, contemplate precipitating
showdown; at the same time he could not afford to remain inactiv
almost within sight of Norwich. While the army made leisurel
preparations to march he sent ahead Norroy King of Arms to proclain
war on the rebels unless they opened the city gates instantly an
submitted. He hoped, indeed, that they would take this fina
opportunity to yield, anxious as he was to avoid unnecessary bloodshe
and to rescue the captive gentlemen unharmed.

On the approach of the herald Kett sent Steward, the deputy mayon
and Alderman Robert Rugge out through a postern to parley with him
In all due form they bewailed their misfortunes, protesting that the
were forcibly prevented from faithfully carrying out their duty to th
King who, they trusted, would appreciate the constraints placed upon
them. They pointed out there were in the city numerous poor, unarme
men who had deserted the camp, 'who besides through fear and con
sciousness of their own wickedness holden guilty, moreover were wear
of their doings, as which had filled the very desire of working mischie
with satiety of their furies', in the light of which the delegation begge
that the Lieutenant General might extend pardon to all who would nov
lay down their arms, 'which would be an eternal memory unt
posterity, and a glory exceeding all victory, if they might carry hom
peace, and their weapons unstained with the blood of civil dissension'
This petition was immediately referred back to Warwick who, concerne
primarily for the security of the kingdom, signified that he would b
pleased to exercise clemency.

When, after a quarter of an hour, Norroy and his trumpeter returne
bearing the general's favourable reply, he demanded that the portculli
should be raised as the first step. This was done; the gates were opened
and 30 or 40 mounted rebels rode out in pairs, and proceeded to escor
him through the streets to Bishop's Gate, and one lying nearest th
camp. There the cavalcade halted, the trumpet was sounded, an
thousands of men poured down the hill from Mousehold. Everythin
was perfectly orderly. The horsemen marshalled them in two line
facing one another between which the herald and his escort advance
slowly for about a quarter of a mile. Hats were removed and th
assembly shouted, 'God save King Edward!'

Reaching the brow of the hill Norroy turned and began to addres
them in stern tones. He rebuked them for the treason they had com
mitted, the atrocities done to the King's subjects, the destruction o
property, and the forgery of laws and commissions, all of whicl
stemmed from the unspeakable wickedness of their hearts. Nevertheless

if they would like natural subjects repent of their misdemeanou and humbly submit themselves to the King's mercy, he would grant to them His Highness' pardon for life and goods, Kett only excepted; if not, he [Warwick] protested with the help in whom his confidence rested that he would never depart out of the place, till, without pity and mercy, he vanquished them with the sword.

At the sound of these words many of the insurgents 'in fear trembled', but the majority fell to reviling the herald, calling him a traitor, and accusing him of speaking not for the King but for the gentry, their enemies, seeking to gull them into apathetic surrender with a bogus amnesty — 'barrels filled with ropes and halters', as some of them described it. Other men insulted him personally, deriding his gorgeous surcoat which they likened to popish vestments. Even those who welcomed the prospect of being let off the hook were none too happy about the terms of the offer.

With Kett by his side Norroy moved further down the line repeating his statement to those who had not yet heard it, until all of a sudden he was interrupted by a dozen or more horsemen who came charging out of the wood yelling that he had come only to bait a trap, and that at this very moment 'our men are killed by the water side'. What had happened was that some soldiers had strayed from the column, still halted on the opposite side of the town, and had come to watch the negotiations from a discreet distance. In Neville's words, 'An ungracious boy, pulling down his breeches showed his bare buttocks, and did a filthy act, adding thereunto more filthy words', provoking one of the troopers for whose benefit the performance was put on to draw his pistol and shoot the wretched youth in the groin. For all we know this soldier had intended to do no more than scare him, and by chance had scored a hit at extreme range.

A tremor of rage swept through the crowd, and it might have fallen on Norroy had not Kett led him quickly away to Sturt Hill. As he conducted his charge down the hill he was overheard to say that he intended to go to Warwick and give himself up in order that he should not remain as an obstacle to his followers freely availing themselves of the amnesty. But the mounted escort restrained him, and a large band gathered round shouting that they would go with him to protect him and if necessary die. This of course would have defeated the whole object of his surrendering himself. The herald, anxious for his own safety, suggested going on alone while Kett went back to calm the tumult; this he did, and led his men back to Mousehold.

As it was now clear to Warwick that the attempt at pacification had failed, he prepared to move against the city. Artillery was brought up to breach St Stephen's Gate which had been closed again. While this operation proceeded slowly — the army had not been provided with a siege train — Steward came forward with the information that there was

a postern nearby called Brazen Doors which, although barricaded wi'
timber and rampired with earth, could easily be forced open. Pionee
were sent forward to deal with it and soon got it open. A detachme
of foot charged in, overran the rebels they encountered, and drove the
back with heavy loss. Meanwhile the guns had smashed the portcul
and the half gate behind it, opening a way for Lord Northampton a
Captain Drury who burst into the town in force and rapidly cleared t
streets, killing many insurgents. Steward himself hastened to Westwi
Gate which he had opened to admit Warwick and another part

By early afternoon the army was in full control of Norwich. Citize
who had holed up in cellars and attics emerged in search of amnest
which they were granted, but otherwise people were ordered off t
streets. In the course of mopping up, some 49 rebels were capture
and hanged that evening. Congestion on the gallows became so gre
that the ladders broke and had to be repaired at the cost of 3*d*. to t
town funds; the funerals cost a further 3*s*. 6*d*.

But there was to be only a brief lull. Confused, sporadic fighti
flared up again and continued for several hours. Although at fi
taken off guard by the vigour of the assault, the rebels soon recover
and counter-attacked, heartened by the fact, which soon becan
obvious, that the quality of many of Warwick's troops was po

A costly mistake occurred while the army was moving into the cit
At about three o'clock the baggage train entered by the Westwick Ga
making for the Market Square. However, instead of turning right
Charing Cross, it carried straight on down Tombland, across Pala
Plain, and out again through Bishop's Gate, up the side of the hill a
into the eager hands of the rebels. Drury, with part of his compan
chased after it and recaptured a number of wagons at the cost of sever
casualties. But much of its load of guns, powder and other munitio
remained in the possession of the rebels — 'greatly rejoicing, for befo
they were utterly unprovided of such things'. A similar incident —
may even have been a different version of the same one — occurr
when much of the artillery train was parked somewhere near Bishop
Bridge ready to be brought into action. It was guarded by a handful
Welsh soldiers who did so little to defend themselves against persiste
harassment that the rebels concluded that they were short
ammunition. A man named Myles succeeded in bringing down t
master gunner with a well aimed shot, and immediately a party carryi
staves, bills and pitchforks, and some who were not armed at all, can
storming down the hill. The Welshmen lost their nerve and bolte
leaving all the guns and ammunition to be driven away in triumph t
the enemy. This episode, which features in Neville's narrative only, m
not be entirely true; like John Hooker he may have been prejudic
against the Welsh and sought to show them to disadvantage. At any ra

the publication of his book provoked a storm of protest, and the book-seller deleted the offending page from most copies.

The insurgents wasted no time in putting the captured guns to work harassing the troops and bombarding the town. But their gunners were untrained and aimed wildly, causing little real damage. Their only real success was to demolish a tower at Bishop's Gate, killing several men who were stationed − or huddled for shelter − in and around it. The real threat came from roving bands which infiltrated the narrow lanes of the city looking for opportunities to ambush small parties of soldiers. A large, well-armed company concentrated in Tombland outside the cathedral; dividing into three groups, one occupied St Andrew's church, another St Michael Coslany, and the third the area near St Simon's and St Peter Hungate, 'by the Elm and about the Hill next the corner' of the building 'late Black Friars'. They surprised a party of soldiers in the vicinity and succeeded in killing three or four gentlemen before reinforcements could be brought up. A hard fight developed as Warwick in person arrived to restore the situation. He advanced in strength through St John's, Maddermarket, to St Andrew's where his force fell into an ambush and was pinned down by a hail of arrows 'as flakes of snow in a tempest', until the indefatigable Captain Drury could bring up his arquebusiers, 100 strong, who raked the densely packed ranks of the rebels with 'a terrible volley of shot (as if it had been a storm of hail)' and routed them, pursuing them through the cathedral and back in the direction of the camp. It was all over in half an hour. At least 100 (one account says 330) rebels lay dead in the streets, and numerous wounded men and stragglers were rounded up lurking under the shelter of the churchyard walls. Drury's losses in these two actions were not insignificant, and that night he paid John Porter, a local surgeon, 33s. 4d. for tending the wounded.

The evening was occupied in making good some of the losses and damage sustained during the day. The smiths of the city cast 320 lb. of shot at a cost of 17s. 11d. The breach near Bishop's Gate was blocked up temporarily, and a special guard under Lord Willoughby posted at this exposed position. The earl of Warwick himself, following the strenuous afternoon and evening, called in at Augustine Steward's house for a drink at about quarter to ten. Some 15 minutes later he left to inspect the perimeter defences and personally supervise the posting of sentinels. Almost simultaneously the rebels returned to the attack, coming in across the river to Conisford Street where they set fire to houses, and corn and other merchandise stored on the staithe. They were soon driven away, but the fires were allowed to go on burn-ing for the rest of the night, the commanders suspecting that the insurgents had intended that the army should get involved in putting them out. Warwick meanwhile concentrated on security for the night.

The walls were fully manned and all but two of the gates blocked up. Every street was patrolled, and flares were kept burning to illuminate open spaces like the market place.

IV

The fire was still raging next morning. All in all, 25 August was a depressing sort of day. Under the pall of smoke which hung over Norwich, Kett's men constantly prowled around Conisford and threatened a fresh attack on Bishop's Gate which the army seemed powerless to fend off. In the eyes of the inhabitants Warwick's situation appeared ominously similar to what Northampton's had been a few weeks earlier, and they worried lest he should meet with the same fate in the event of which their homes would once more been exposed to sack. Towards midday a deputation of citizens waited on the general to point out that he was greatly outnumbered and that the city, with all its gates broken or burnt down, was barely defensible. They advised him to withdraw to a position of greater security to await reinforcements. His reply was that he would either save the city from the insurgents or sacrifice his life defending it. Then, in a dramatic gesture he called on his officers to draw their swords and each to kiss the other's, after which they all made the sign of the cross and swore a solemn oath to conquer or go down fighting.

The chivalric ritual was characteristic of the man. It is true that its archaic mystique served the immediate purpose of impressing the bourgeois, as well as inducing a sense of spiritual exaltation in the nobles and gentlemen who took part in it. But it also held a deep significance for their leader who throughout his life had devoted himself to the knightly ideal, seeking distinction in the tournament, an enthusiasm he had shared with Henry VIII who had steadily promoted him through a succession of offices. At the same time there was nothing of the Don Quixote in him, for he had proved himself a fine soldier and a commander of real ability. His first campaign, the duke of Suffolk's invasion of Picardy in 1523, had provided an object lesson in pointless warfare. His next experience, 20 years later, came as Lord Admiral commanding the fleet with telling effect in the systematic devastation of Scotland. The following year saw him directing the successful siege of Boulogne, while as governor of the town in 1545–6 he conducted an equally brilliant defence. Most recently, as second-in-command in the campaign of 1547, he was considered by many to have been chiefly responsible for the victory at Pinkie.

There was another side to this complex and enigmatic man. Reared in the hard school of Tudor politics he had learned early how to disemble. At the age of seven he had been orphaned when the youthful Henry VIII had courted public acclaim by sacrificing the head of Edmund Dudley, the hated minister of Henry VII. Although the stain of treason had subsequently been removed from the family name, the young John Dudley had needed to tread warily. (Even so, more Dudleys were decapitated than members of any other family in the sixteenth century. In addition to his father, John himself, his son, Guildford, and his daughter-in-law, Lady Jane Grey, perished on the scaffold; three other sons were condemned but reprieved, while to round things off, the youngest, Robert, earl of Leicester, was to be widely suspected of encompassing the death of his first wife.) Throughout the Protectorate, Warwick gives the impression of standing watchfully by, biding his time, never revealing his thoughts. Bombast was foreign to his nature, so, one feels, was self-importance; the fabrication of a genealogy to link himself with the extinct Sutton family, former Barons Dudley, was a fairly commonplace piece of vanity, harmless and not without a degree of utility. Later on, as dictator in all but name, he was to refrain from claiming the style of Protector for himself, contenting himself with a ducal coronet to ensure precedence over his Council colleagues. As with his rival, Somerset, it is incredible that no adequate biography of him exists.

Warwick did not bother to explain his strategy to the citizens, if indeed he did to anyone else; even the King's journal reads: 'he was so weak that he could scarcely defend' Norwich. This, probably, was nothing less than the truth. Drury's and Malatesta's were his only efficient infantry, and time and again on 24 August they had retrieved the situation — xenophobia must have inhibited the chroniclers from allowing the Italians any credit. The English levies were as ineffectual as the Welsh. If he had any mercenary horse he was not going to fritter them away in street fighting, unlike the marquis of Northampton who casually led a small column of mounted men into narrow alleys where they were unable to manoeuvre. He had used this infantry, 5,000 or so, and artillery to occupy the city, and now the most that could reasonably be expected of them was to hold it; half trained though they were, behind even makeshift defences they must at least have been the equal of the sketchily armed rebels. Secure in the knowledge that the arrival of the German veterans was at most a matter of hours, he was not going to risk his plans being leaked to the enemy by divulging them prematurely. In forcing his way into Norwich he had struck an immediate and telling blow both in recapturing the second city of the realm and in cutting off Mousehold from its main source of supplies, not to mention the support of the dissident element in the population. Kett, on the other hand, was now in the position where he was forced either to attempt to regain control of the city or leave the hostile army complete

freedom to attack him at the first favourable opportunity. Realis
that his adversary had all along been committed to maintaining
relatively passive stance, Warwick judged that he could be counted
to react wildly to controlled pressure systematically applied on t
fronts: from the infantry garrisoning the city, and also from the hor
at least 2,000 strong, which he sent to scour the countryside, cutti
off rebel foraging parties and steadily tightening the blockade of t
camp itself. In fact it was now Kett who was struggling in a trap, r
Warwick.

Although the insurgents continued to make demonstrations in so
force against the river bridges on 25 August, they displayed l
aggression than on the previous day and were driven off fairly easi
The biggest threat was posed by an attempted attack across Whitefri
Bridge which Warwick, therefore, ordered to be demolished: t
rebuilding subsequently cost the city £2 6s. 8d. It was now possible f
the first time to do something about billeting the soldiers, and some
the inhabitants who had previously concealed their possessions n
produced them so as to be able to entertain their guests the better. T
commander-in-chief quartered himself on Steward. Once again the nig
was disturbed by alarums and excursions, but all attacks were beat
back and were not renewed the next morning.

As the Lieutenant General sat dining at Steward's table about no
on 26 August a great noise of firing broke out. This time it was not t
insurgents, but the landsknechts entering the city and announcing th
coming in characteristically flamboyant fashion. Now that he h
von Walderden and his 1,100 highly trained infantry he could go ov
to the offensive.

While morale in the city soared, it slumped in the camp
Mousehold. Kett, realising the game was up, decided to abandon t
camp and retreat. Neville makes the curious suggestion that it was k
intention to attack before he could be gravely weakened by desertion
But the truth is that Mousehold, although impregnable to assault l
Warwick's numerous cavalry, had become untenable. Food was runni
low; some of the rebels, it was said, had tasted nothing but water f
three days. To stay would be to starve. Further, the story runs, at tl
moment when things already looked ominous, a snake leapt from tl
heart of a rotting tree into Mrs Kett's bosom, to the consternation
her husband and everyone else who saw it happen, and in an age ridd
with superstition it was instantly interpreted as an evil omen. But r
matter what manifestations of the occult may have stirred him, Kett
real problem now was how to put as many miles as possible between h
rabble and Warwick's army. Again, it is said that the direction of tl
retreat was dictated by superstition, by the rhyming prophecy,

> The country gnoffes, Hob, Dick and Hick,
> With clubs and clouted shoon,
>   Shall fill the vale
>   of Dussindale
> With slaughtered bodies soon. . . .

The truth is that they just set out to march northwards. No doubt there was a general belief that they would meet their destiny at Dussindale, that there they would beat down the enemy with their rustic weapons and put the boot in to finish them off. But the wiser heads, certainly Kett himself, knew that oracles are always ambiguous, and had little doubt about the identity of the slaughtered bodies.

And so the six weeks' occupation of Mousehold was brought to an end. The camp, with a great quantity of stores, was set on fire, 'the smoke rising from so many places distant from one another, seemed to bring night almost upon the whole skies, and covered the plains with thick darkness'. The Norfolk peasants marched away with '20 ancients and ensigns of war', taking with them the prisoners they had been holding in Surrey Place. It required the rest of the day to remove the guns and ammunition carts, and to block the roads in their rear. They did not go far, a couple of miles at most, though exactly where they went is not certain. The whereabouts of Dussindale have long since been forgotten, perhaps deliberately. All we know is that it was an open position, lacking any natural defences, which they made shift to protect as best they could with entrenchments and sharpened stakes set in the ground — swine feathers — to ward off cavalry charges.

V

Warwick made his preparations methodically, without haste. The next morning, 27 August, he marched out of Norwich to attack Kett with all his horse, the Almain foot, and the artillery, perhaps 4,000 men in all, leaving the English foot in Norwich, including Thomas Drury's, and even Malatesta's, bands which, having borne the brunt of the fighting hitherto, were certainly in need of rest: Drury's losses for the whole campaign totalled 60 men, nearly a third of his original strength. Although not large, the striking force was carefully picked and thoroughly reliable.

There was one final appeal for peace. Ahead of him Warwick sent a delegation led by Sir Edmund Knyvet and Sir Thomas Palmer to offer the rebel host the opportunity to surrender and escape being massacred. Their appeal evoked only a resolute shout of, 'No!'

The troops were eager for the fray. Warwick rode along the front and addressed them, exhorting:

That they should valiantly invade the enemy, and cast no doubt bu repute and take the company of rebels which they saw, not for men but for brute beasts imbued with all cruelty. Neither let then suppose that they were come out to fight, but to take punishment and should speedily require it at the hands of those most ungraciou robbers; that they should lay even with the ground, afflict, punish and utterly root out the bane of their country, the overthrow o Christian religion and duty. Finally [that the rebels were] most crue beasts, and striving against the King's Majesty with an irrecoverabl madness.

Having spoken he signalled for battle to commence.

The rebels had drawn themselves up with their prisoners placed i front, chained together like condemned felons. For some minutes th royal army hesitated to attack. Then Kett's master gunner, Myles, whe had already proved himself to be a crack shot, took aim at the Roya Standard. The ball crashed through the standard bearer's thigh and hi horse's shoulder, mortally wounding both of them. Immediately the landsknechts opened fire, a devastating volley which shattered the rebels' ranks, throwing them into utter confusion, in the middle o which the captive gentlemen made good their escape: why they were not decimated is not explained! Now Warwick hurled his cavalry inte the confused mass, 'whereupon, instead of abiding the encounter they [the rebels] like sheep ran away headlong, as quickly as they could' Here and there knots of more resolute men rallied,

> returning speedily from their flight, they with deadly obstinacy withstood our men a little while; such, however, was the force o: the shot, and the eagerness of our men to rush upon them (for like unbridled horses, being greedy of the victory, they broke into the host of the enemy) that Kett's army being beaten down and over thrown on every side (with the hot assault) were almost with nc labour driven from their standing.

It was not a battle but a massacre. Kett (in Neville's ungracious words fled from the field with five or six men:

> As he had been a bold leader in wickedness, so he showed himself a cowardly commander on the battlefield; for when he saw everythin going against him . . . being . . . agitated by the consciousness of hi exceeding villainy . . . he secretly fled from the battlefield.

The royal horse pursued the broken peasants, hacking them dowr mercilessly. An estimated 3,500 were slain,[2] and many hundred: wounded. At length, as the troopers paused to reform their ranks, the remnants began to rally, realising that flight could not save them, anc resolved 'that they had rather die manfully in fight, than flying to be slain like sheep'. There was an abundance of discarded weapons lying ready to hand on the ground; they set stakes in the earth and laagered carts and wagons. Then they drank to each other in token of good fortune, offered prayers and made solemn vows to conquer or die.

Still anxious to avoid needless bloodshed, Warwick sent forward his herald to offer them pardon. The answer was that they would willingly surrender if only they could be confident of safety, but recent experience of the cruelty of loyalists had convinced them that the offer was a deception on the part of the nobility who intended to send them all to torture and death: 'And then in truth, whatsoever might be pretended, they knew full well and perceived this pardon to be nothing else but a cask full of ropes and halters, and therefore die they would.' Saddened at this, Warwick offered to go and speak to them in person. The insurgents replied that 'if that were done they would believe, and resign themselves to the authority of the King'. And so he rode forward to where they stood, and the herald read out the proclamation of amnesty. At about four o'clock in the afternoon they laid down their arms, crying 'God save King Edward!' and it was all over.

Warwick's losses were slight. It may well have been that the majority of casualties were sustained by the prisoners of the rebels both during the opening fusilade and the subsequent mêlée, for Neville wrote that it was 'on record ... [that] many gentlemen and some of the chief of the City were slain in this tumult, and heat of the fight: although they gave money and great rewards to the soldiers to spare their lives'. Surviving parish registers of the city record the burial of four gentlemen killed during the insurrection, although two of them, bearing the Welsh names of Rice Griffin and Morgan Corbet, are likely to have been serving with the army: George Hastings, who had been buried on 26 August, must have fallen during the street fighting. Roger, the son of Charles Knyvet, was said to have been killed in the camp.

While the soldiers took away the spoil they had collected and sold it in the Market Square, and regaled themselves with the two barrels of beer — it couldn't have gone far — which the grateful municipality supplied at a cost of 1s., Kett fled to Swannington, eight miles distant. There, his horse spent, he took refuge in a barn in which a wagon load of corn was being unloaded. He was discovered and taken to the house of a Mr Riches in the village where he was left alone with only a child of seven years to watch him, but 'had not the spirit to depart while Mrs Riches was fetched from church, whom, though she rated for his misdemeanour, yet did he pray her of contentation and to have meat' that is, he begged her to hold her peace and give him food. At four the next morning he was brought to Warwick by a party of 20 men who had been sent to fetch him, and who, as Neville would have it, found him hysterical with fear: more probably it was delayed shock following the shattering events of the day before.

VI

The Norfolk rising was over. Warwick kept his word: there was r
general proscription, no reign of terror. There would have been
the local gentry had had their way; after their despicable conduct
the hour of crisis they were full of fire now that the danger had passe
But Warwick cooled them down:

> There must be measure kept, and above all things in punishmen
> men must not exceed. He knew their [the rebels'] wickedness to I
> such as deserved to be grievously punished, and with the severe
> judgment that might be. But how far would they [the gentry] g
> would they ever show themselves discontented and never please
> Would they leave no place for humble petition? none for pard
> and mercy? Would they be ploughmen themselves and harrow the
> own land?

There were mutterings, and attempts to exact revenge under the clo
of legal process. Sir Thomas Woodhouse, in a letter to his broth
described how gentlemen were pressing Warwick for grants of the rebe
property, and daily levelling accusations against this man and tha
Ralph Symondes had made a great complaint against Turcock, who,
turned out, had only been in the camp for a few days at the beginni
of the stir, after which he had gone to Newcastle until after the batt
Nevertheless, the sheriff had seized his goods, and only Woodhouse
intercession with Warwick had saved his life. Woodhouse denied havi
lodged any complaints himself, in spite of having been, as he claime
despoiled of 2,000 sheep, all his bullocks and horses, and most of h
corn. Further, his life had been threatened because he had accompani
the army to Dussindale — while other gentlemen had skulked in Norwic
The town ruffians had sent a letter to Sir Thomas Clere threatening hi
if he went too, and adding that they meant to shoot Woodhouse wi
half hacks in the event of Warwick being defeated.

There were, of course, some punishments to be handed out. Warwic
spent two weeks at Norwich mopping up. A court was set up in t
castle the day after the battle. The ringleaders who had been taken
arms were condemned and led out to Mousehold to be hanged on t
Oak of Reformation. Kett, his brothers, and several others we
dispatched to London to stand trial.

Meanwhile there was great rejoicing in Norwich. A solemn thank
giving was held in St Peter Mancroft on 29 August, and afterwar
27 August was proclaimed a holiday for all time, a day of prayer, wi
a sermon to be preached in the market place. It continued to be observ
at least until 1667.

Echoes of the commotion were still to be heard for some month
On 21 September, Robert Burnham, clerk of the parish of St Gregor

was haled before the mayor, accused of uttering the words, 'There are too many gentlemen in England by five hundred.' He then turned to the court: 'Ye scribes and pharisees! ye seek innocent blood! but if I cannot have justice here I shall have it of better men, and I ask no favour at your hands.' On 30 September, William Mutton, a painter, abused the mayor for imprisoning Burnham, and was ordered to be stood in the pillory with his ears nailed to it. At the same sitting Edmund Johnson, a labourer, was alleged to have told Mr Chandler's servants that if Kett were hanged it would cost another thousand lives. Some weeks later still, Ralph Claxton boasted to Thomas Wolman that he had been out with Kett, whom he admired, and that 'he trusted to see a new day for such men as I was', while John Rooke had been heard in the house of Marian Lelly in St Botolph's predicting the formation of as large a camp as ever had been on Mousehold by Christmas, or least in the spring, this time in support of the Lord Protector. But these were no more than the bitter valedictions of disappointed and defeated men; their wishes fathered no deeds.

Chapter 13
The Reckoning

I

The city of London received the news of the overthrow of the Norfo rebels with caution, and did not relax its guard for some days. T manning of the gates continued until 10 September when the gu borrowed from the Tower were returned, and things were not co pletely restored to normal until the aldermen were released from th nightly patrols on 16 September. Yet the situation remained ten the spectre of civil strife was not finally laid.

Warwick returned from Norwich by 10 September when he resum his seat at the Council board. Already at odds with Somerset, believed that he had been deliberately kept short of men and suppli and clashed with the Protector anew when his application for t reversion of a couple of offices in favour of his son, Sir Ambro Dudley, who had served with distinction in Norfolk, was turned do and they were given to Thomas Fisher who was merely one Somerset's secretaries. Other Councillors were more than disillusion with the Protector's increasingly dictatorial conduct and seeming capricious decisions. He regularly snubbed them, giving way to su violent outbursts of temper that only his friend, Paget, dared offer a criticisms, and even these produced no effect. Grudges of a mo specific character were by now being nursed by a growing number his colleagues who, significantly, included nearly everyone who h held commands in the field. Sir William Herbert had suffered from t anti-enclosure policy. Northampton had been rebuffed when he h sought assistance in resolving his marital problems. The equable Russ had had more than enough of being treated as an incompetent. T latest reprimand he had received starkly illuminates the insensitivi and faulty judgment which brought Somerset to the point at whi every decision he took was wrong. Among the prisoners was a certa Robert Paget of whom little is known except that he was apparently brother of Sir William Paget. Somerset, to whom the case had natura been referred, insisted that he should be executed because in 'su treason and rebellion as this it behoveth us most of all to show different justice, especially considering that we have not spared our own brother'. When, a month or so later, snide remarks to the effect that he had butchered his own brother yet spared his friend's for political advantage warned him that his orders had been ignored, Somerset wrote again to Russell demanding instant execution. The wonder is that William's loyalty remained unshaken.

Personal considerations apart, it was impossible to feel confident of Somerset's capacity to rule. The worst fears had been amply justified by events. Although, after initial blunders, he had handled the crises of the summer efficiently enough, the credit accrued to the men who had led the armies to victory. Further, his whole foreign policy had become non-existent since drifting into war with France. Mercifully the anticipated French invasion had not materialised, but the campaign in Scotland was no longer even a pipe dream, having been cancelled by the end of July. The northern war was finished. Early in August a searching report had demonstrated the impossibility even of holding on to Haddington, save at an unacceptable cost, and after an agony of indecision, the Protector gave the order for evacuation in mid-September. This accomplished, lack of funds dictated the speedy paying off of the army and the abandonment of the scheme to unite the two kingdoms.

Within days of his return, Warwick began consultations with other Councillors at meetings lasting far into the night, in the privacy of his home at Ely Place. With regular sessions of the Council reduced to little more than a formality, the real deliberations were going on here, their purpose above all being to win over the Catholic members. All of these naturally deplored the trend to Protestantism, and Warwick, keeping his true beliefs to himself while known to be reactionary in most matters, doubtless insinuated the prospect of a retreat towards orthodoxy. There were overtures also to the Princess Mary, and the possibility of making her regent did not go unmentioned. The adherence of most of the moderates was already assured; officials for the most part and concerned primarily for efficient administration, they needed no persuasion that a change of government was overdue. Trimmers like Lord Chancellor Rich could be counted on to mount any bandwagon.

Cut off from the definite knowledge of what was afoot, there was little Somerset could do except wait on events. He could not confront Warwick now that the earl had command of a large army which was beginning to enter London, while he himself had been forced to relinquish control of the mercenaries, leaving him with nothing but his household retainers. The soldiers, the foreigners especially, had not yet been paid, and it was Warwick who was pressing their claims, writing, for example, on behalf of the gallant Captain Drury whose band had lost 60 men killed in Norwich and was owed two months' wages. Somerset had no funds to pay them off; until paid they would not

disband, and until then they would obey Warwick. The best t
Protector could do was to publish a proclamation ordering all troop
in particular those in and around London, to proceed immediately
the Border or whatever other commands they were assigned to. (
2 October he signed an order for pay so that they could depart, but
was too late.

By 30 September the situation was looking ominous with t
majority of the Council remaining in London backed by the power
Warwick's army, and the Protector at Hampton Court with his ro
nephew and a rump of five Councillors, including Paget and Cranm
The attitude of the western commanders had now become cruci
Russell and Herbert were many miles away, advancing imperceptibly,
at all, ignoring Somerset's appeals for haste 'for matters of importanc
Within the next few days it became evident that the Catholics h
joined forces with Warwick and that action could be postponed
longer. Matters came to a head on 5 October with the circulation
inspired rumours that Somerset had sold Boulogne to the French –
distortion of the fall of a few strongpoints – and diverted moneys d
to the troops into his own pocket. The Protector proclaimed a summo
to all loyal men to assemble at Hampton Court to defend the King a
himself against 'a most dangerous conspiracy', ordered those support
he still had to raise as many troops as they could, and dispatched
urgent appeal to Russell and Herbert to join him at once.

The morning of 6 October brought intelligence of large conce
trations of troops in London, preparing to move. For a mome
Somerset prepared to fight it out at Hampton Court, arming 500 of
servants from the royal storehouse, and attempting to organise t
peasants who, in response to his appeal of the previous day, had co
to defend their 'good duke'. He sent Sir William Petre to London
open negotiations. The secretary, perhaps already planning to defe
took a copy of the summons to Russell with him. This, coupled w
the Protector's appeal for a *levée en masse*, gave Warwick am
justification for acting, and the same day the Councillors in Lond
effectively constituted themselves as the government.

When no reply came from London the Protector realised t
Warwick's party had determined to resort to force and there was ve
little he could do to oppose them. The appeal to the country had
course been a bluff. He dismissed his ragged army of 4,000 virtua
unarmed peasants, and late in the evening retired to Windsor with t
King, a little farther away from Warwick's army, a little nearer Russel
He dashed off a final letter to the Lord Privy Seal appealing to him
show the part of a true gentleman and of a very friend'.

During these critical days the western army was advancing
leisurely stages, punctuated by numerous rest days, while t

ommanders watched developments and pondered their course of
ction. Accompanied by a cavalry escort, Russell and Herbert had
eached Andover where Somerset's letter was delivered to them. They
ook their time to compose an answer, probably sleeping on it, for it is
lated 8 October. Coldly they contrasted the Protector's stance with
hat of Warwick's party, accusing him of seeking to precipitate social
var in furtherance of his personal ambitions. Determined at all costs to
void further bloodshed, they had reached the conclusion that the
Council majority was in reality the party of peace:

> We are out of doubt the devil hath not so enchanted nor abused
> their wits that they would consent to anything prejudicial and
> hurtful to the King's most royal person, upon whose surety and
> preservation . . . the state of the realm doth depend.
>
> And having consideration of their honours' discretion and their
> continual truth unto the Crown, we believe the same so assuredly
> as no other argument may dissuade from the contrary.

And while this chilling rebuff went on its way they halted the army at
Wilton, Herbert's place in Wiltshire, where it was just arriving, a
lecision which allowed them simultaneously to dissociate themselves
rom the confrontation, to avoid exerting direct pressure on Windsor,
ind yet to interdict Somerset's communications with his territorial base
n the West Country. The last was perhaps the most important con-
ideration: on 9 October, Russell informed his colleagues that 5,000 or
5,000 peasants in those parts were on the point of rising in support of
he duke and that in order to deal with the situation he had had to call
out the gentlemen of Hampshire and Wiltshire and send to Bristol for
cannons.

Confident of growing support, Warwick refrained from advancing
igainst Windsor, while continuing to isolate his adversary. Sheriffs and
ustices of the peace were commanded to ignore Somerset's warrants, to
evy no forces except on the Council's orders, and in general to see that
people stayed at work and remained calm. The Council further published
i proclamation cataloguing Somerset's crimes and announcing his
leposition. Significantly, the signatures of the absent Russell and
Herbert were included with the rest; indeed by this time all people who
nattered were flocking to Warwick's standard. Even Somerset could
low see that he was powerless, trapped between the armies of Russell
ind Warwick, and that the best he could hope for was lenient treatment.
He offered to negotiate, undertaking to accept whatever terms could
pe agreed: he also wrote privately to Warwick to remind him of their
ong-standing friendship, enclosing a plea nominally from the King.
Finally, on 10 October, he agreed to the Council's demand that he
ubmit himself to the laws of the realm, accepting the assurance of their
emissary that no harm should befall him. Paget and Cranmer gave an

undertaking that the King would not be removed from Windsor. The Council had already ordered 500 horse to stand by in case it should be necessary to employ force, but in the event the final scene proved a mere formality. On Wednesday, 11 October, Sir Anthony Wingfield and Sir Anthony St Leger rode down to Windsor and made a ceremonial entry into the castle. They placed Somerset under arrest, and in the name of the Council took over the custody of the 12-year-old King who was suffering from a heavy cold. The Protectorate was at an end.

A few days later Somerset was escorted to London and confined in the Tower where he was held for several months until the new government had fully established itself and the country had returned to tranquility. Shortly afterwards he was permitted to resume his seat on the Council.

II

Changes in government made no difference to the fate of the leaders of the rebellions. They went on trial together before a Special Commission in Westminster Hall on 11 November, their first and only fleeting contact. Equally the architects of the Protector's downfall, their motives had been diametrically opposed, for while Kett had sincerely believed himself the agent of the government's policy, Arundell and his associates had set out deliberately to resist it and couldn't have cared less what became of the régime so long as they got what they wanted.

Russell had already examined the prisoners taken in the West and had sent up to London the obvious ringleaders together with several more held on suspicion. Ten were interrogated by Sir Edward North, Sir John Baker and Sir Richard Southwell, members of the Council. They admitted nothing, but five were able to give tolerably convincing accounts of their conduct in consequence of which interest was narrowed to Arundell, John Winslade, John Bury and Thomas Holmes who were examined again on 22 October by the Lord Chancellor, Sir John Mason and Sir Thomas Smyth. Although very possibly subjected to torture they still insisted that they had been compelled to join the rising and refused to implicate the others. As there was insufficient evidence and their part in the affair had been unimportant the Council ordered the release of five on 1 November. Pomeroy was lucky for his prank at the battle of Clyst could easily have brought about the decisive defeat of Russell's army, but he was the sort of man it was difficult to take seriously; besides he had given himself up voluntarily, as had two more, named Harris and Wise. William Winslade's youth told in his favour; it is conceivable that his father volunteered a confession in change for his life. The fifth man, Fortescue by name, may have owed his escape to good family connexions. Coffin may also have been captured although nothing further was heard of him; it is possible that he was released but more likely that he died of wounds sustained at King's Weston. Another five men were released on recognizance: Humphry Bonville, Winslade's brother-in-law, Richard Roscarrok who was related to Arundell by marriage, Thomas a Leigh of St Mary Week, the servant who had once sued Arundell for withholding his pay, Thomas Downish of Crediton and John Prideaux of Tavistock.

The case against the four remaining prisoners from the west rested on the testimony of a man named Kestell, possibly James Kestell of Kestell whose son was married to the daughter of John Coffin of Northledge, possibly the rebel leader. He had already made a clean breast to Russell who had sent him on to London with the recommendation that

he came in of himself and in the midst of the hottest stirs he sent his secret advertisement to Mr Godolphin and other gentlemen of so much as he knew of Arundell's proceedings and the rest . . . to whom for the honesty we have perceived in him in all his declaration we shall heartily pray you to be good Lord accordingly.

He had acted as Arundell's secretary — against his will, it is hardly necessary to add; it is worth remarking that although he disappeared after turning King's evidence an obscure Jesuit of the same name died many years later at Coimbra in Portugal.

The trials did not take long — treason trials never did. Robert and William Kett pleaded guilty and craved mercy, the rest were convicted, and the sentence of the law for treason pronounced.

On 29 November the Ketts were delivered into the custody of Sir Edmund Wyndham, sheriff of Norfolk, and two days later were brought back to Norwich and confined in the Guildhall. On the morning of 7 December Robert was taken out and drawn on a hurdle to the castle. There he was bound in chains and hoisted by a rope round his neck to a gibbet mounted on the battlements, 'and there hanged for a continual memory of so great villainy until that unhappy and heavy body (through putrefaction consuming) shall fall down at length'. It was widely believed that William would be granted mercy, for he had at one point submitted to Northampton and been sent back to Mousehold to persuade his brother to yield. But he had given information of the smallness of Northampton's force and its weak position, and so, although his personal contribution to the revolt had been small, he was held responsible for the rejection of the offer of pardon and the resulting débâcle on the Palace Plain. The day after Robert's execution he was taken to Wymondham and hanged on the great west tower of the church which the family had laboured to

preserve for the town. It is not recorded whether lawyer Flowerde
came to enjoy the edifying spectacle.

Arundell, Winslade, Bury and Holmes were allowed a few wee
more to live, until on 27 January 1550 they were taken from the Tow
by the Constable, Sir John Gage, an unwavering Catholic, and drawn
hurdles through the streets of the city to the gallows at Tyburn whe
they were hanged, and while yet living were cut down, their entra
ripped out and burned before their eyes, and finally their heads we
struck off by the hangman and their bodies quartered — 'the head a
quarters of each of them [to] be placed where our lord the King sh
appoint' as a deterrent to other traitors. Among the throng lining t
route to the scaffold that raw winter morning stood two servants
Winslade, one who had been with him upwards of 10 years, the othe
mere lad of 19, faithful to the end.

There still remained in the Tower a few not directly involved in t
rebellion whom the government suspected of being disloyal at hea
They included Doctors Moreman and Crispin whose preaching was
much admired in the West Country and whose release the rebels h
demanded. The former was detained until the end of Edward's reig
the latter died in confinement in the autumn of 1551. Following
examination by the Council on 27 July 1549, Sir John Arundell
Lanherne had been released on bail of £4,000 (his brother, Sir Thoma
and Sir Thomas Stradling of Glamorgan standing as sureties)
condition of his remaining within one mile of the City and its subur
unless given leave by the Protector to pass beyond the limits. Sin
subsequently Lord Russell was unable to dig up any concrete eviden
against him he was discharged from bail on 1 November. Shortly befo
Christmas he and Sir William Godolphin were each bound over in t
sum of £1,000 to keep the peace pending the settlement of a dispu
between them, probably, as Rowse suggests, related to Arunde
dealings with his cousin Humphry which Kestell had passed on
Godolphin. Very soon afterwards he found himself back in the Tow
evidently on the information of Godolphin who was in good standi
with the government. Sir Thomas Arundell was also arrested
30 January 1550. When Somerset was restored to the Council at t
beginning of April he did his best to obtain better treatment for the
with the result that John's wife was permitted to visit him, and bo
were allowed more liberty within the Tower itself. However, there w
no sign of them being released, so they refused to pay for their fo
on the ground that they were being wrongfully detained. In its tu
the Council, in April 1551, placed them in 'strait' confinement again
prove that they were being held justly. Six months later Thomas w
brought before the Council, admonished and bailed. Within a fortnig
the duke of Somerset himself was arrested on the information of o

Thomas Palmer that Thomas Arundell had told the duke that the Tower was 'safe'. Two days later Arundell was re-arrested and accused of plotting with other prisoners the assassination of Warwick (now duke of Northumberland). The charge was flimsy and the jury failed to agree until they had been shut up all night without food, after which they brought in a verdict of guilty. Arundell was beheaded on 26 January 1552, four days after the ex-Protector had himself been executed on a trumped up conspiracy charge. His opponents had kept their word, technically. They had done him no harm, just given him the opportunity to incriminate himself!

Sir John Arundell persisted with his 'rent strike' until on 26 June 1552 he successfully applied to the King's Bench for bail and was released. He sat once more in Parliament in the reign of Mary, but the poor health of which he had complained at the time of the commotions had perhaps worsened during his confinement; he soon withdrew into private life and died in 1557, a victim maybe of the influenza epidemic which ravaged the country at that time. The Arundells of Wardour, descendants of his brother, have never ceased to be Catholics.

Two men were penalised for what they had not done during the rebellions. William Rugg, bishop of Norwich, was thoroughly incompetent, and corrupt even by the tolerant standards of public life at the time. Wanting in any moral authority, he had been unable, indeed had made no effort to exert any sort of leadership in his diocese. The uncovering of financial irregularities made it possible to force his resignation towards the end of the year. Bishop Veysey of Exeter was of course an octogenarian, but in many years he had scarcely set foot inside his diocese, leaving the management to a deputy, while devoting his time to his home town of Sutton Coldfield where he is remembered as the founder of the grammar school. In his case, however, negligence could be construed as contributory to the makings of rebellion, and consequently he was deprived in 1551 — the new government may have waited a bit to see if he would die — in order to make way for Miles Coverdale who must have been deemed worthy of reward for his services as chaplain to Russell's army; as an active reformer he was an obvious choice to straighten out the religious problems of Devon and Cornwall.

II

After the risings the inquest. 'The causes of sedition must be rooted out', wrote Robert Crowley afterwards; he said nothing about the cost. On the narrowly financial side, a contemporary statement of account put the cost of suppressing the two rebellions at £28,122 7s. 7d., no inconsiderable charge on the government's already strained resources. I may even have been higher since it is uncertain whether this include the wages of the mercenaries which probably amounted to som £10,000 for the three month period which covers the emergency. I the long term, of course, the cost to the nation in terms of damage t be made good was a good deal higher. The account includes £2,800 fo miscellaneous charges such as breaking down bridges which the variou local communities no doubt were left to rebuild at their own expense The toll of plunder and wanton destruction is anyone's guess.

No one thought to count the number of dead. The Venetian envo told his government that it amounted to 10,000 or 11,000, a figur which is as good as any, especially since it has to cover the man smaller disturbances which occurred. Mere aggregation of the frequentl conflicting estimates of the rebels' losses in battle is inconclusive. It i generally accepted that 3,000, or thereabouts, were killed at Dussindale losses in the earlier, smaller scale fighting in Norwich may be additional Casualties in the fiercely contested battles in Devonshire must hav been at least as great,[1] making it probable that some 6,000–7,000 me were killed in action. This sheds some light on the obscure subject o the 'white terror' in Cornwall, not to mention the aftermath of othe commotions. Information about executions is generally vague: Warwic hanged 49 men the day he entered Norwich, Grey staged a doze exemplary executions in Oxfordshire – how many other men wer strung up where they were caught? – and a good many of the 10 prisoners taken at King's Weston were similarly dealt with. There is a almost complete silence on the losses sustained by loyalist forces Northampton may have lost as many as 100 men at Norwich; Captai Drury was said to have lost a full third of his 180 men. In general w are left with the impression that those troops who bore the brunt o the fighting were armoured well enough to escape with minor wound in most cases, and since it is probable that most rebels were killed whil in flight, not forgetting the massacre of prisoners at Clyst St Mary, i may be taken as reasonably certain that the death roll in the govern ment forces fell well short of 1,000.

In a nation of less than 3,000,000 the aggregate loss of life wa immense. To accept a figure of 10,000 or thereabouts is to say tha the equivalent of the whole population of Rutland, the smallest county was wiped out in the space of a few short weeks. In twentieth-centur values it would work out at some 165,000 men,[2] a scale of casualtie such as the major battles of the First World War produced.

The causes of revolt were not rooted out. The rebels were, at leas in the West Country. The Prayer Book Rebellion had come virtuall out of nowhere; like a comet it had flashed across the sky and wa burned up, smashed. Elsewhere the landowners, the sheepmen, ha won. Yet within a year or two the boom in wool came suddenly to an end, and although inflation continued for another century, matters improved somewhat. as rising prices stimulated an expansion of corn growing. In the short term, moreover, pressure was eased temporarily by the influenza epidemic of 1556–8 which reduced the population slightly. Enclosures did not cease, nor disputes about individual cases. On occasion there were bigger demonstrations, a rising of Buckinghamshire peasants in 1552, and widespread disorders in the Midlands in 1607, but never again did popular revolt reach the scale of 1549.

The two rebellions of 1549 followed remarkably parallel courses. Each began as a spontaneous stirring of the peasantry – petty tradesmen in the case of Bodmin. Each was mishandled by the authorities in much the same way. Unthinkingly it was taken for granted that the unsophisticated commons were manipulated by clever, unscrupulous agitators and could be recalled to their senses by the combination of a few specious promises with a token show of force. Ignorant of the minds of those they ruled, it did not enter the heads of the governing class that the spirit of revolt was born of a wave of intense emotion. Like almost all insurrections they were instinctive surges of deeply felt injustice sparked off by accident. Leaders appeared subsequently. Each was propelled along by a series of provocative half measures which helped to convert it into a full scale rebellion which necessitated the mobilisation of the military resources of the state to crush it.

Each rebellion, furthermore, polarised in a manifestation of peasant antagonism against the gentry. Where there were powerful territorial magnates able and determined to act decisively, no rising developed: in Somerset the combination of the bishop of Bath and Wells and Lord Stourton proved irresistible. But in both Norfolk and Devonshire the old established temporal magnates had previously been eliminated, and, coincidentally, the local bishops neglected their sees, the one supine, the other an aging absentee. The gentry, the magistracy, found themselves leaderless and divided. Accustomed to the individual pursuit of selfish ends, they did not trust one another: in Devon they could not be sure that some of the most influential ones were not in sympathy, even in collusion, with the insurgents. Worse, they felt isolated and betrayed by the government, their government; and the Privy Council itself was torn apart by personal antipathies.

There the similarities end. Although they took place almost simultaneously there was never the least hint of communication, much less collaboration between the two risings. Not only were they geographically isolated, their ideologies remained poles apart. There was indeed one other common characteristic, but by its very nature it accentuated the dichotomy – the provincialism which so deeply permeated men's thinking and limited their horizons. Robert Kett set out to enforce the

law in Norfolk, and to that end took over the administration of th
shire. He never sought to go outside its boundaries; he never wanted t
If other counties had similar problems it was up to them to adop
appropriate remedies. The westerners did perhaps plan to march o
London, but primarily, one suspects, to win concessions for themselve
rather than to salvage the cause of Catholicism in general. True, the
called for the reinstatement of Cardinal Pole, at least the final list c
demands did, but they never attempted to secure the support of th
Lady Mary which would have seemed the obvious course — not that sh
can be imagined welcoming the unsolicited championship of th
mutinous lower orders. They made little or no attempt to explo
manifestations of hostility to the Prayer Book in other souther
counties, or to organise a network of revolt which, indeed, must surel
have evoked as little response as Kett's half-hearted move to drum u
support in Suffolk.

But even without the handicap of regional exclusiveness they woul
have needed leaders of outstanding political ability to forge a commo
cause, so radically different were their objectives. In Norfolk religio
was not at issue; complaints about the Church were confined to th
shortcomings of its ministers. Protestantism was firmly establishe
among the rebels; it never occurred to them to enlist the sympathy c
Mary even though she was living not far away, under house arrest a
Kenninghall in Suffolk. In utter contrast, the western rebellion wa
resisting the imposition of the *Book of Common Prayer,* and did nc
concern itself with economic questions at all, despite the facil
assumptions of most recent historians, following the lead of A. F. Pollar
who clearly felt disconcerted by the problem of accounting for a revol
motivated by faith and soon switched to the more congenial subject c
agrarian discontent. It is true that the social mix of both lots c
insurgents was much the same, but there the resemblance ends. If th
Prayer Book Rebellion was anti-gentry it was because many gentleme
had associated themselves with Protestantism, rather than the othe
way round: the westerners made only one demand relating to th
gentry, the significance of which is not altogether clear.

Because of its isolated nature and refusal to conform to any con
venient pattern the Western Rising puzzles some historians. They not
it briefly, gingerly, deck it out with attributes it did not possess, seek t
make it more complex than it really was, before passing on to de
(more confidently) with Norfolk, compared to which it appears a
irrational phenomenon, as indeed it was. In reality it is Kett's rebellio
that should provide the puzzle. What distinguishes it from a score c
other localised agrarian risings in the spring and summer of 1549? Th
answer is nothing, except that it lasted longer, produced a systemati
schedule of grievances, and terminated in a massacre. There was c

course the commanding personality of its leader. But the other revolts collapsed before leaders of stature had time to emerge, and it is pertinent to ask whether even Kett would be remembered had he and his followers been suppressed by the local authorities. It was the timing of this rebellion rather than its character that determined its course. By the time it began the other had been in progress four weeks, and the Council had taken the decision to commit a substantial part of its slender reserves. With the Oxfordshire rising following almost immediately and the remaining southern counties looking like exploding at any moment, still more troops were drawn in. The calculated risk was taken to leave Norfolk to itself while the West was dealt with first. It had to be taken. Kett, as it turned out, posed no direct threat to the government; his action was, as Professor Bindoff points out, 'a great sit down strike', nothing more.

In complete contrast the rebels of Cornwall and Devon were waging war. Whether the Protector and Council got as far as drawing this distinction we do not know, but they cannot have failed to note Kett's passive stance, and plan accordingly. And the risk was amply justified by the fiercely contested fields of Fenny Bridges, Clyst St Mary and Sampford Courtenay. These were real battles, decided only by the superior armament and discipline of continental mercenaries, compared with which Dussindale was a tragic farce; the defence of Norwich was half-hearted, and Northampton brought about his own defeat. Grey of Wilton's admiration for the valour of the Cornishmen may be accepted at its face value. They fought for what they believed in, religion and racial identity. Kett's followers had no such inspiration. Men will die for an ideal but not for material interests. It was this difference that made the Prayer Book Rebellion the more dangerous of the two, indeed, bearing in mind the shaky condition of the government, much the most serious of the century. They had the men, and to some extent the arms, but above all they were determined to fight. The ruthlessness with which the dying embers of revolt were stamped out in Cornwall bears witness to the alarm it engendered, and contrasts starkly with Warwick's comparatively lenient treatment of Norfolk.

Able to flourish until a decisive victory had been gained in the West and Exeter relieved, the Norfolk rebellion was granted a further three weeks' respite while the government redeployed its forces. After that Warwick had a walkover against farmers and labourers who had never wanted to fight in the first place, but had been driven into a posture of rebellion by the government's blunders. Once they realised that Warwick meant business their one idea was to get away; to all intents Dussindale was a rearguard action. It was anything but unusual for people to come together and brandish weapons, but rare indeed for there to be any serious intention of using them. In this respect the

rising bears comparison with the Pilgrimage of Grace which also marke‹
the climax of an accumulation of economic and social grievances, eve‹
if in the event it was precipitated by indignation over the dissolution o‹
the monasteries. But once it had been taken over by the gentry, wh‹
added political objectives, it ceased to be an exclusively peasant affai‹
It ended when the gentlemen reached an accommodation with th‹
Crown and deserted the peasants, who promptly dispersed, havin‹
presumably never seriously contemplated armed conflict. If, as there ‹
reason to suppose, the gentry had exploited the grievances of th‹
people in order to foment revolt, the pilgrimage had more in commo‹
with peasant risings in France than with the Norfolk revolt whic‹
was overtly anti-gentry.

The fact that some of the attributes of rural protest movement‹
down the ages have tended to be recurrent has, naturally enough‹
encouraged the formulation of general theories of peasant revolt. Ye‹
comparisons can be pressed too far, and attempts to fit English insur‹
rections — to say nothing of others — into a single all-purpose matri‹
regardless of complex social realities, have not escaped criticism‹
Certainly the 168 years which separate them is enough to raise doubt‹
about the utility of comparing 1549 with 1381. A similar difficult‹
arises in relation to the Leveller movement of the 1640s.[3] Few of th‹
disturbances which were a frequent occurrence in the interim amounte‹
to more than a localised bread riot among the poor in periods of deart‹
and high prices.

Certain characteristics common to the wave of European revolt‹
between the fourteenth and seventeenth centuries were unquestionabl‹
present in 1549. Organisation had improved, objectives were mor‹
clearly articulated than in the past, and the outbreak was mor‹
extensive, at least in so far as the two major rebellions, their difference‹
notwithstanding, took place simultaneously against a background o‹
nationwide unrest. The rebels, moreover, suffered from the commo‹
handicap of lack of military experience. The usual recourse of enlistin‹
minor gentry and mercenary soldiers was imitated superficially in th‹
Prayer Book Rebellion. However, the role of the well-born participant‹
can be overestimated, while Humphry Arundell was an officer, unlik‹
the rank and file landsknechts — a species unknown in England — wh‹
organised and led the peasants of Germany. No armigerous gentleme‹
supported the Norfolk rising, nor was there a place for them if it wa‹
not really conceived as an armed insurrection. Kett himself was n‹
more than a borderline case.

Yet these are externals. The innate dissimilarities are more impressive‹
Late medieval revolts increasingly challenged the social order, under‹
mined social values; the economic and social aims of the Germa‹
Peasants' War of 1525 originated in novel religious ideas. In contrast‹

not only did the Prayer Book Rebellion seek to reverse the Reformation, the social order was irrelevant except to the extent that it determined the form and content of religion. The position of the Norfolk rebels was more complex. A distinct influence of the Twelve Articles of Swabian peasants, 1525, can be inferred since they had circulated widely in print. Yet not more than three out of 29 demands can rightly be termed borrowings: the two relating to the election of competent clergy, and the liberating of bondmen on the ground that their freedom had been purchased by the Crucifixion. Moreover, apart from this solitary and somewhat perfunctory reference, appeal to ancient custom and precedent took the place of Christian principles; in short, the devotional content was subsidiary. The vital difference was that Kett's people wanted to preserve, indeed restore, traditional society. Where the Germans were radical the English were conservative, reactionary even. In fact the rebellion in Cornwall, tinctured as it was with Celtic particularism, seems to bear a closer family likeness to the counter-revolutionary rising of the Bretons of La Vendée in 1793.

There is, furthermore, the crucial question of the relative situation of the peasantry in different countries. In the first place there is no reason to doubt that Englishmen did enjoy superior material conditions to their neighbours, the French especially. As to serfdom, England, where it had all but disappeared, was moving in the opposite direction to most of central and eastern Europe where it was spreading rapidly, frequently being imposed on the peasants for the first time. Kett's articles voiced the complaints of small property owners who objected to shouldering obligations appropriate to those of greater wealth and status.

Against a background of increasing radicalism on the continent, the conservatism of the English in 1549 looks anachronistic. For that matter it appears also to interrupt the continuity of popular protest which some scholars claim to trace through the centuries from the revolt of 1381, through the Lollards of the fifteenth century to the Levellers of the seventeenth and beyond, undeterred by the long intervals which separate these manifestations. The anomaly, if there be one, could equally originate in an initial misapprehension, the crediting of peasants as a type with any radical, or revolutionary, impulse at all. The tradition which idealises, indeed sentimentalises, the peasant may be contrasted with Émile Zola's unflattering portrait of him in *La Terre*. Communist successes in underdeveloped Asiatic countries have, it is true, been hailed enthusiastically as vindication of the peasantry as a revolutionary class; the verdict of history may conceivably be different. While awaiting it we may ponder the fact that the French in 1789 and the Russians in 1918 turned their backs on revolution the moment they had expropriated the landlords. Experience suggests that the peasant aspires to nothing more ambitious than to own a plot of land and be left in peace on it – no more and no less than the average sixteenth-century Englishman wanted.

Circumstances conspired to doom the English rebellions from the outset. The rigidly localised character of the Norfolk one condemned it to isolation and made its downfall inevitable. Under different conditions the western one might have succeeded in blowing a faltering government off course, but peasants, however valiant, could not hope to defeat professional soldiers, and they had the bad luck to pick the one time in the whole Tudor age when such forces were present in the country. Besides, they denied themselves one essential weapon – ruthlessness. Whatever drove them on, they were ordinary, decent folk at heart. Not for them the callous butchery of scores of victims selected at random; they killed only in battle. Of course a lot of people must have suffered rough handling; of course there was looting. But not more than one or two individuals were slaughtered in cold blood. Tales of nameless atrocities were born of hysteria and certainly fostered by offical propaganda; a 'letter' from an anonymous Devon gentleman, which circulated in pamphlet form, was very likely a government inspired fabrication. The upper class was handicapped by no such inhibition, and won. It is significant that it was Humphry Arundell who was alleged to have projected the massacre of the prisoners held at Launceston, and the townsmen who thwarted him. Successful revolutionaries are not renowned for humanitarianism.

Surprised by the outbreak of revolution in Paris in 1848, the republican leader Auguste Ledru-Rollin confessed ruefully: 'I am their leader, therefore I must follow them.' All the events of 1549 bear witness to the spontaneity of the uprisings. Although the government and its apologists insisted that the Prayer Book Rebellion was fomented by priests, the record, sparse as it is, suggests the opposite, showing Mr Harper being forced by his parishioners to say Mass, and Robert Welch intervening to prevent the incendiary bombardment of Exeter. While, among the laymen, Arundell's precise contribution remains obscure, Kett was certainly drawn in more or less by accident. Once installed, their ability to influence the course of events naturally increased and their limitations were correspondingly exposed. Both failed to hold on to the initiative. Arundell perhaps fell victim to his own professionalism which inhibited him from bypassing Exeter as the Cornish rebels had done with impunity in 1497. The effect on the 'quavering quiet' of counties further to the east of the appearance of his army was never put to the test. There was in the West a total neglect of political objectives. Kett, too, was politically naïve. His diagnosis and prognosis of the ailments which afflicted the peasant community of Norfolk were admirable, but he showed not the least comprehension of the realities of national politics. In both cases the rank and file knew well enough what they wanted, but the leaders to whom they turned did not know how to get it, the one relying exclusively on naked force, the other on 'non-violent' protest.

Notes

Introduction

1 J. D. Mackie, *The Earlier Tudors* (1952), pp. 489–90.
2 A. G. Dickens, *The English Reformation* (Fontana edn, 1967), pp. 305–6.
3 See for example, A. Fletcher, *Tudor Rebellions* (1968), and D. M. Loades, *Politics and the Nation, 1450–1660* (1974), pp. 204–13, who on the slenderest of evidence insist on attributing to the Western Rising motives other than ideological ones.
4 M. L. Bush, *The Government Policy of Protector Somerset* (1975).
5 C. G. Cruickshank, *Elizabeth's Army* (2nd edn, 1966), *Army Royal* (1969); L. Boynton, *The Elizabethan Militia, 1558–1638* (1967); J. J. Goring, 'Military Obligations of the English People, 1511–1558' (unpublished University of London thesis, 1955).

Chapter 3 Protest and Provocation

1 Hooker makes this out to be the Pavia campaign of 1524–5, but this clearly is too early to square with the fact that he must have been at least 13 when sent to France; besides England was at war with France, whereas by 1528 they had become allies.

Chapter 4 Half Measures

1 This is the only reference to such a person; he cannot be identified.

Chapter 6 War of Words

1 Thomas Fuller, *Church History of Britain* (1845 ed.), ii, p. 322.

Chapter 7 The Norfolk Rising

1 The only source for the letter is Sir John Hayward's *Life and Reign of Edward VI* (1632). However, while the assumption is that he was

citing a MS. which is no longer extant, the absence of any other reference to so controversial a proposition suggests that he may have read too much into his source.

Chapter 8 The Battle of Fenny Bridges

1 The absence of reference to pistoleers in the various contracts of service and accounts may well be due to English conservatism in the military art not having caught up with the latest developments.

Chapter 9 Fiasco at Norwich

1 M. A. S. Hume asserted that no Spanish troops served in Norfolk.
2 Estimates vary: Sotherton says 40 soldiers were killed, the King, 100. Ford says 100 on each side; Neville, some soldiers and 140 rebels. The register of St Martin's at the Palace Plain records the burial of Sheffield and 35 others.

Chapter 10 Clyst St Mary and the Relief of Exeter

1 There is reference for extra pay for mercenaries in Norfolk only.
2 A recent housing development on this site seems to have obscured the previous lie of the land to some extent.

Chapter 12 Dussindale

1 This assumption is based on the fact that those Germans who were presumably still in the environs of London did not reach Norwich until 26 August by which date the ensigns serving with Russell would have had just sufficient time to march back from Devonshire. Suggestions that troops were withdrawn from the army in the North cannot be sustained; there is no evidence that any of von Walderden's command even formed part of it.
2 Very possibly an exaggeration; it may be the grand total for the whole rebellion.

Chapter 13 The Reckoning

1 A. L. Rowse's attempt to minimise casualties at Sampford Courtenay, *Tudor Cornwall* (1941), p. 281, is based on a misreading of the MS. of Russell's report.
2 This point is made by W. K. Jordan, *Edward VI: the Young King* (1968), p. 493; he also accepts the Venetian estimate.
3 It is too soon to evaluate Brian Manning's interpretation of the revolution, *The English People and the English Revolution, 1640– 1649* (1976).

Select Bibliography

1 Sources

The Prayer Book Rebellion
The narrative source is John Vowell, alias Hooker, *The Description of the City of Exeter*, ed. W. J. Harte, J. W. Schopp and H. Tapley-Soper (1919), part 2, pp. 55–96, supplemented by his 'Life of Sir Peter Carew', *Archaeologia*, xxviii (1840), pp. 96–119. Communications from the Privy Council to Lord Russell, with other papers, were edited by N. Pocock in *Troubles Connected with the Prayer Book of 1549*, Camden Society, new series, xxxvii (1884). Most of Russell's letters are lost; his report on Sampford Courtenay is in the British Library, Harleian MS. 523. Richard Carew's *Survey of Cornwall* (ed. 1769) contains additional material.

Kett's rebellion
The earliest account was written by Nicholas Sotherton, an eye-witness, and entitled 'The Commoyson in NO[folk]', Harleian MS. 1576, ff. 251–9. Alexander Neville's *De Furoribus Norfolciensium Ketto Duce* was published in 1575, and translated by Richard Wood, 1615. F. Blomefield, *History of Norfolk*, iii (1730), has further material.

Military
Muster returns for various dates are in the Public Record Office, Exchequer, E 36 and E 315, also State Papers, SP 1. Contracts for mercenary bands, SP 46, vol. 2. Details of native forces and pay, Enrolled accounts, E 101/531/39, and Declared accounts, E 351/13, 43, 215, 217, 221. See also, *Acts of the Privy Council*, ed. J. R. Dasent, vol. ii (1890); Historical Manuscripts Commission reports, *Rutland MSS*.

Social and economic
Quantitative statements are based chiefly on Lay Subsidy Rolls, PRO, E 179, especially those for 1524–5; also on surviving muster books for 1522, see above, which incorporate much detail relating to the distribution of wealth. Many of the conclusions based on them are drawn from the writer's unpublished researches.

Other printed documents and calendars include *Letter and Papers, Foreign and Domestic, of the Reign of Henry VIII; Calendar of State Papers, Domestic, 1547–1580; Calendars of State Papers, Foreign; English Historical Documents*, vol. v, *1485–1558*, ed. C. H. Williams (1967); *Tudor Economic Documents*, ed. R. H. Tawney and E. Power, 3 vols (1926); J. Strype, *Ecclesiastical Memorials*, 3 vols (1822); *The Chronicle and Political Papers of King Edward VI*, ed. W. K. Jordan (1966); P. F. Tytler, *England Under the Reigns of Edward VI and Mary*, 2 vols (1839); *Tudor Royal Proclamations*, ed. P. L. Hughes and J. F. Larkin (New Haven, 1964); Historical Manuscripts Commission, *Bath MSS;* Charles Wriothesley, *Chronicle*, ed. W. D. Hamilton, Camden Society, new series, xx (1877); *Discourse of the Common Weal*, ed. E. Lamont (1893).

2 Secondary Works

There are fully documented studies of each rising. F. W. Russell, *Kett's Rebellion in Norfolk* (1859) is an excellent piece of work. Frances Rose-Troup's *The Western Rebellion of 1549* (1914) is thorough but marred by a somewhat sentimental approach; A. L. Rowse's readable account in his *Tudor Cornwall* (1941) provides a corrective. The definitive analysis of the Norfolk rising is S. T. Bindoff's penetrating *Ket's Rebellion, 1549* (Historical Association pamphlet, 1949). A. Fletcher's short accounts in *Tudor Rebellions* (1968) are conventional and add nothing to the subject.

The most recent general history of the period is W. K. Jordan, *Edward VI: the Young King* (1968). M. L. Bush, *The Government Policy of Protector Somerset* (1975) supersedes previous work on this subject.

The classic survey of rural conditions is R. H. Tawney, *The Agrarian Problem of the Sixteenth Century* (1912); however, much of it is now outdated and it has been severely criticised by E. Kerridge, *Agrarian Problems in the Sixteenth Century and After* (1969). S. T. Bindoff deals succinctly with social and economic conditions in *Tudor England* (1950). Cornish society is surveyed by Rowse, loc. cit. On Exeter see W. G. Hoskins, 'The Elizabethan Merchants of Exeter' in *Old Devon* (1966) and W. T. McCaffrey, *Exeter, 1540–1640* (1968). See also J. Cornwall, 'The People of Rutland in 1522', *Transactions of Leicestershire Archaeological Society*, xxxvii (1963), 'The early Tudor Gentry', *Economic History Review*, 2nd series, xvii (1965), and, on population, 'English Population in the Early Sixteenth Century', ibid., xxiii (1970). I hope shortly to complete a study of the structure of society and the distribution of wealth in this period. For inflation see R. B. Outhwaite, *Inflation in Tudor and Stuart England* (1969), and E. H. Phelps Brown and S. V. Hopkins, 'Six Centuries of the Prices of Consumables', *Economica*, xxiii (1956).

C. Oman, *The Art of War in the Sixteenth Century* (1937), is a standard work. C. G. Cruickshank, *Army Royal* (1969) and *Elizabeth's Army* (2nd edn. 1966) are invaluable; also J. Millar, 'The Landsknecht: His Recruitment and Organisation with Some Reference to the Reign of Henry VIII', *Military Affairs*, October 1971. I am much indebted to Jeremy Goring's unpublished thesis, 'The Military Obligations of the English People, 1511–1588', University of London, 1955.

Index